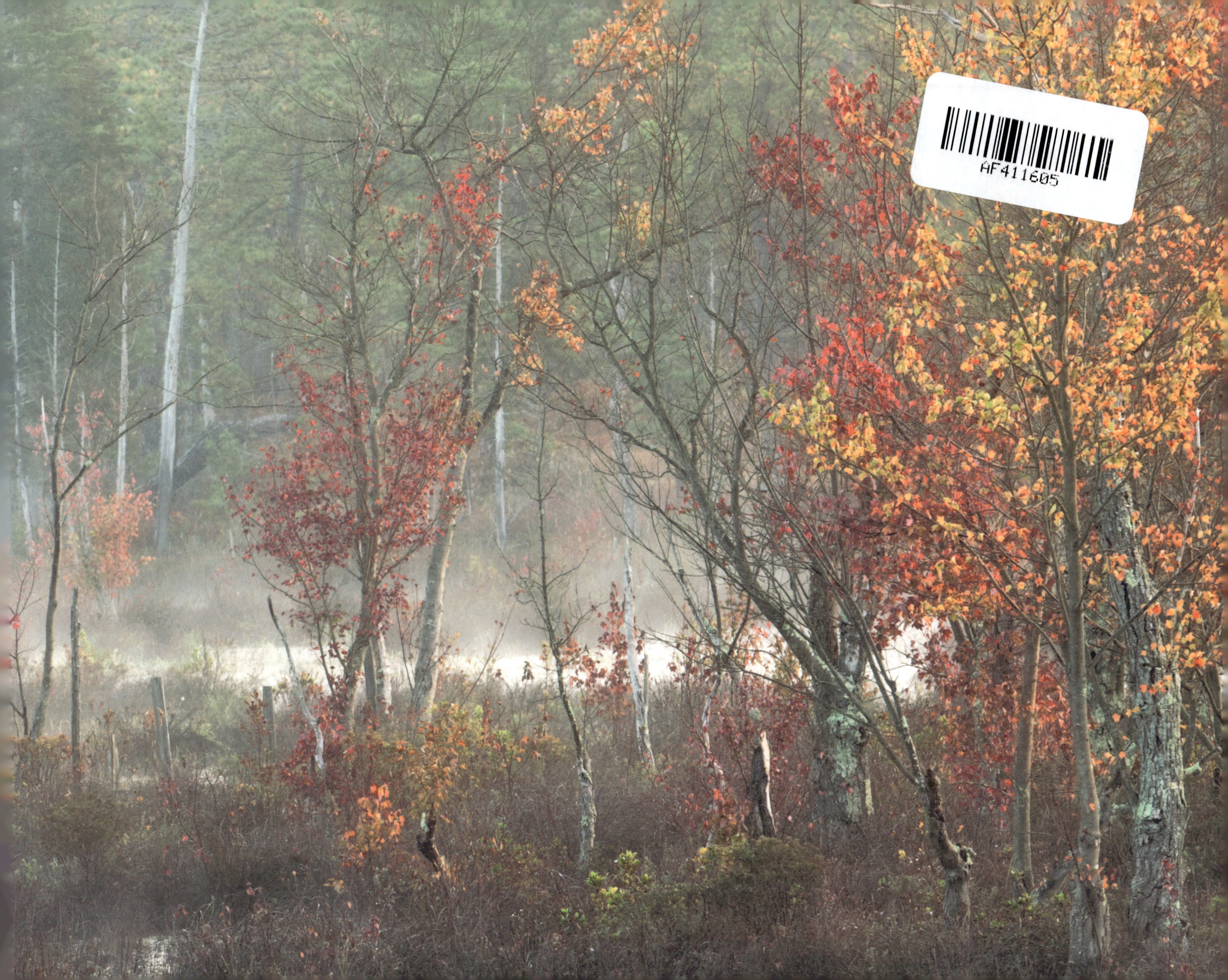
AF411605

ALBERT D. HORNER

PINELANDS

New Jersey's Suburban Wilderness

Schiffer Publishing Ltd

4880 Lower Valley Road • Atglen, PA 19310

Copyright © 2015 by Albert D. Horner

Library of Congress Control Number: 2015930298

Designed by John P. Cheek
Type set in Perpetua

ISBN: 978-0-7643-4881-5
Printed in China

Published by Schiffer Publishing, Ltd.
4880 Lower Valley Road
Atglen, PA 19310
Phone: (610) 593-1777; Fax: (610) 593-2002
E-mail: Info@schifferbooks.com

For our complete selection of fine books on this and related subjects, please visit our website at www.schifferbooks.com. You may also write for a free catalog.

This book may be purchased from the publisher. Please try your bookstore first.

We are always looking for people to write books on new and related subjects. If you have an idea for a book, please contact us at proposals@schifferbooks.com.

Schiffer Publishing's titles are available at special discounts for bulk purchases for sales promotions or premiums. Special editions, including personalized covers, corporate imprints, and excerpts can be created in large quantities for special needs. For more information, contact the publisher.

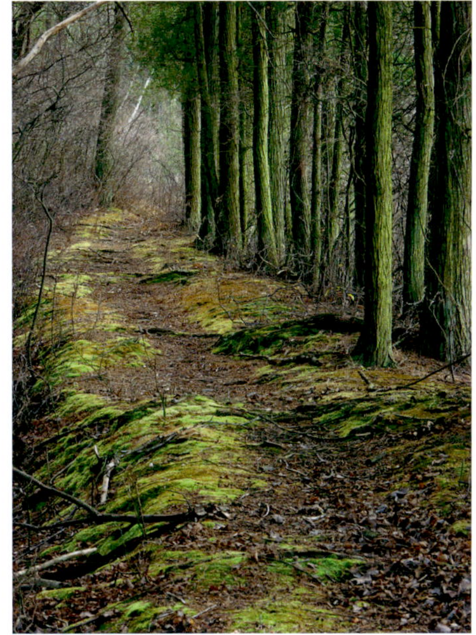

Cedar Path

*This book is dedicated to the many women and men who devote
their lives to preserving and protecting our natural heritage.*

EPIGRAPH

"In the final analysis it is the citizens of New Jersey who will decide the ultimate fate of the Pine Barrens. It is our responsibility to pass this wilderness heritage on, in its natural state, to our heirs."

—HOWARD BOYD, NATURALIST AND AUTHOR OF *A FIELD GUIDE TO THE PINE BARRENS OF NEW JERSEY*

"In wilderness is the preservation of the world."

—HENRY DAVID THOREAU

"My greatest dream is to capture the beauty of the New Jersey Pinelands National Reserve, and then, have those images help preserve it."

—ALBERT D. HORNER, PHOTOGRAPHER

CONTENTS

FOREWORD

When first exploring the New Jersey Pine Barrens, I found the experience exciting—and disconcerting. This place looks and feels strikingly different from other forests. The peculiar combination of sand, pines and oaks, red-to-black meandering streams, lichen-covered openings, stream-side savannahs dense with orchids and asphodel, dwarf forests—to capture just some of the habitats—are more varied, beautiful, and interesting than most naïve observers would think possible in New Jersey. Albert Horner's art captures both the beauty and the peculiarity of the Pine Barrens.

Albert came to me and my colleagues at the Pinelands Preservation Alliance when he saw that we shared a common goal—to save the Pine Barrens by getting people interested, attached, and engaged. We mounted a successful exhibition of Albert's work and began a partnership that has grown over the years as he documents the sublime beauty of the Pines, and the hideous dimensions of human abuses of the land and water.

Art, especially writing and photography, has played a vital role in the story of how the Pine Barrens has—so far —been saved from destruction by suburban sprawl. In the 1960s, when people who loved the Pines began to organize to rescue the region from an enormous airport-cum-new-city development endorsed by the governor of the day, John McPhee's seminal book, *The Pine Barrens*, brought people across the United States to see, usually in their mind's eye rather than in person, the fascination of the region and its culture. Photographs and films were essential tools of early activists as they made presentations to community groups, met with officials in Washington and Trenton, and testified at Congressional hearings. *National Geographic* published two important pieces in the 1970s. Political leaders, lead by then-Governor Brendan T. Byrne and Congressman James J. Florio, took up the cause. Finally, in 1978 Congress passed Section 303 of the National Parks and Recreation Act, and in 1979 New Jersey passed the Pinelands Protection Act, together creating the nation's most innovative and effective regional growth management program.

Albert's work is helping all of us who cherish the Pine Barrens to keep the flame alive. His photography allows those who have not been able to visit in person, or who have not explored all of the Pine Barrens' different habitats, to experience its beauty, serenity, and variety—sparking the kind of attachment so many of us have for places we have not seen but need to know still survive and flourish. Albert's work also brings people like me, who know the Pine Barrens well, to a greater awareness of perspectives, colors, light, and life within the forests.

I hope everyone who enjoys this book also appreciates that the Pine Barrens is highly *accessible*. This, of course, is an asset and a vulnerability. More than 20 million people live within sixty miles of the preserve, and innumerable paved and sand roads crisscross the forests due to its history of settlement and exploitation since the colonial era. This means people of all abilities can experience this unique wilderness, whether they are hikers, kayakers and canoeists, strollers, or need to stay close to a vehicle. To experience Albert's vision through your own eyes, you may need to get up very early in the morning, but you can do it.

I love to look at Albert's photographs. But I also value his work as an activist because it is an incalculably valuable agent of conservation. Whether he is communicating the transcendent beauty of a bend in the Mullica River on a Fall morning, or documenting the depredations of reckless off-roaders on public conservation lands, his work helps people understand why the New Jersey Pine Barrens is so valuable, and so vulnerable.

Carleton Montgomery
Executive Director
Pineland Preservation Alliance

PREFACE

This monograph has been a dream of mine since I started seriously recording the magnificent landscape of the New Jersey Pinelands National Reserve. Morning after brilliant morning, while setting up my equipment, I would say to myself, "Why am I the only one here to see this?" The more I photographed, the more I became an advocate for the Pine Barrens. By publishing this book, I am hoping more people will become aware of this wonderful natural resource and work toward preserving it for generations to come.

ACKNOWLEDGMENTS

First I wish to thank my wife, Diane, for never complaining about my pre-dawn stirrings on the days I go out to shoot, the endless camera equipment purchases, the late arrivals home, and my tramping around the house in muddy boots, but instead praising my work and making it all worthwhile.

Ralph Dahl and Barbara Spector for their insightful haikus and poems that have added a rich dimension to my images.

Pinelands Preservation Alliance, directed by Carleton Montgomery, and the New Jersey Conservation Foundation, led by Michele S. Byers. Both individuals, and their organizations, have worked tirelessly to preserve and protect the Pinelands and many other thousands of acres in this almost built-out state. Without their efforts I am convinced New Jersey would be one huge parking lot.

Schiffer Publishing, for believing that this book was important enough to publish and distribute.

And, of course, to all the family, friends and patrons who continually support my work and encourage me to live my dream of making fine-art photographic images.

INTRODUCTION

For many of us, New Jersey's Pine Barrens need no introduction. For those who know it, this special landscape has inspired great love and passion.

Most people, however, don't even know that this wondrous part of New Jersey even exists—a place that covers more than twenty-five percent of the state, overlies 17 trillion gallons of fresh water, and is home to hundreds of rare plant and animal species, including the Jersey Devil!

Albert Horner's photographic essay is an invitation to discover, explore, and fall in love with the Pine Barrens. His photos capture the essence of its beauty and mystery, and will undoubtedly encourage new visitors to adopt the Pine Barrens as their own intimate wild haven.

In an era of cellphones, iPads, and virtual reality devices, how can we keep people attached to nature? What sparks a sense of curiosity and wonder in this technological age? How can we be sure that future generations will love the land as we do today?

Photographs are a powerful visual tool, and Albert's book is just what is needed to spark curiosity and desire. His images capture the astonishing richness of the colors, light, and textures of a myriad Pine Barrens landscapes—rivers and streams, misty bogs, lakes, spongs, and cedar swamps—in all seasons and times of the day.

I was lucky to land deep in the Pine Barrens fresh out of college from the Rocky Mountains of Colorado. I was grieving for the mountains, but the Pine Barrens took my breath away. I got "sand in my shoes" in no time and have been in love with the Pine Barrens ever since. Apple Pie Hill, the Forked River Mountains, Arney's Mount, and many other "mountains" became intimate friends as I spent hours exploring and getting lost in the vast pine forests and miles of sandy roads.

It's a place where timelessness and wildness seep into your senses and entice you back time and time again.

John McPhee explored the Pine Barrens forty years ago, and was so inspired that he wrote *The Pine Barrens*, one of his most popular books. His words changed the course of history for the Pine Barrens and I hope that Albert's photographs will continue that trajectory.

Michele S. Byers
Executive Director
New Jersey Conservation Foundation

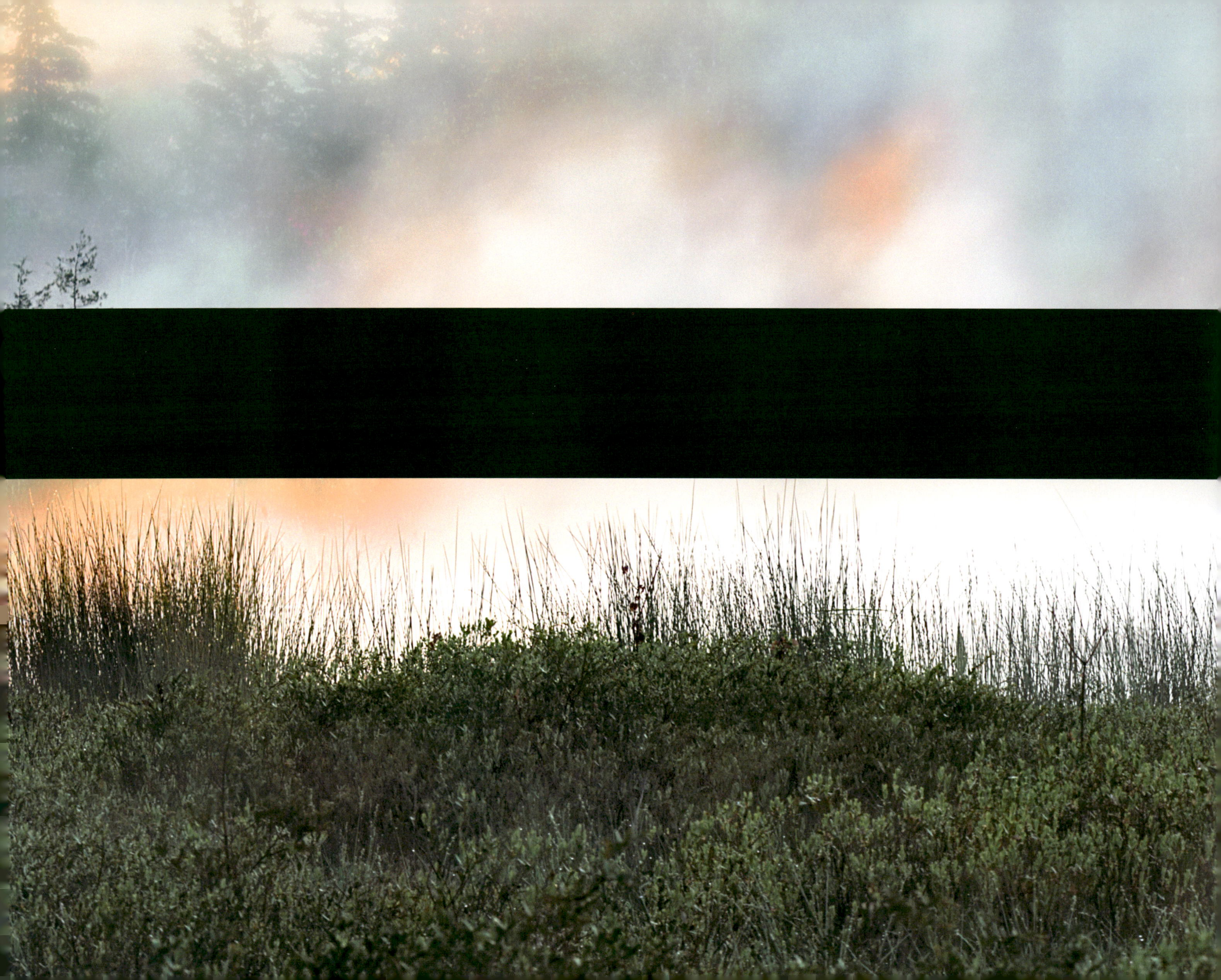

PINELANDS

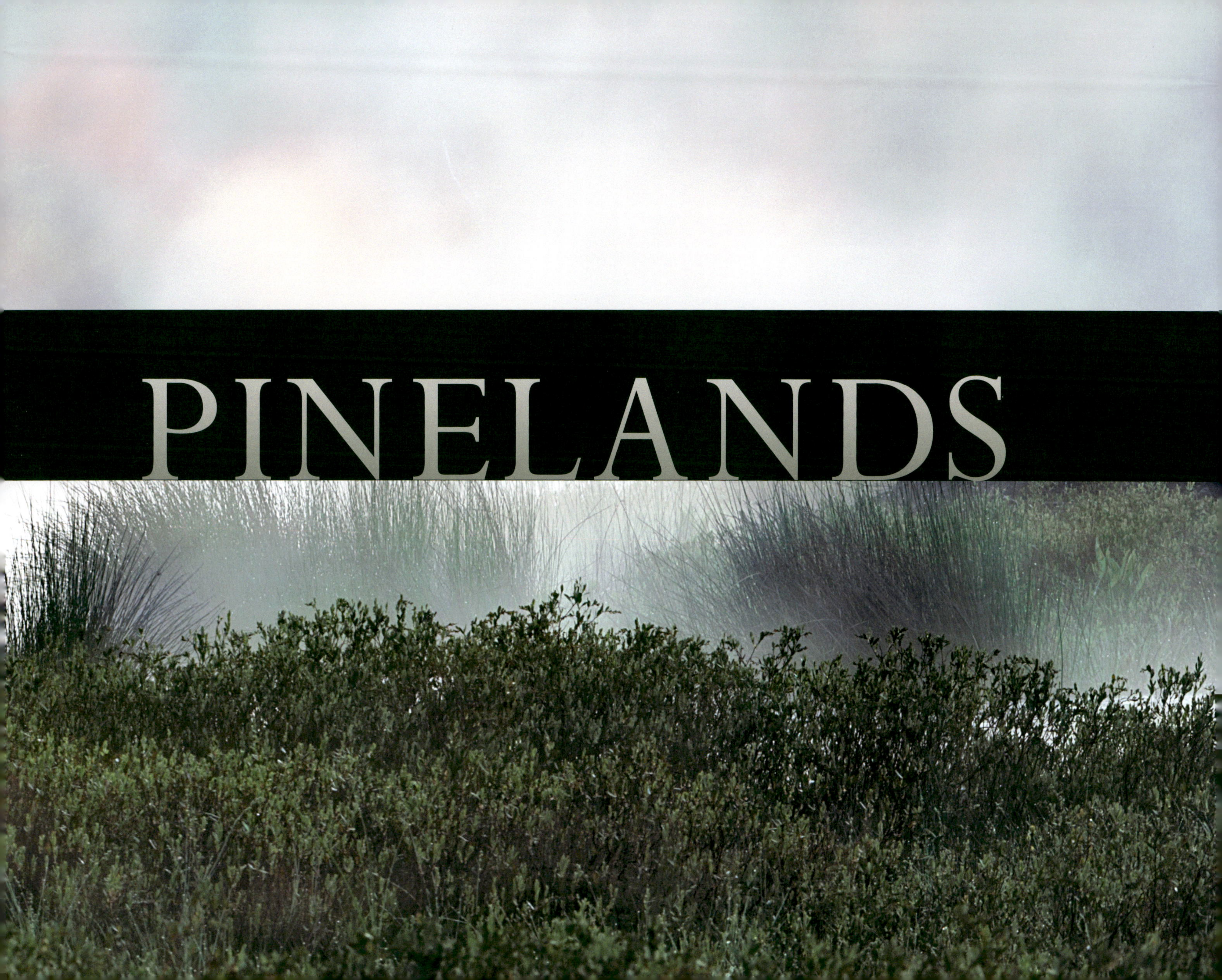

"The love of wilderness is more than a hunger for what is always beyond our reach; it is also an expression of loyalty to the earth, the only home we shall ever know; the only paradise we ever need—if we only had the eyes to see."

—Edward Abbey

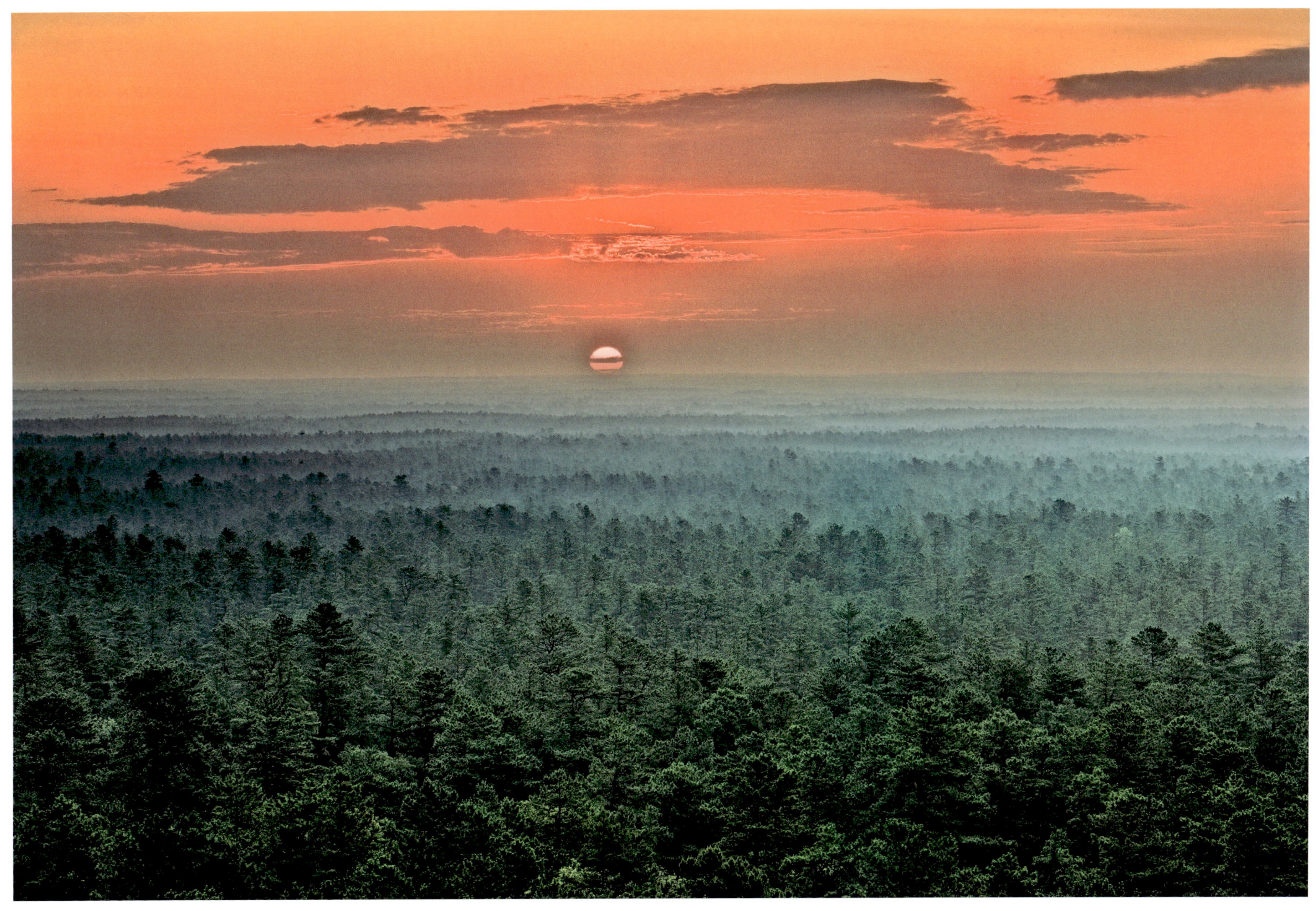

Sunrise, Apple Pie Hill, Chatsworth

—BLACK ELK

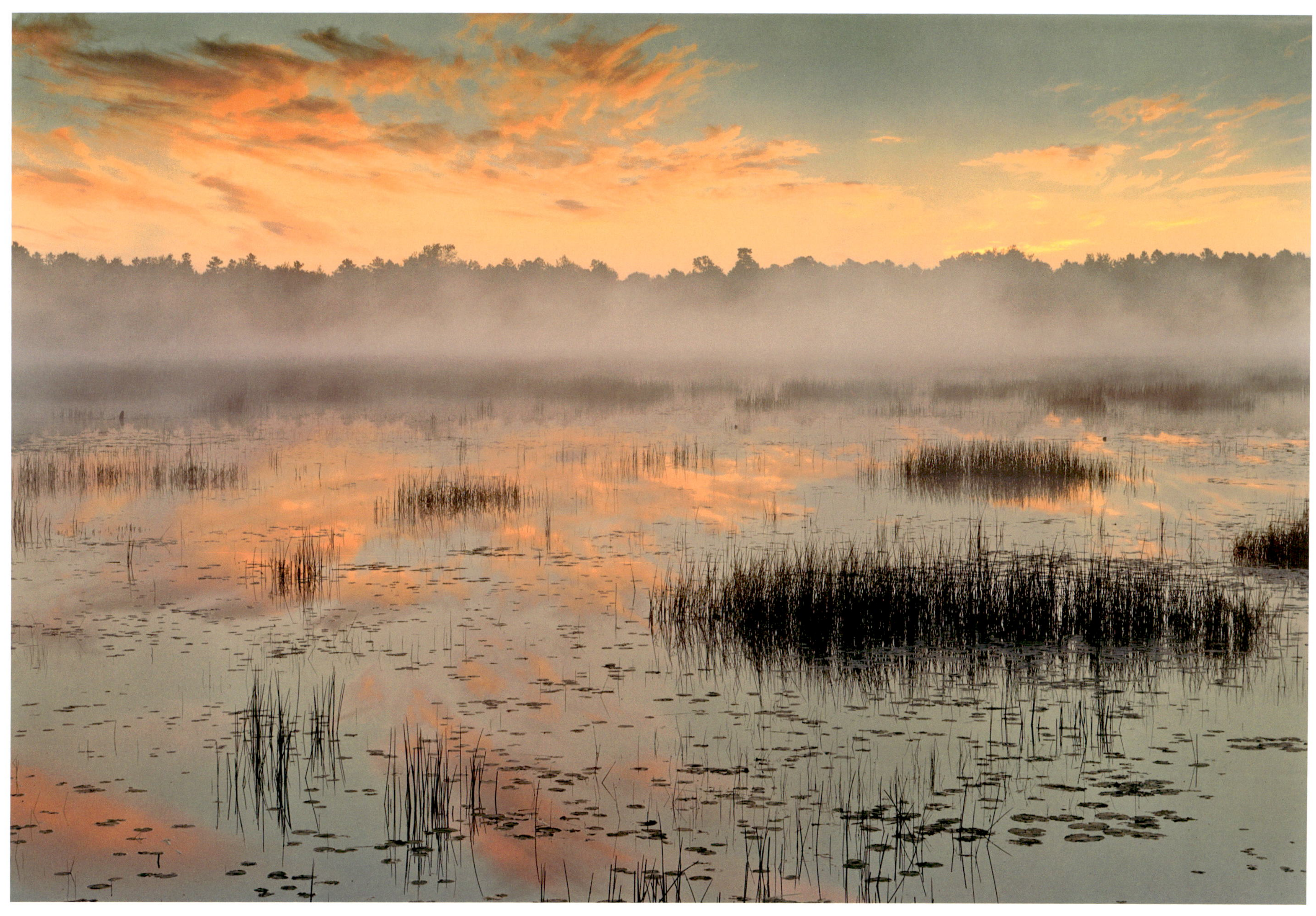

Reflections, Franklin Parker Preserve

An abandoned old bog
shabby and useless
bears a half-moon beauty

—RALPH DAHLE

Half Moon Bog, Friendship Bogs, Wharton State Forest

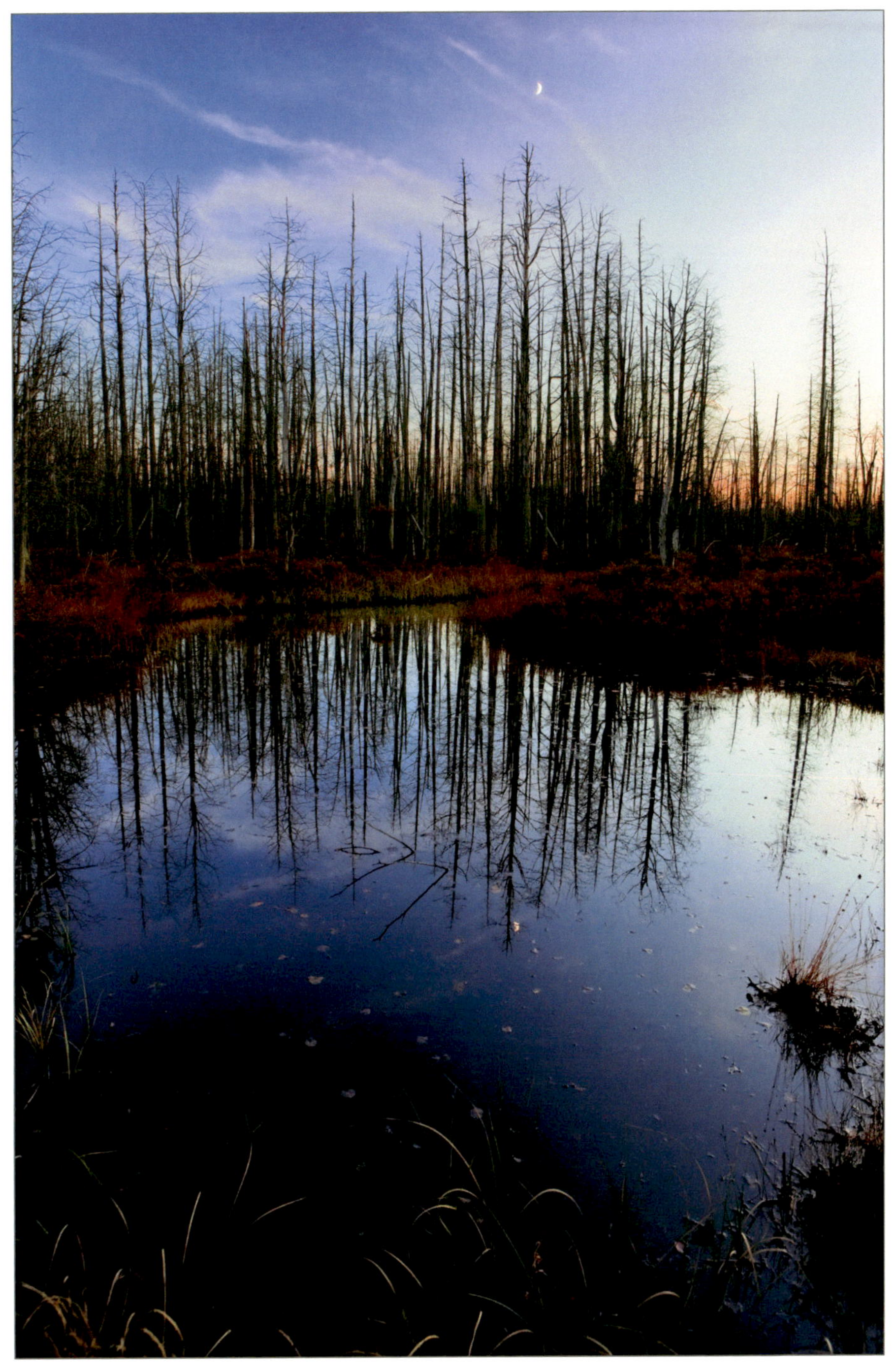

"*Nature always wears the colors of the spirit.*"

—RALPH WALDO EMERSON

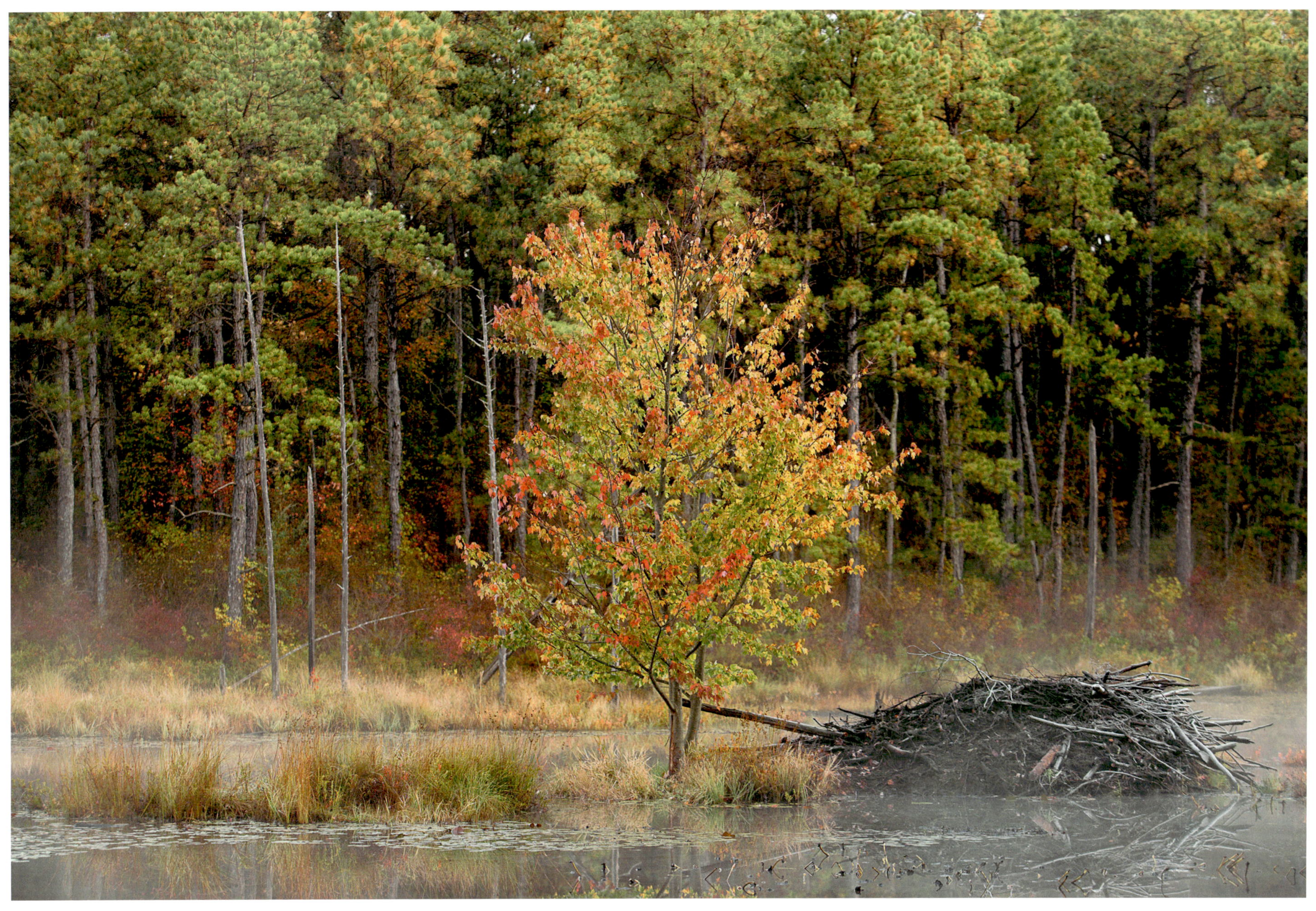

Robert's Branch Pond, Wharton State Forest

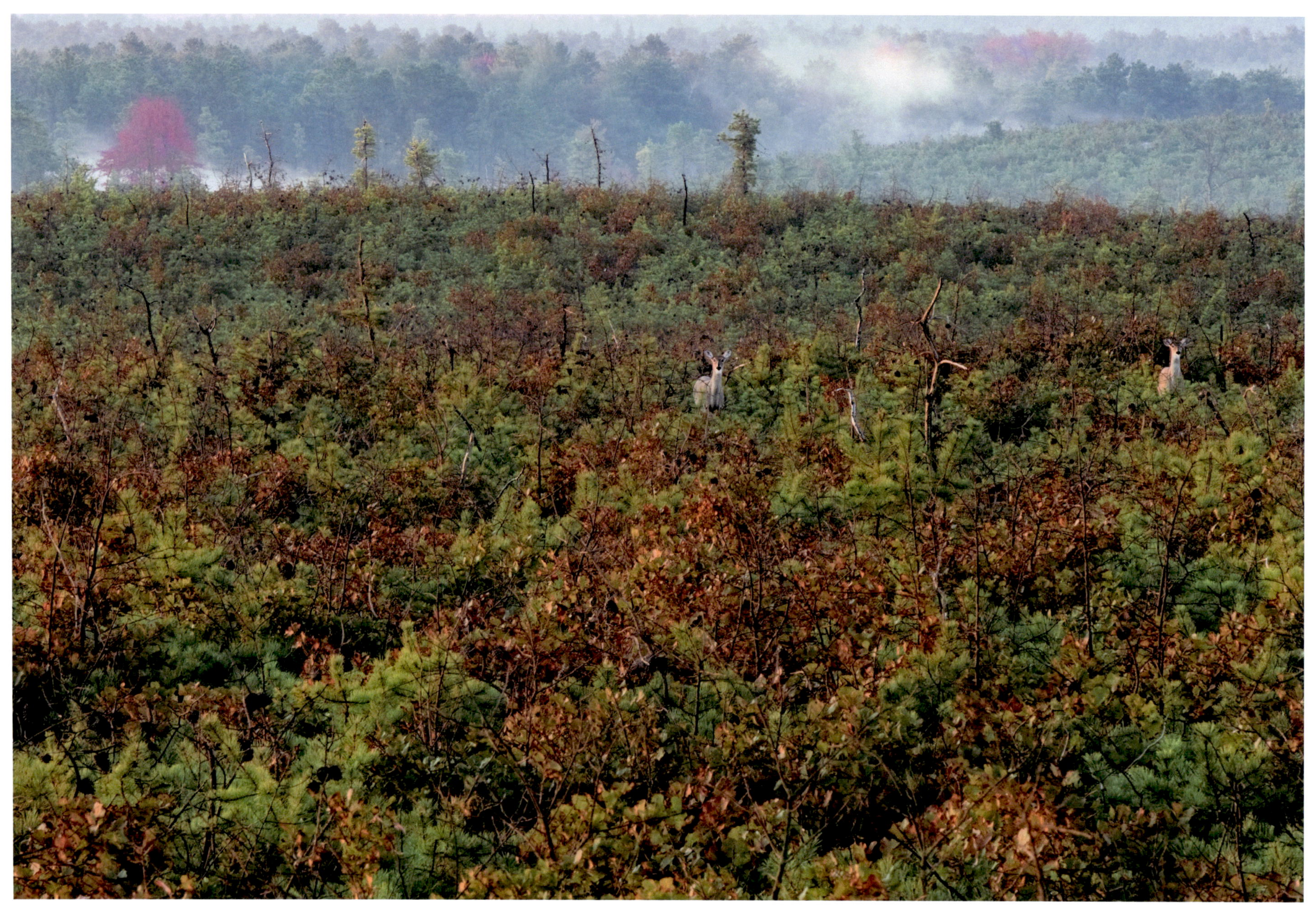

East Plains Deer, The East Plains

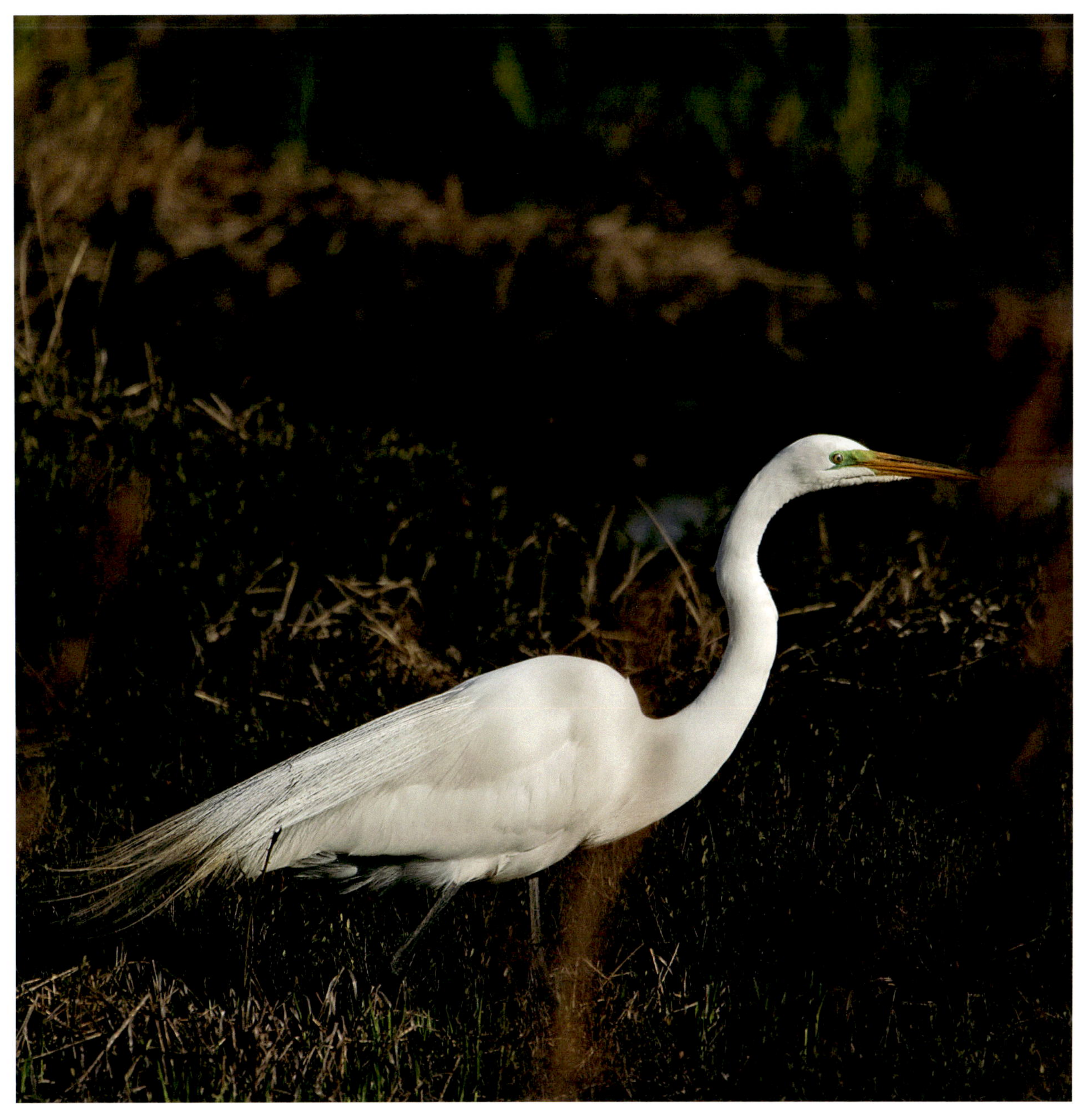

Great Egret, Franklin Parker Preserve

A ceiling of trees
cascades over riverbanks
showing off their colors

—Barbara Spector

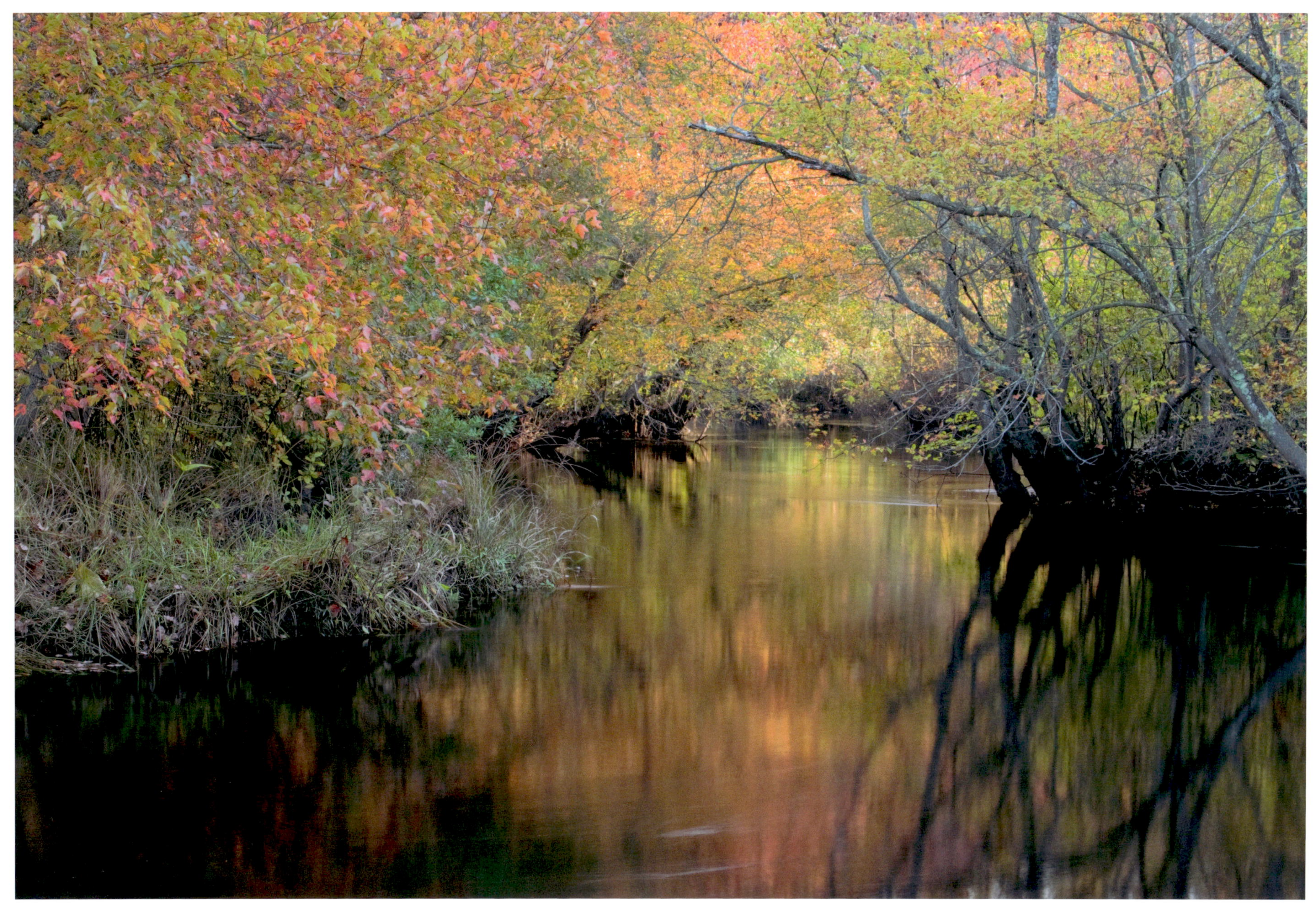

Batsto Canopy, Batsto River, Wharton State Forest

Pastel pastoral
a mist-driven dawn
washes out an autumn sky

—RALPH DAHLE

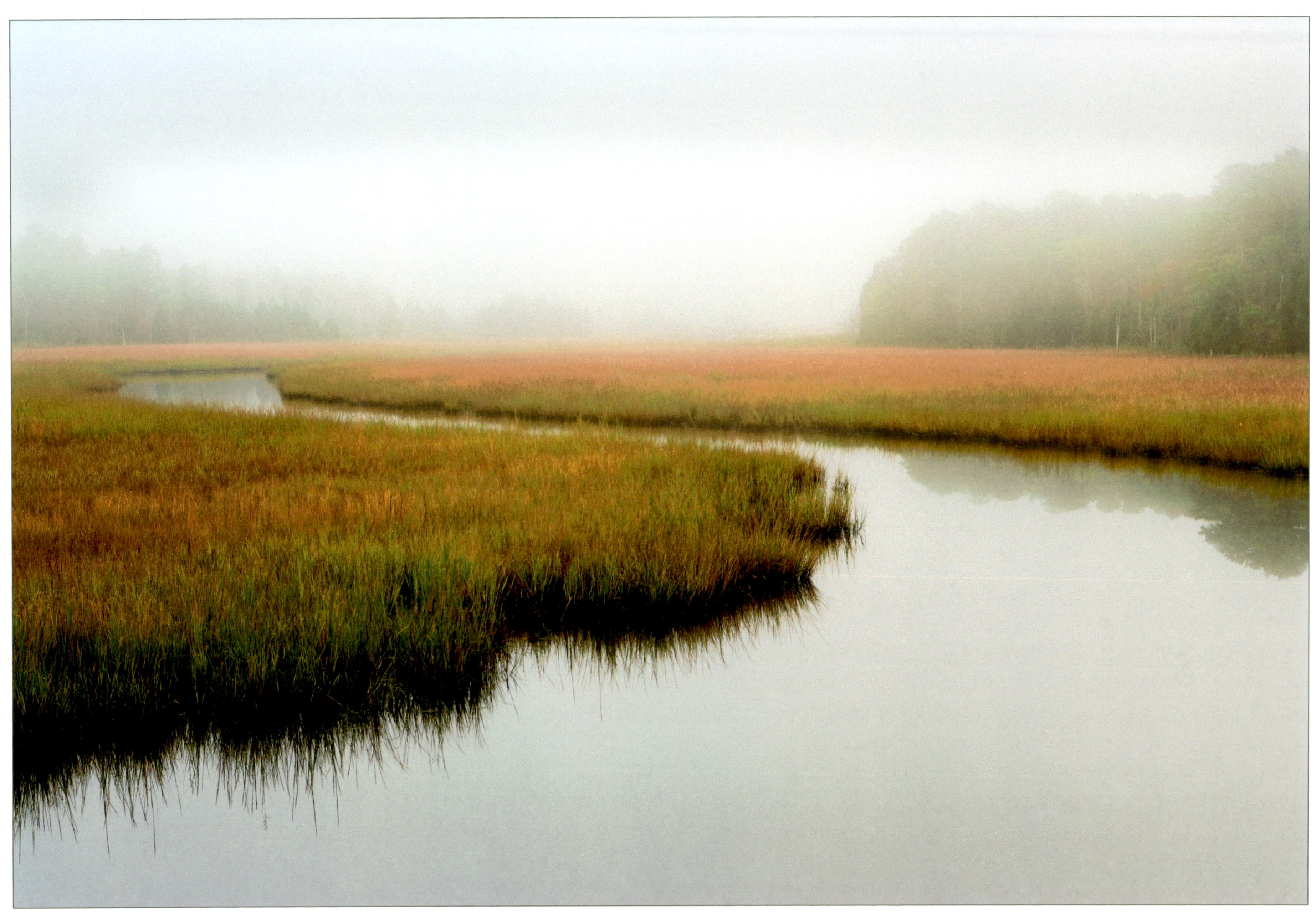

Job's Creek, New Gretna

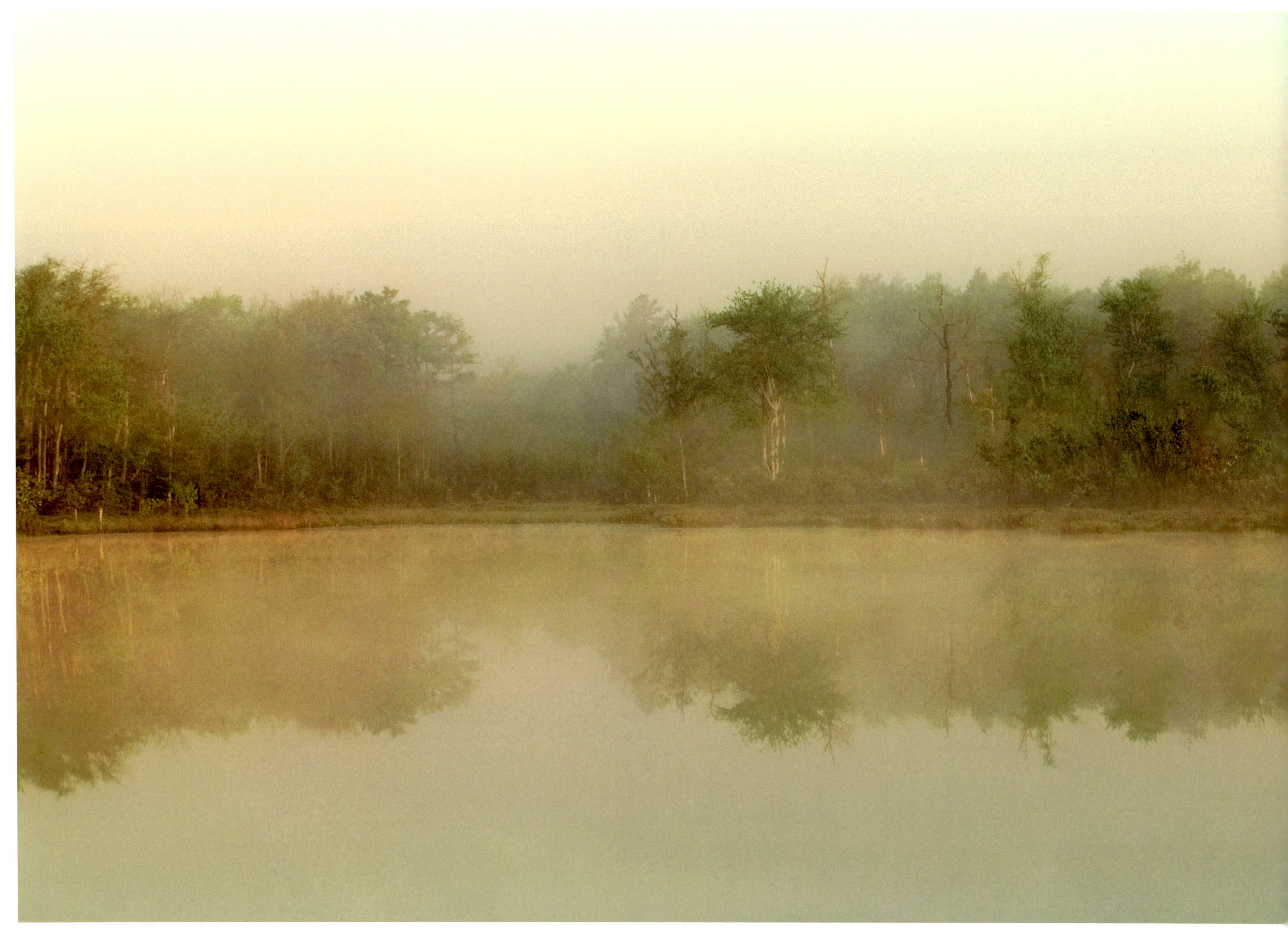

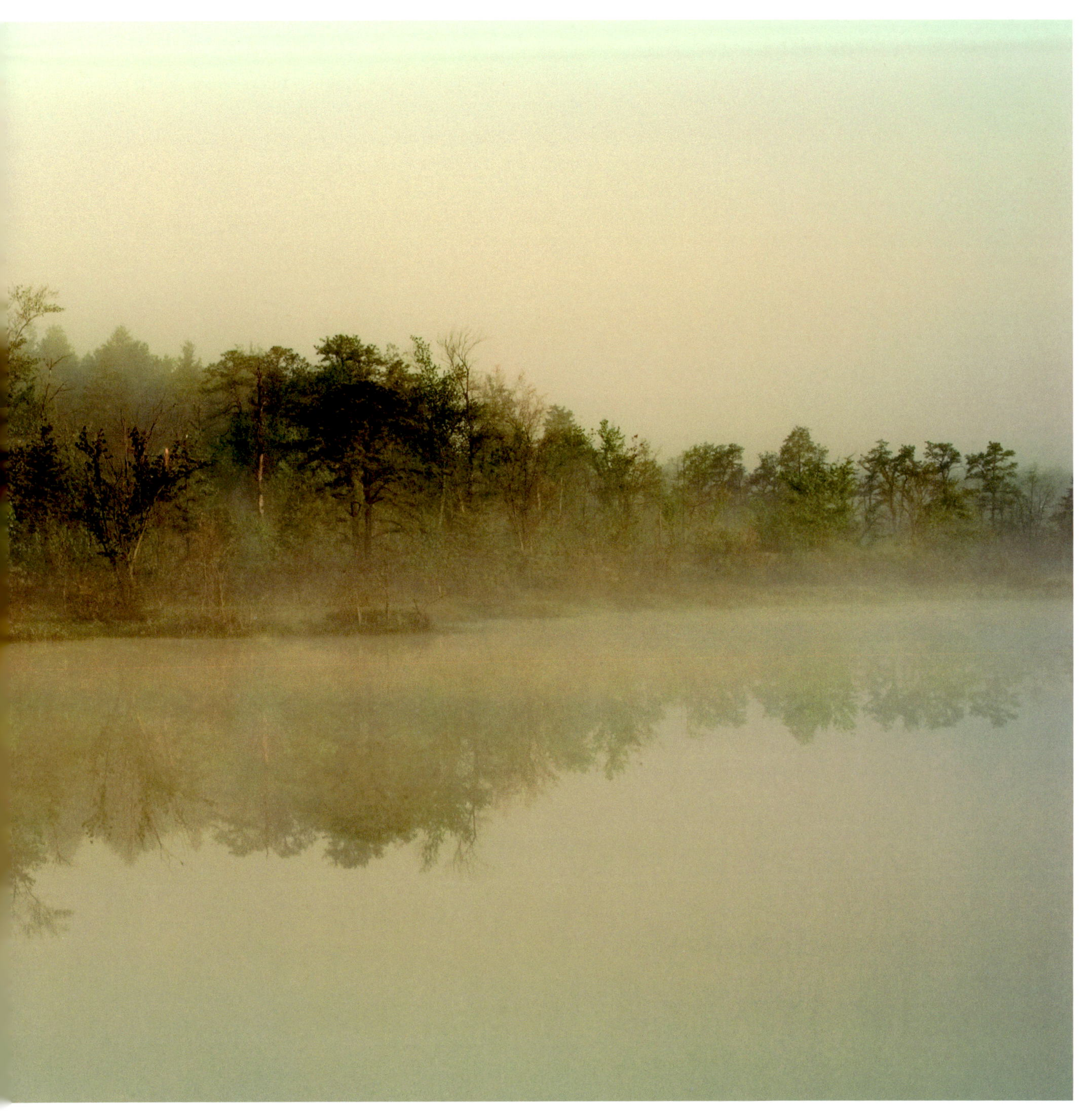

Breaking Through, West Jersey Cranberry Meadows

“Land really is the best art.”

—Andy Warhol

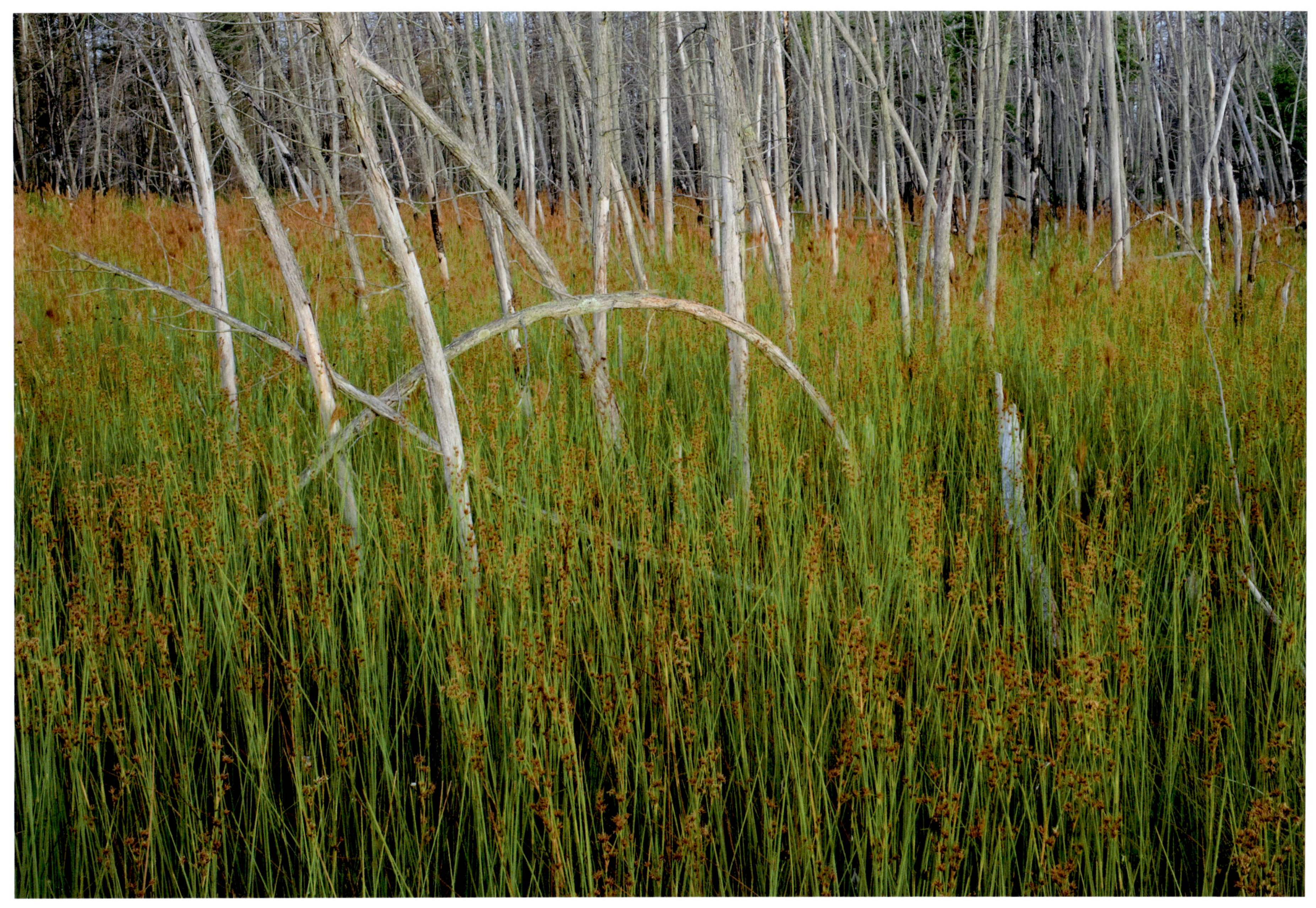

Savanna, Mullica River, Wharton State Forest

Autumn's cedar maze
so lost
in the thick of it

—RALPH DAHLE

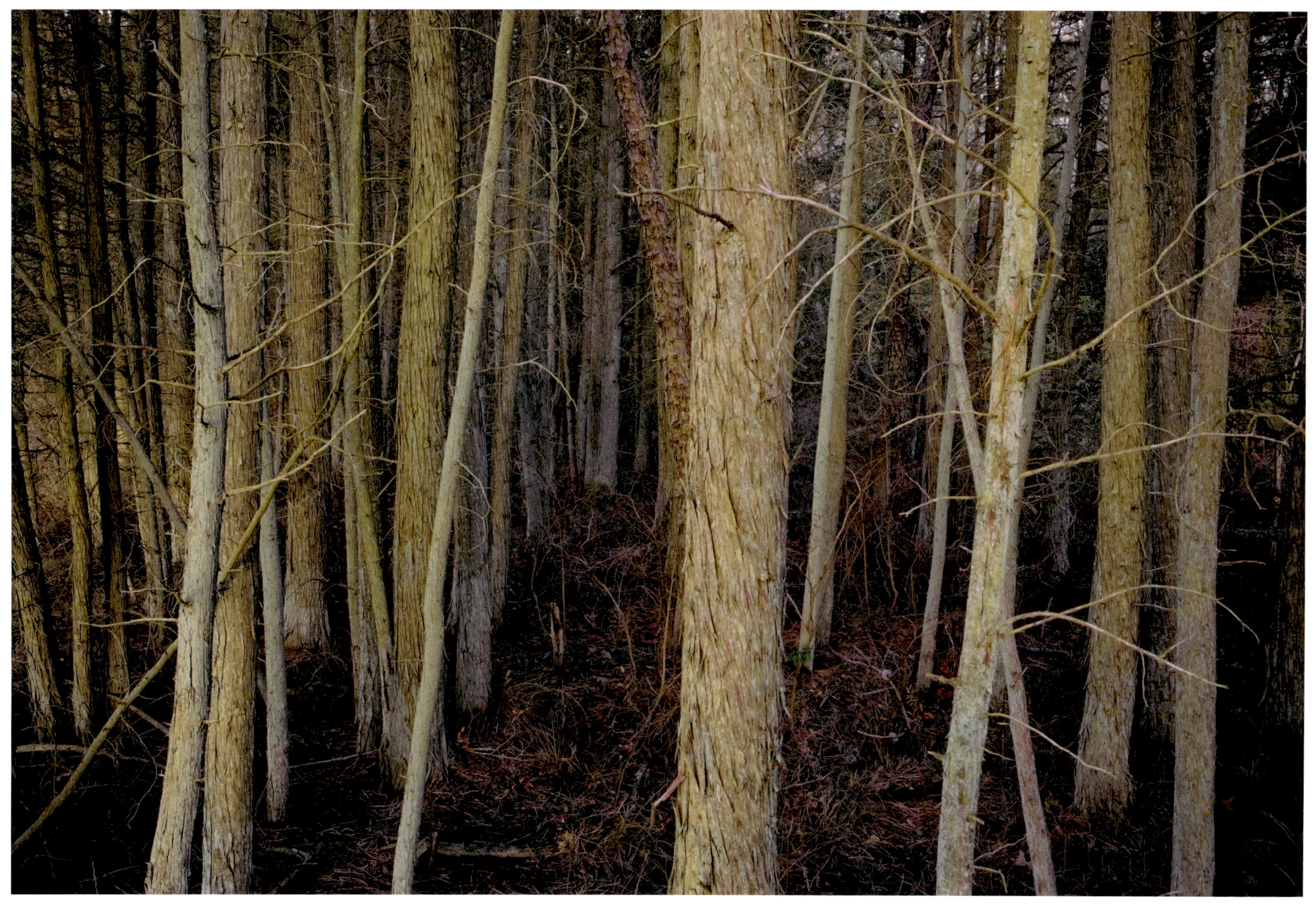

Cedars at Calico Ridge, Oswego River

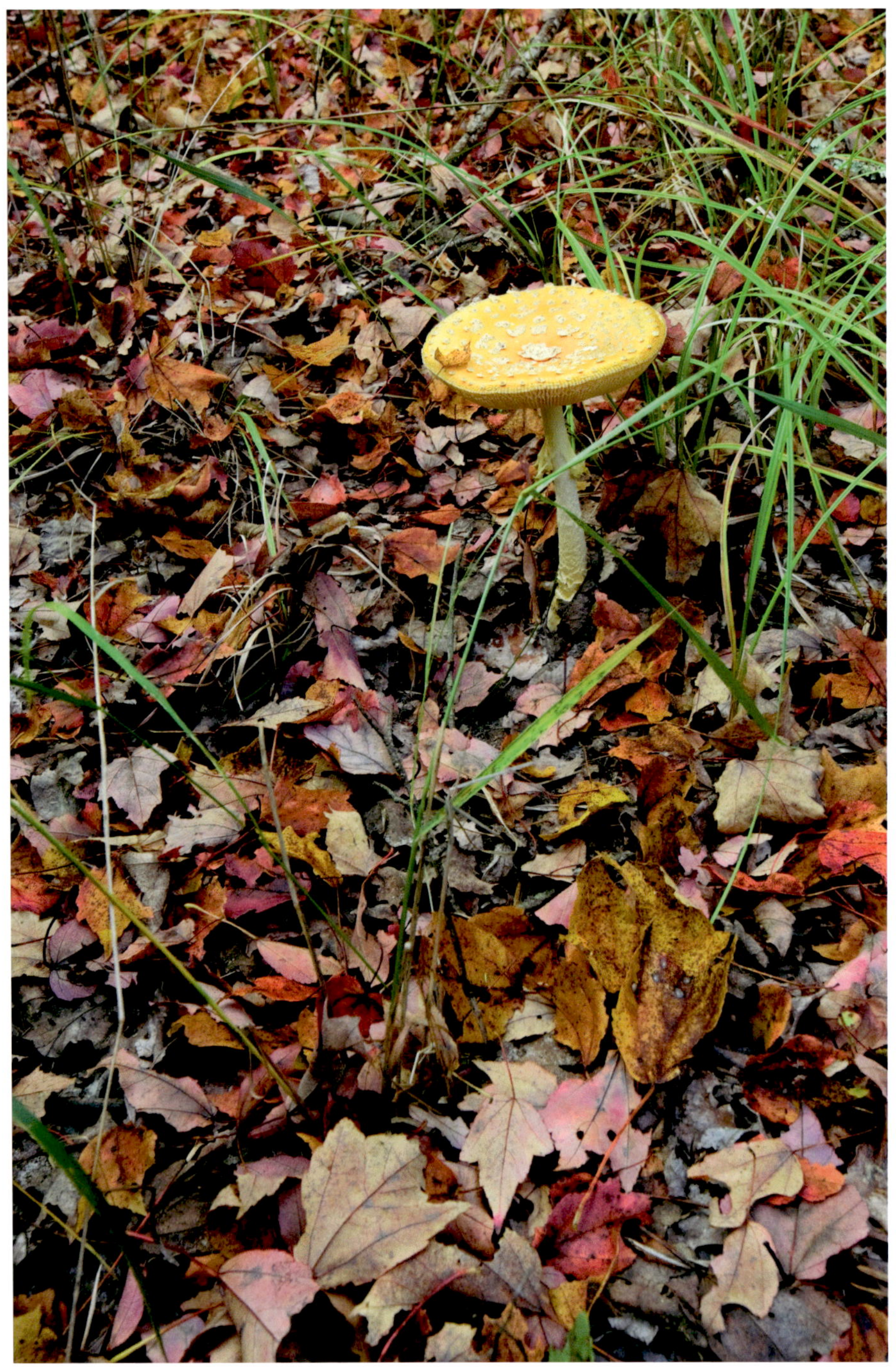

Shroom, bank of the Batsto River

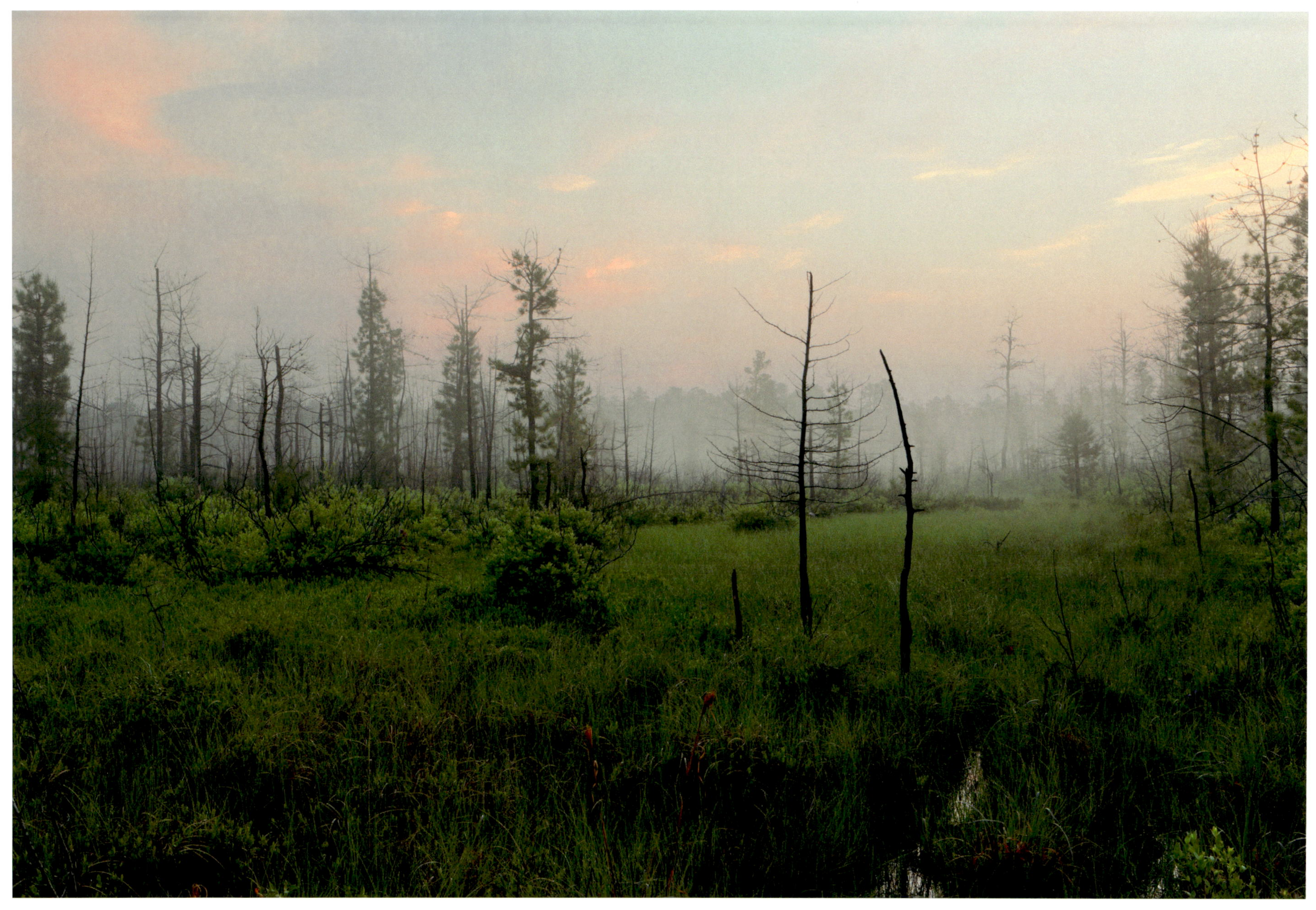

Pinelands Lowlands, Mullica River, Wharton State Forest

Beauty is buried
here beneath blackened remains
to burgeon next Spring

—Ralph Dahle

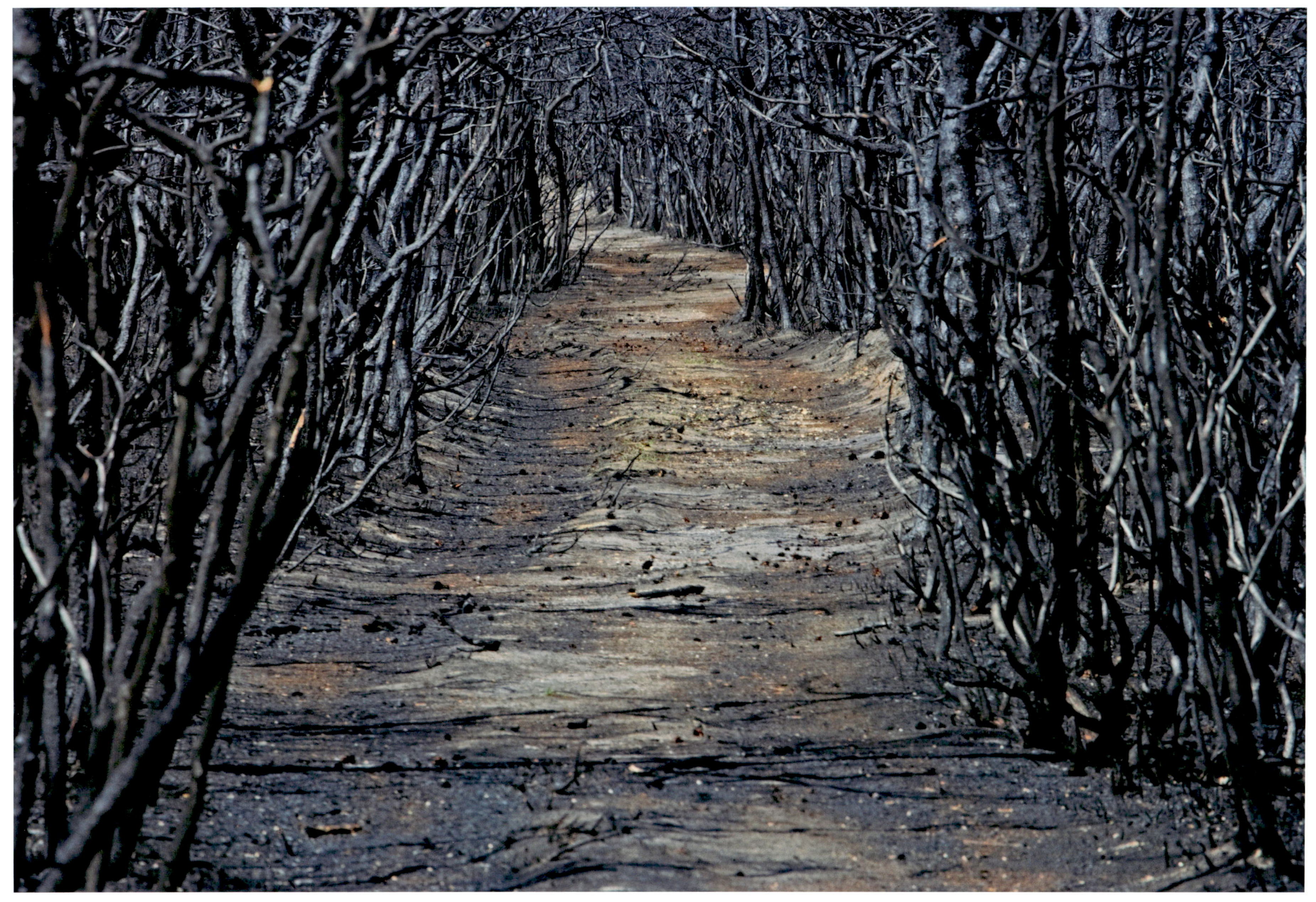

Fire!, The East Plains

Grass rushes fast, first
To gold those young trees haloed
Fore an ancient green

—RALPH DAHLE

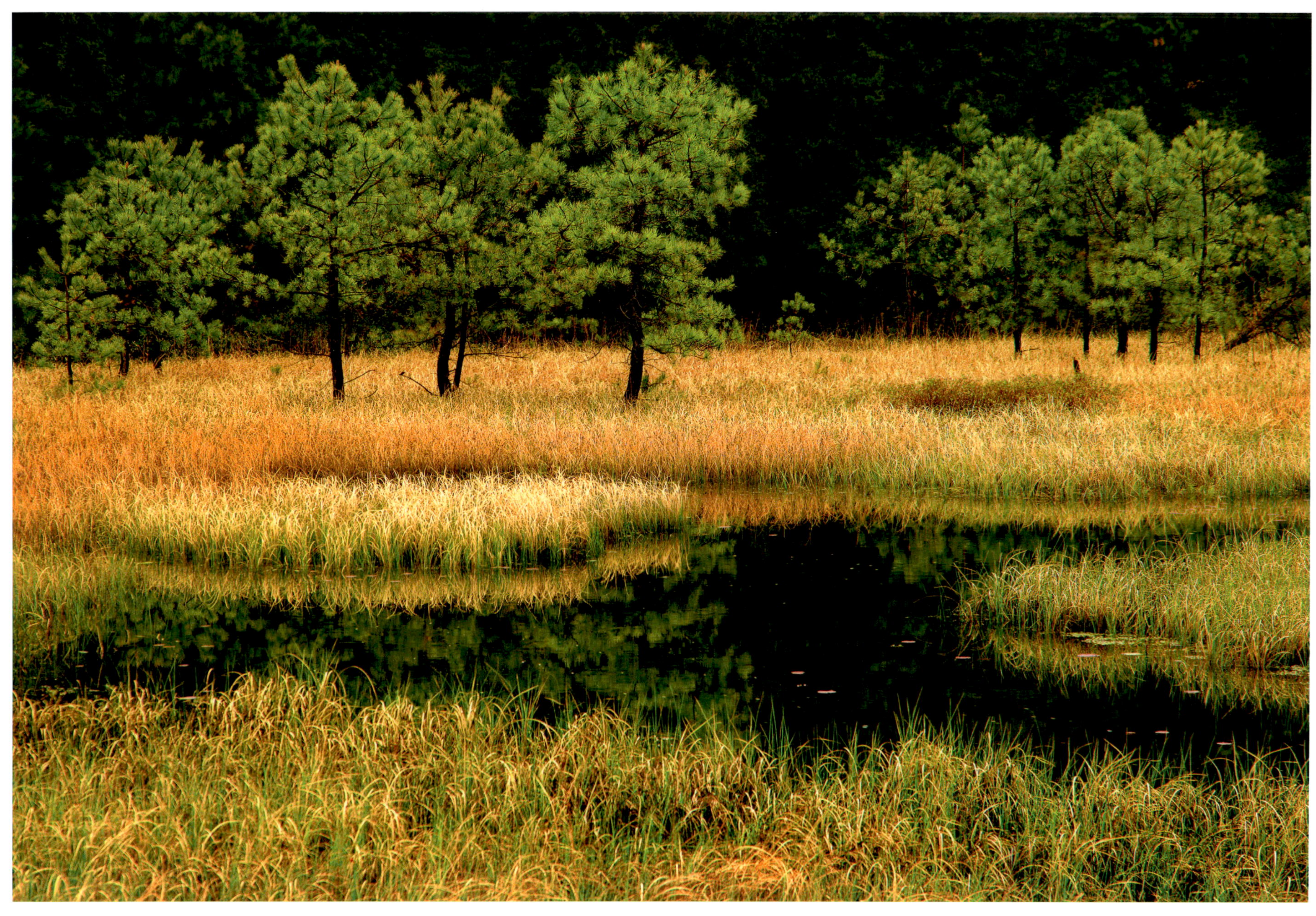

Friendship Trees, Friendship Bogs, Wharton State Forest

"*If we do not begin to preserve them [native wildflowers],
the time will come when they will become extinct and
live only in history.*"

—THEODORE PAYNE

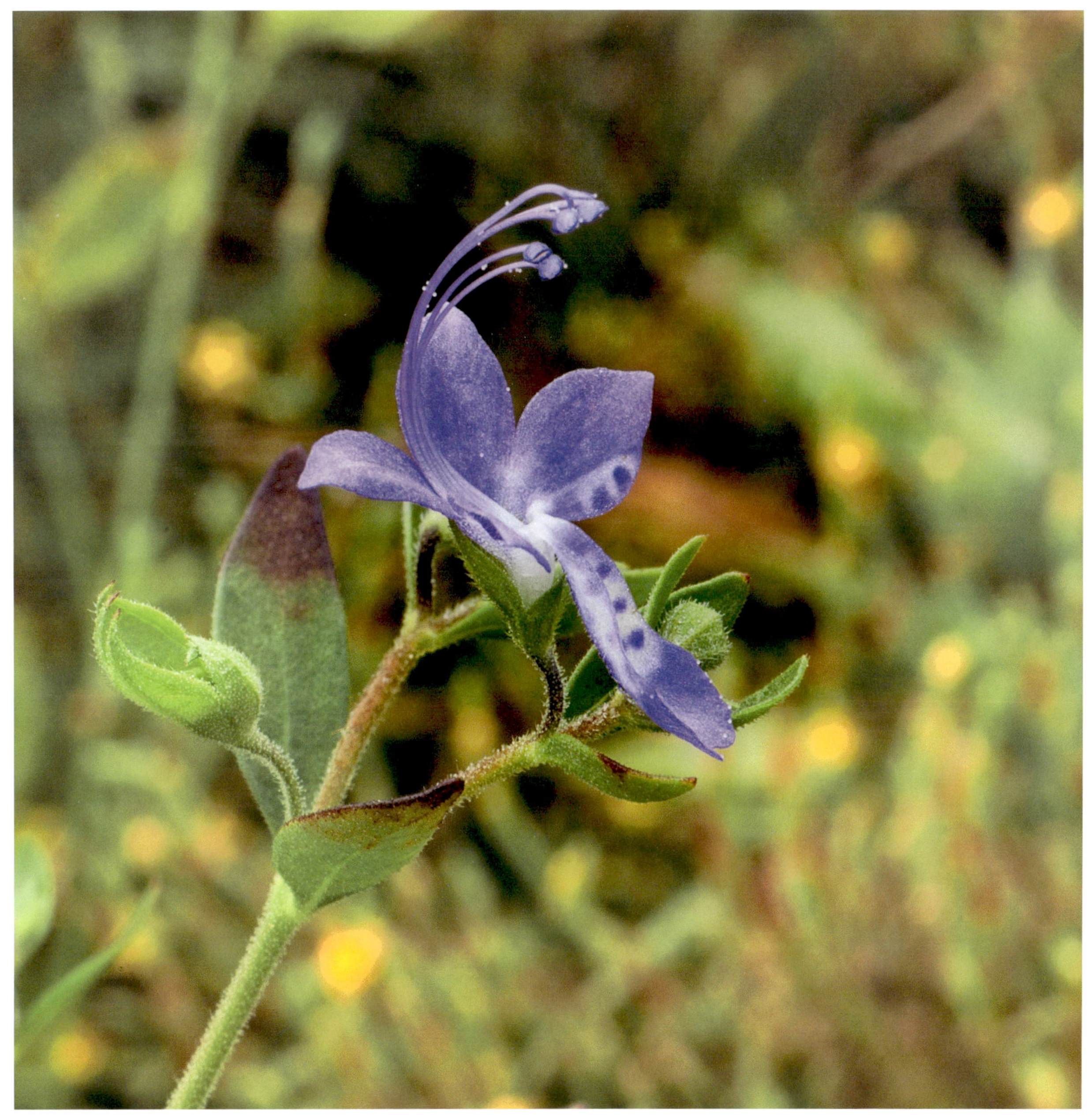

Blue Curl, Franklin Parker Preserve

Moored in morning mist
a beaver lodge holds
living beauties

—RALPH DAHLE

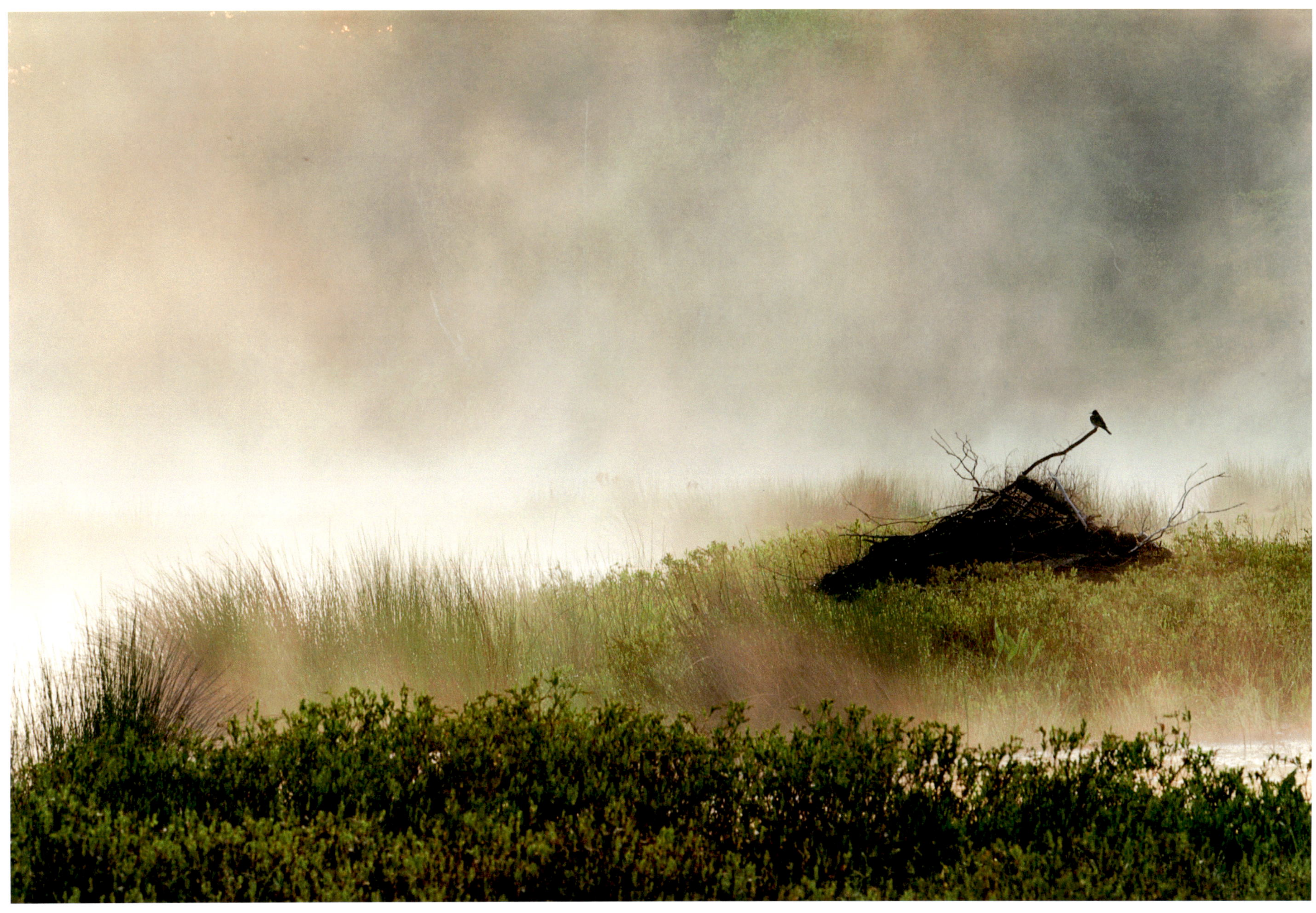

Meadows Beaver Morning, Chatsworth

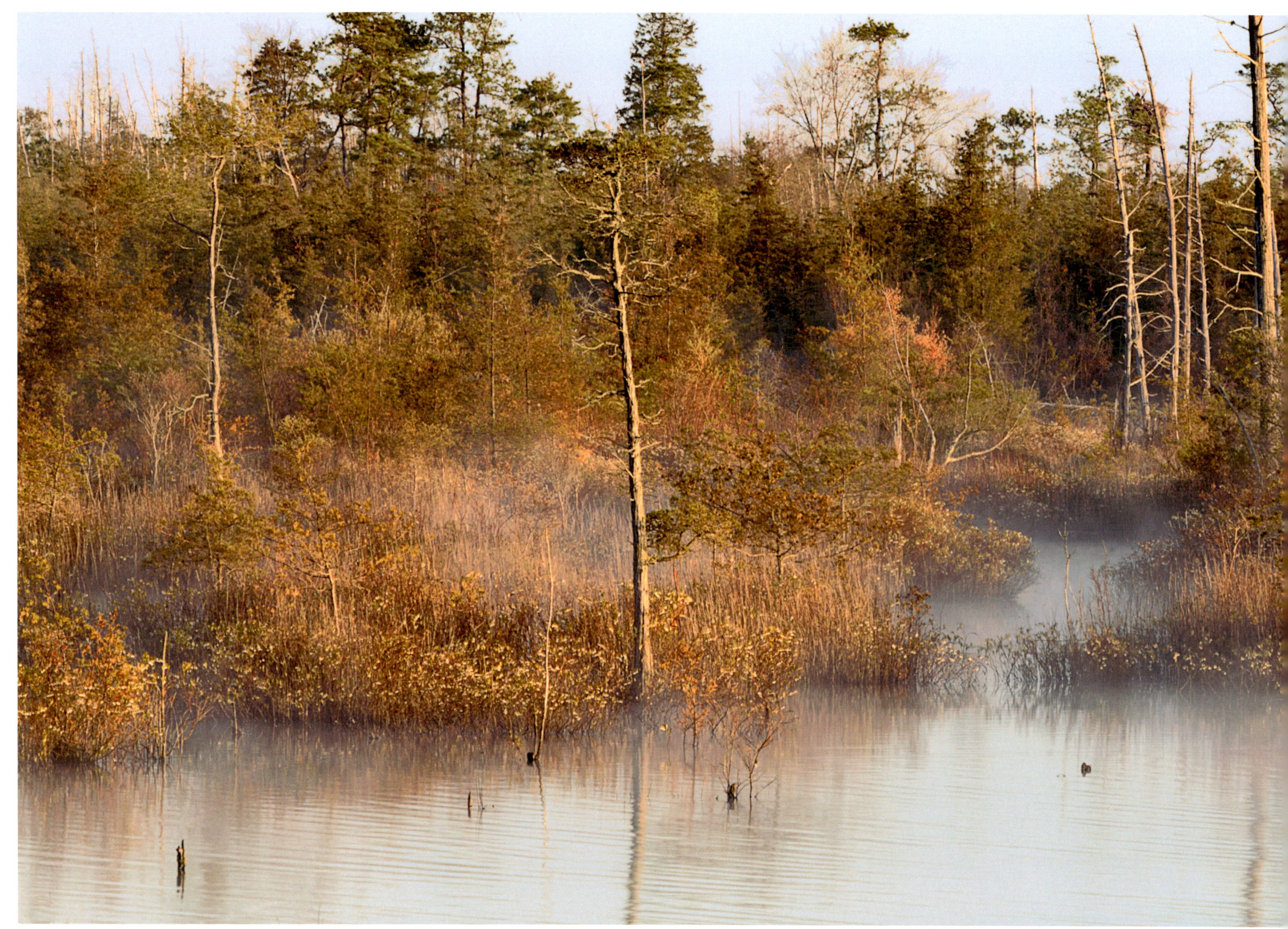

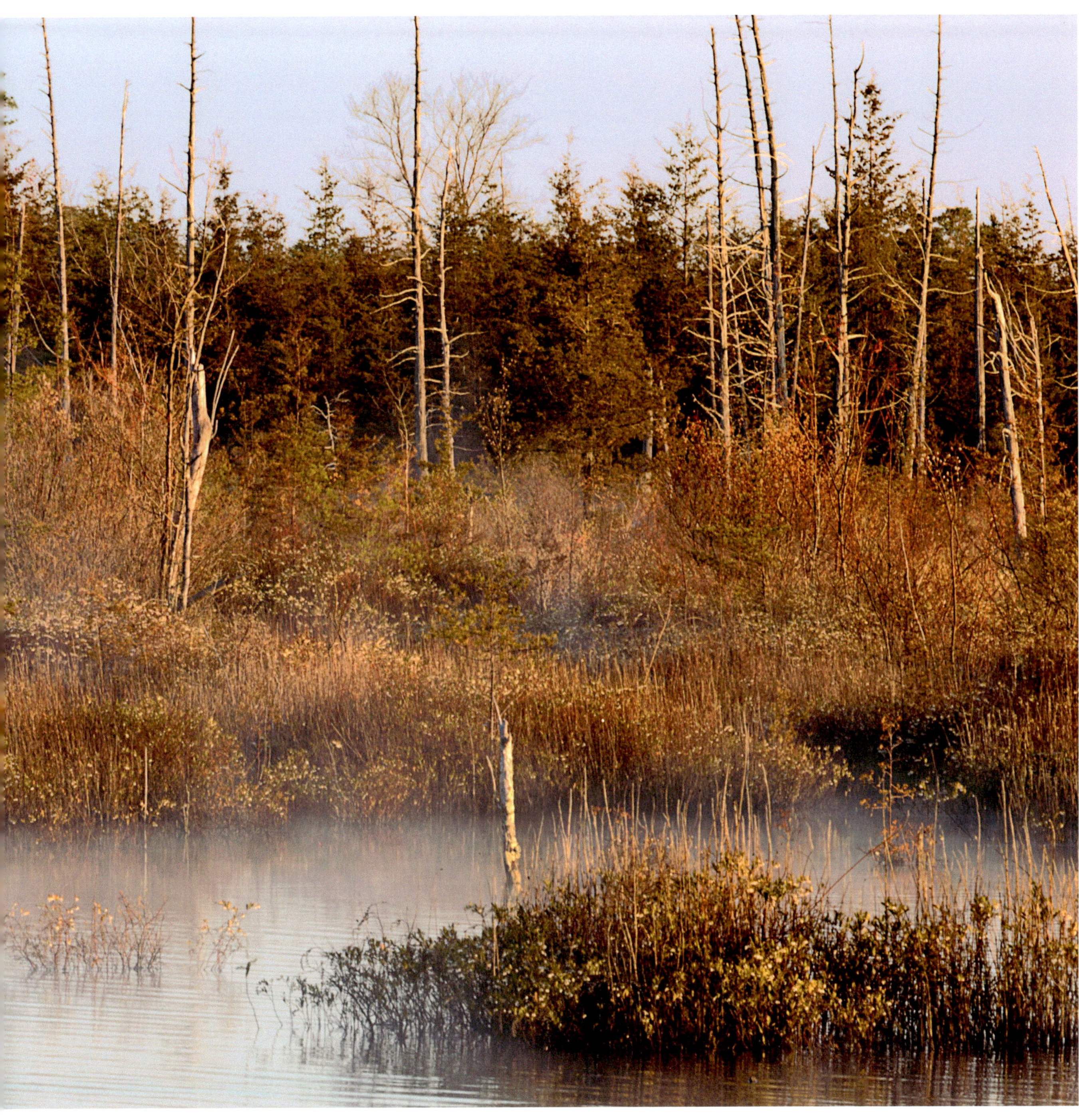

Spring Bog, Wading River

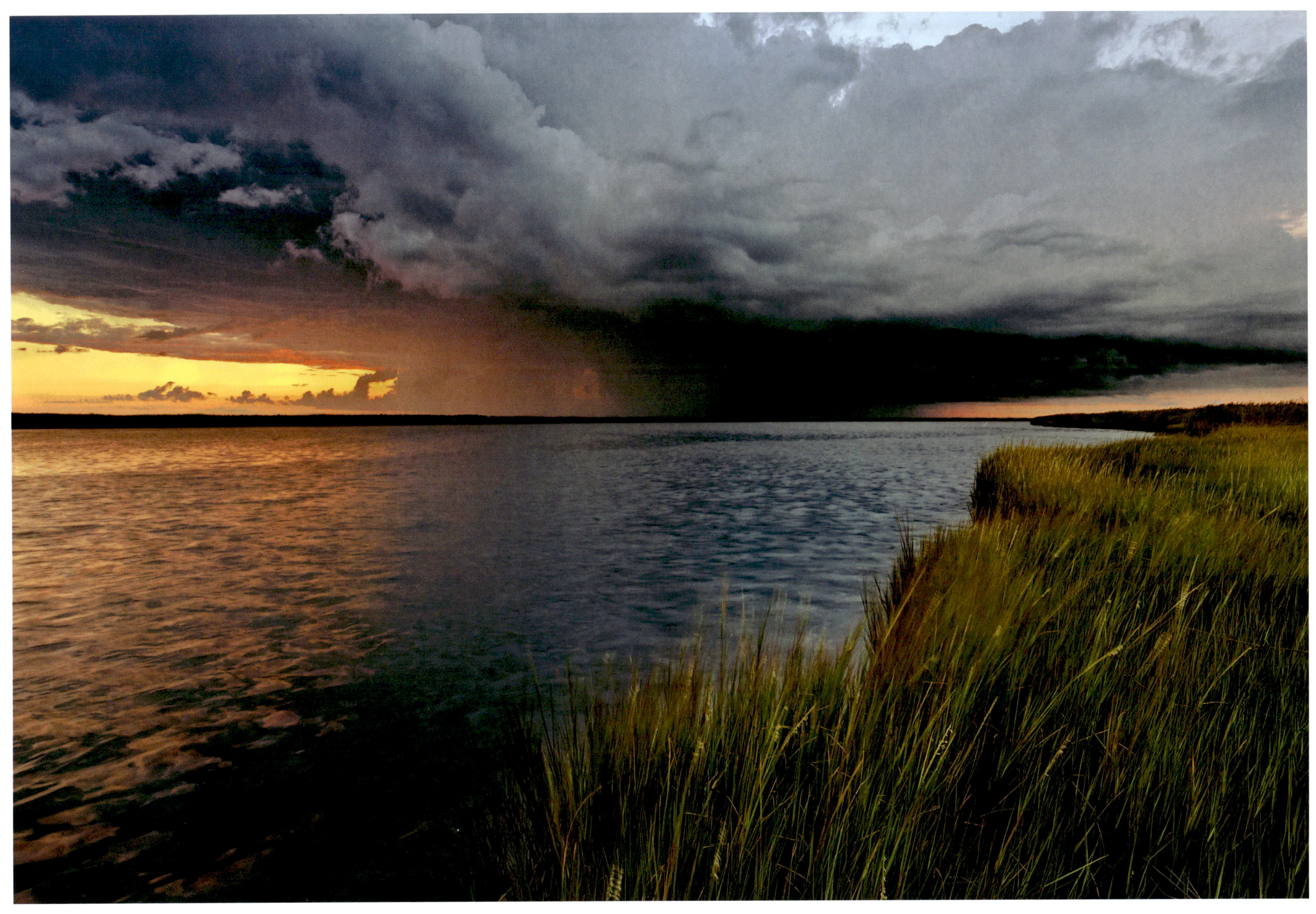

Retreating Storm, Clark's Landing

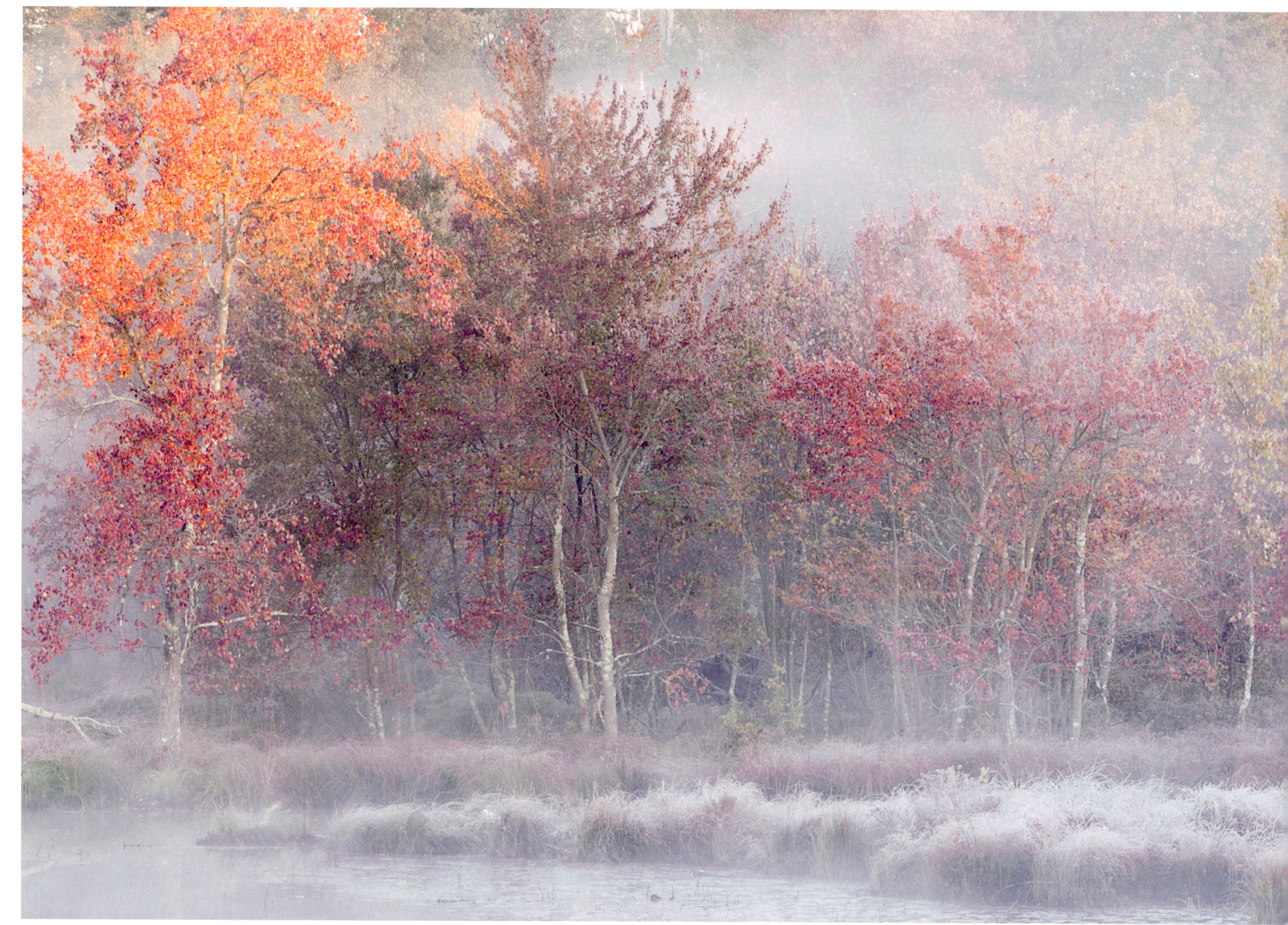

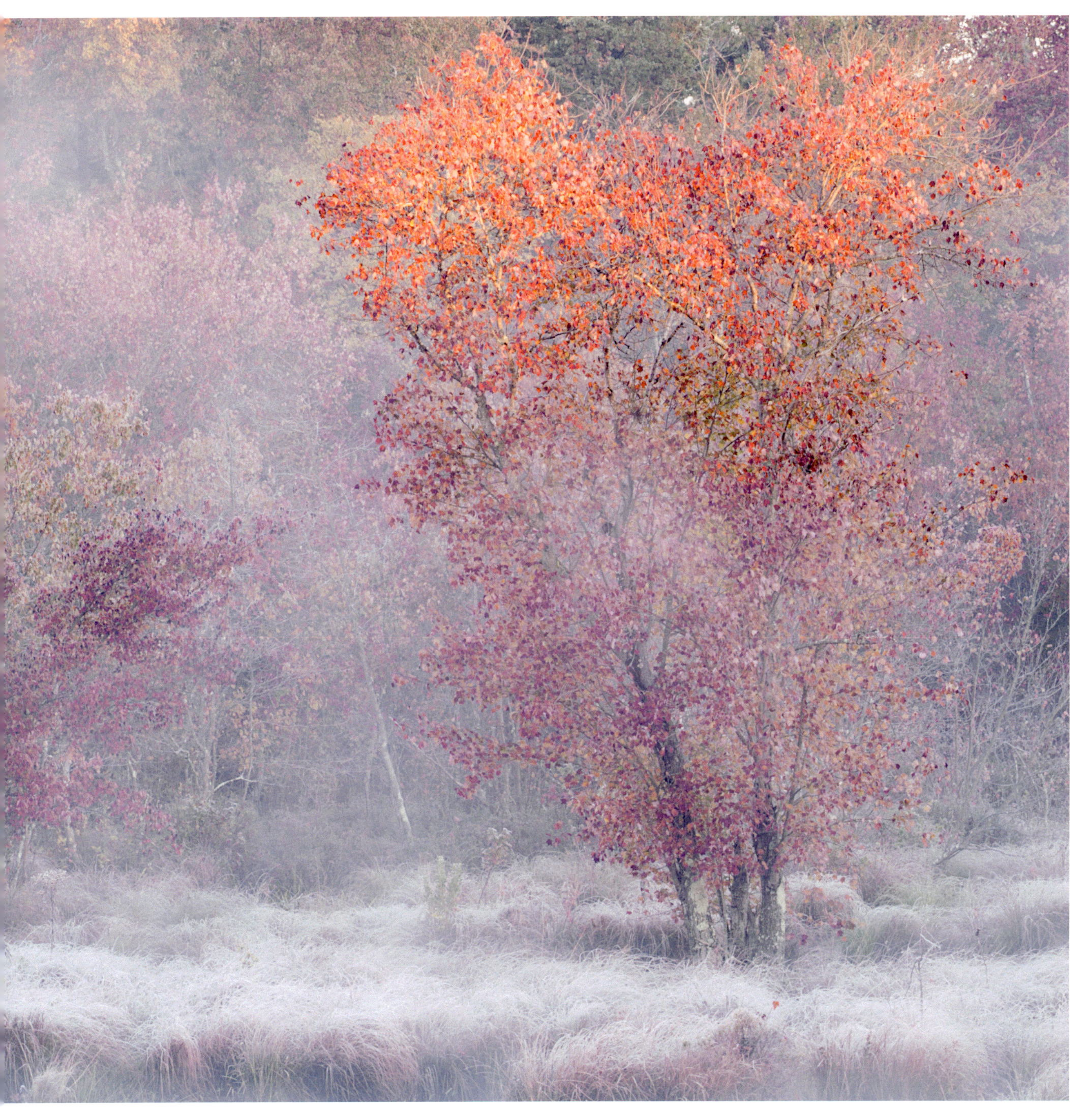

Mullica Maples II, Mullica River, Wharton State Forest

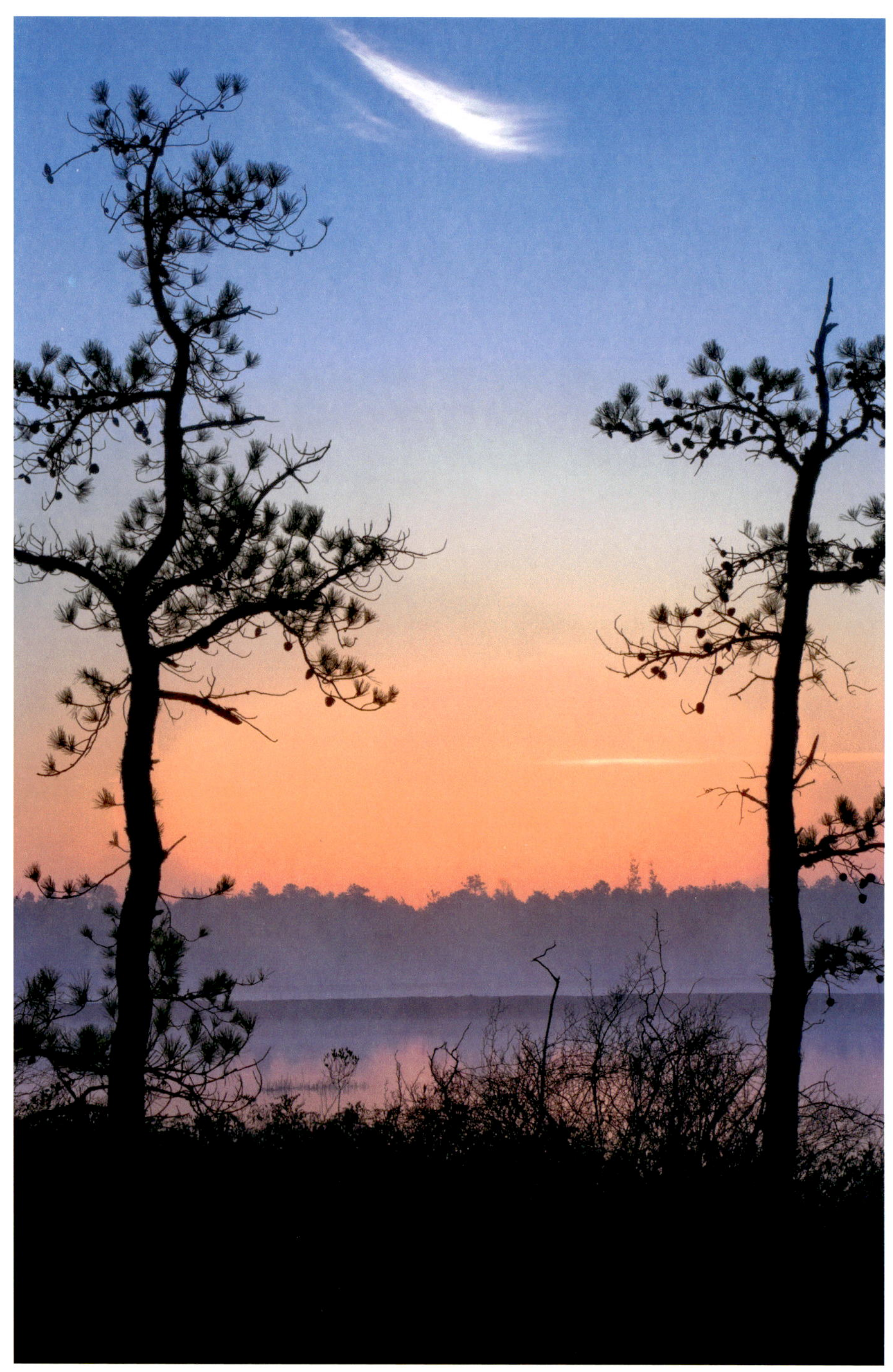

Between Two Pines, Woodland Township

Morning on Chatsworth Lake, Franklin Parker Preserve

*Autumn's last act
the masks of summer
down*

—RALPH DAHLE

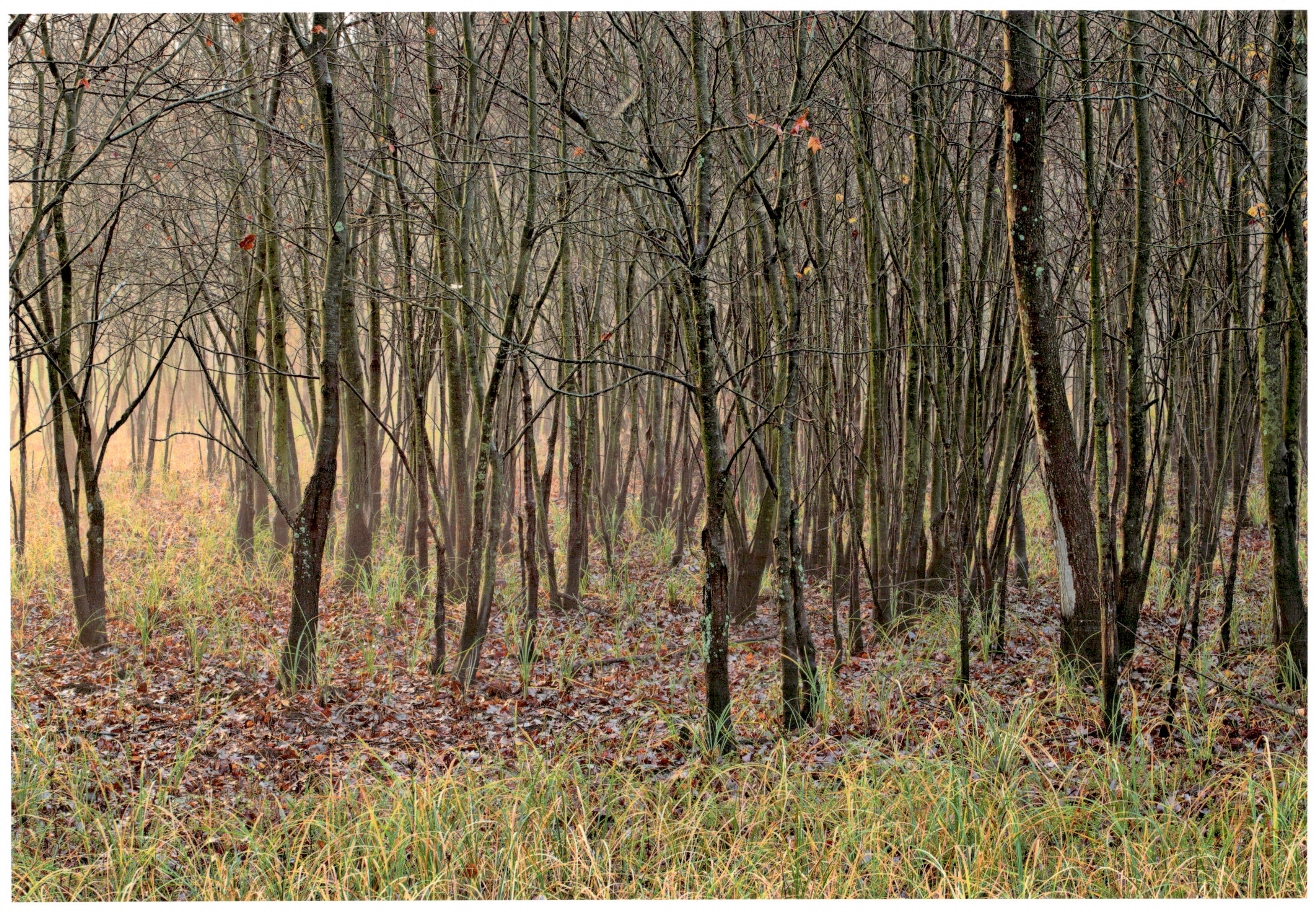

End of Fall, West Jersey Cranberry Meadows

"Earth laughs in flowers."

—Ralph Waldo Emerson

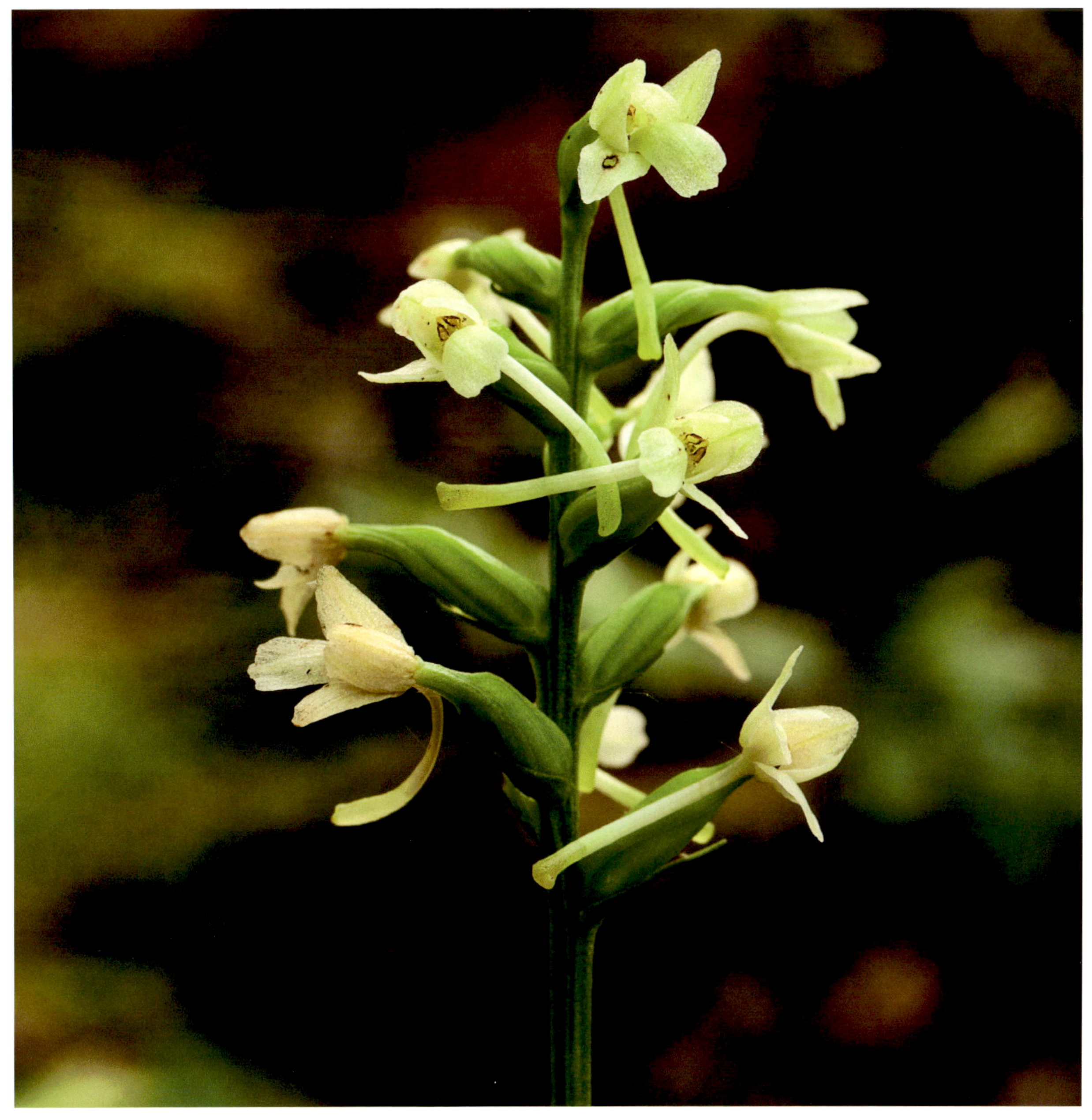

Green Wood Orchid, Pemberton Township

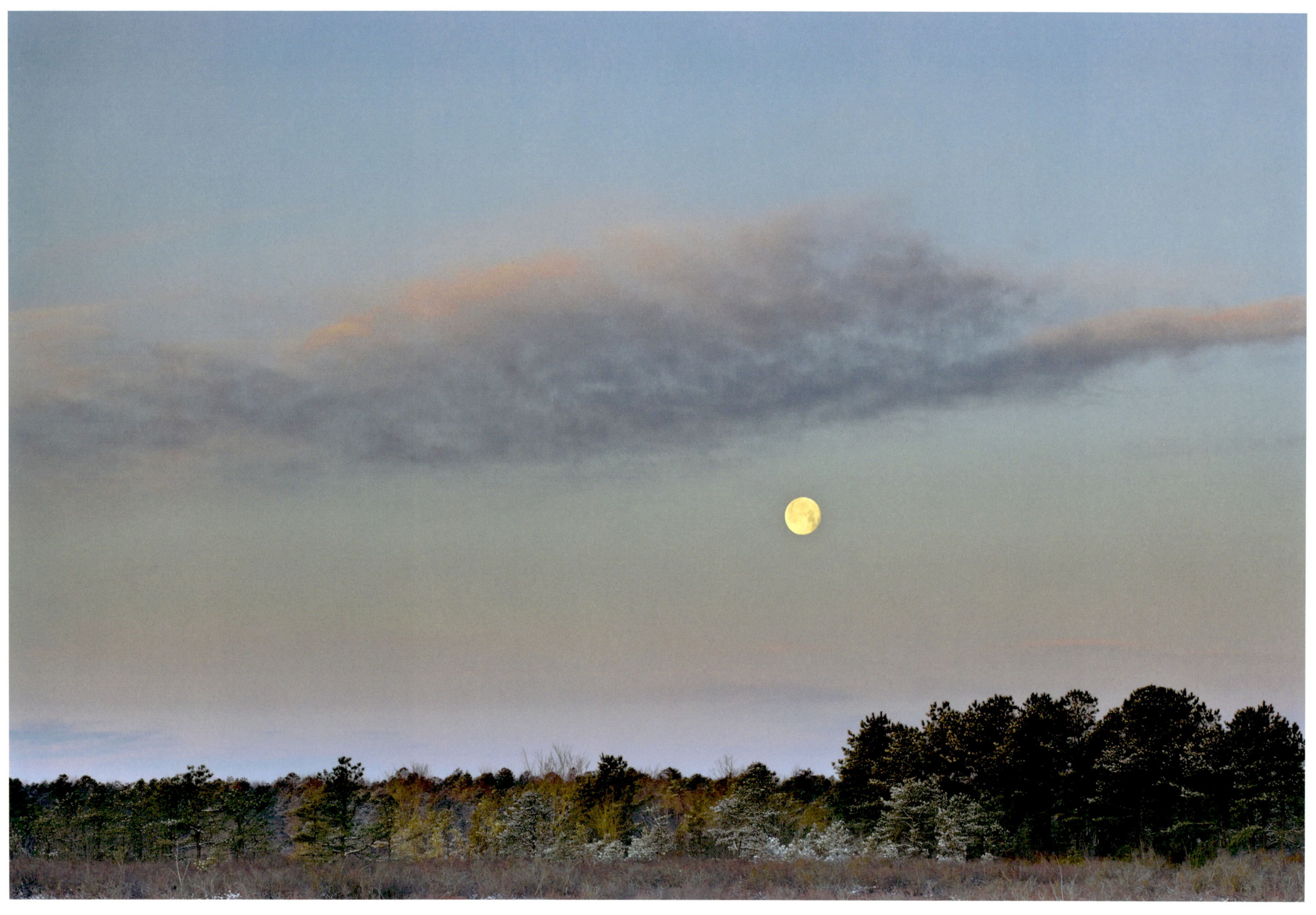

Falling While Rising, West Jersey Cranberry Meadows

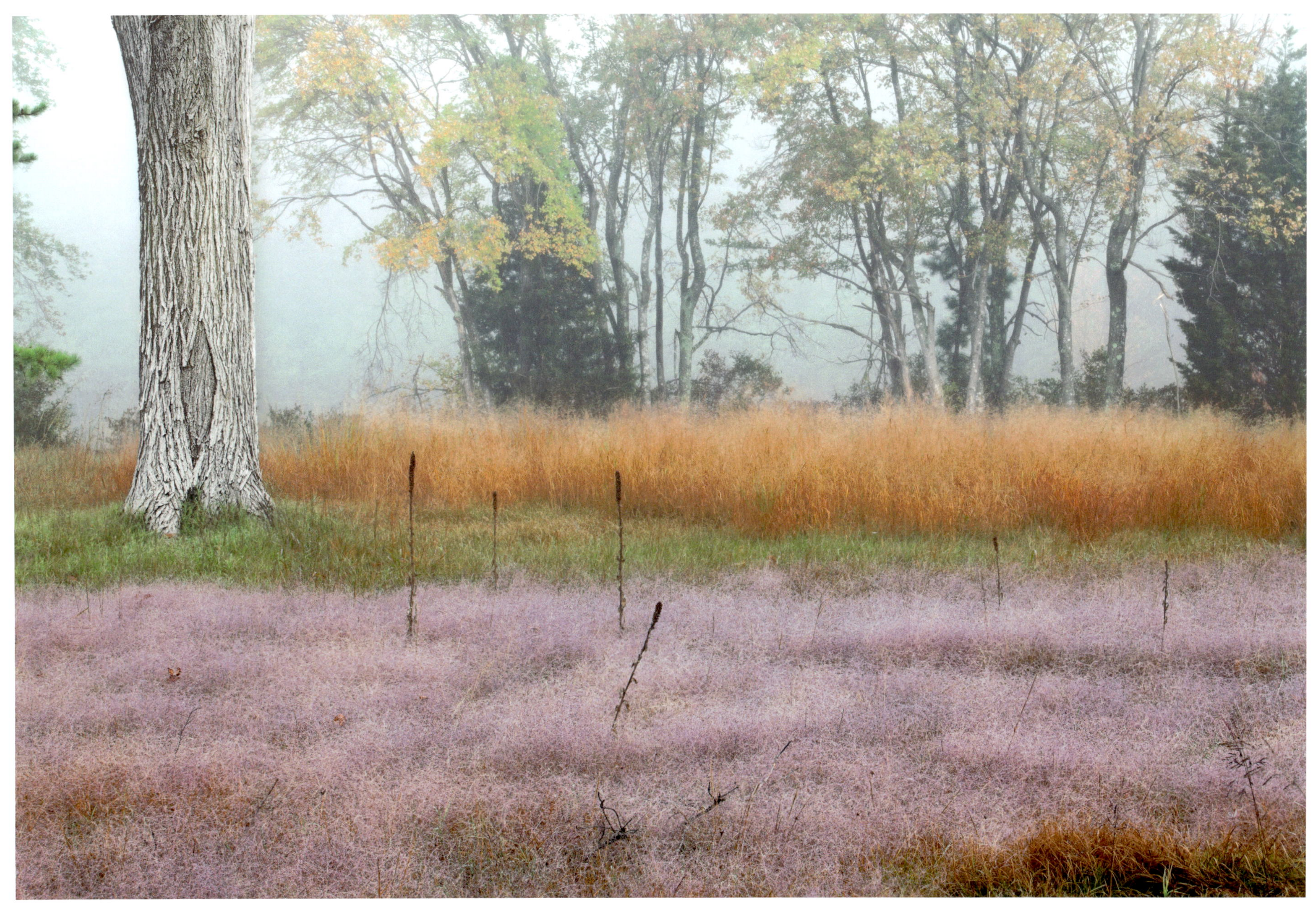

Trunk, Friendship, Wharton State Forest

*One Atlas lies slain
amid the yellowing ferns
of another Fall*

—RALPH DAHLE

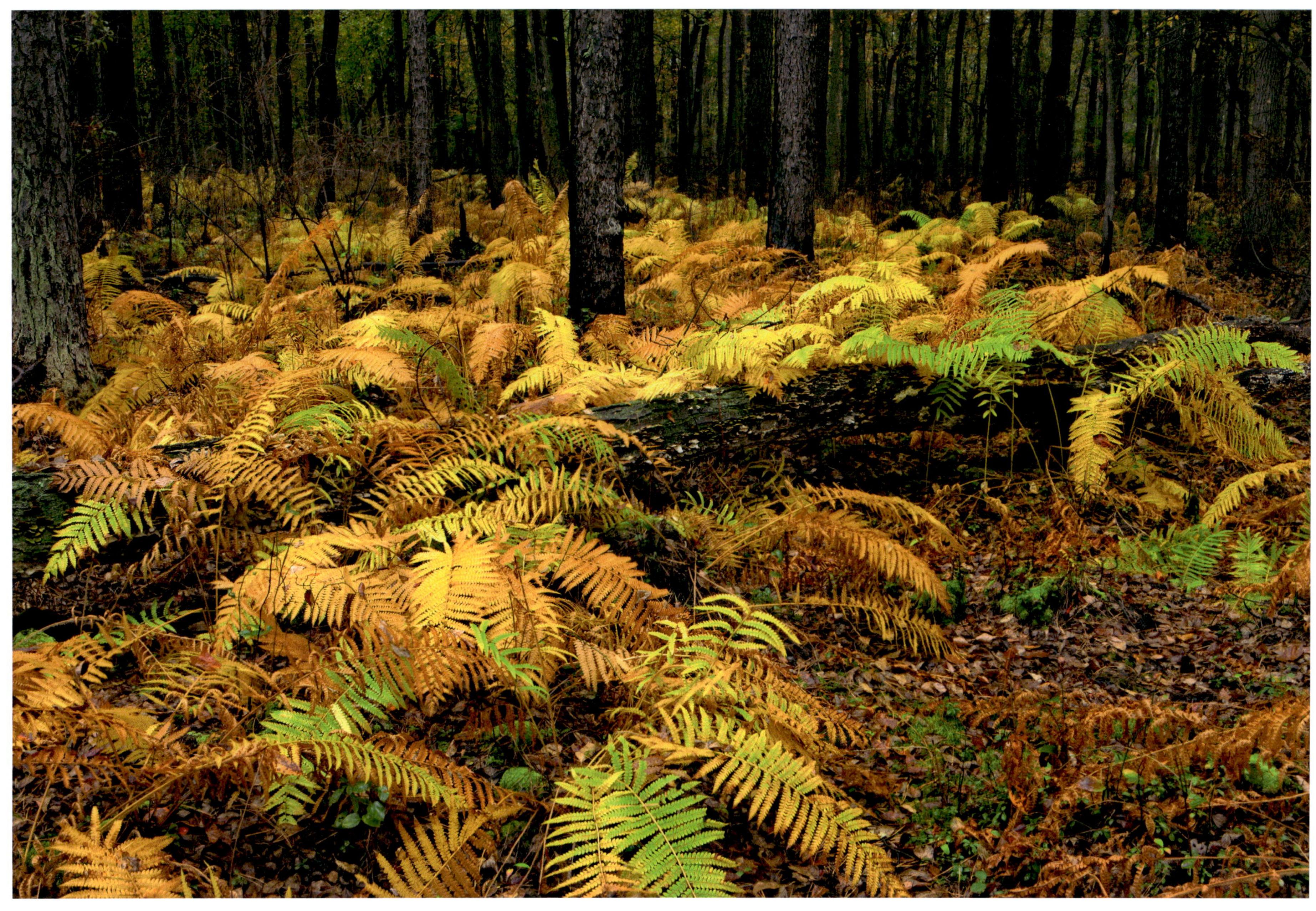

Ferns, Shamong, Wharton State Forest

—BARBARA SPECTOR

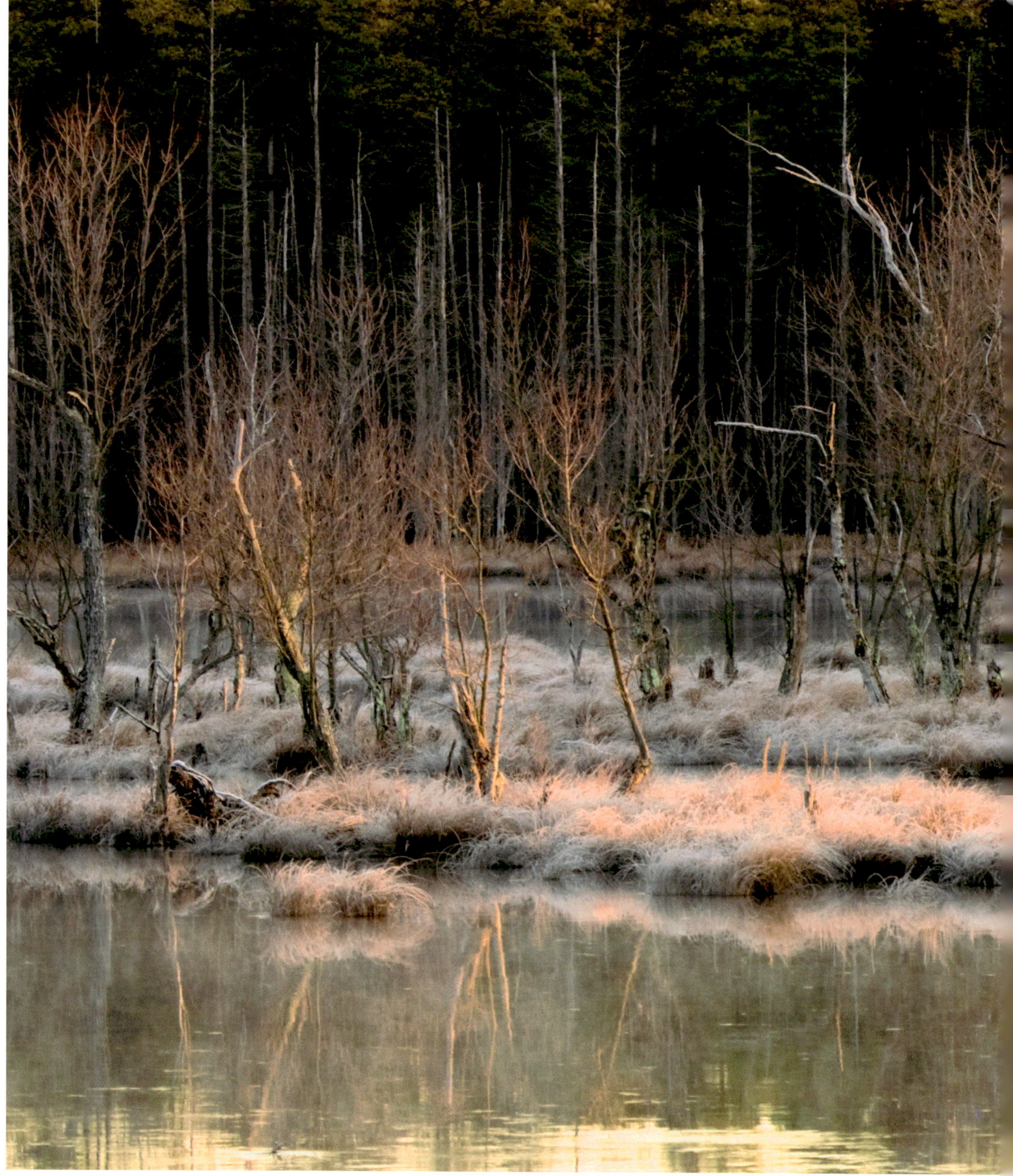

Lodges, Mullica River, Wharton State Forest

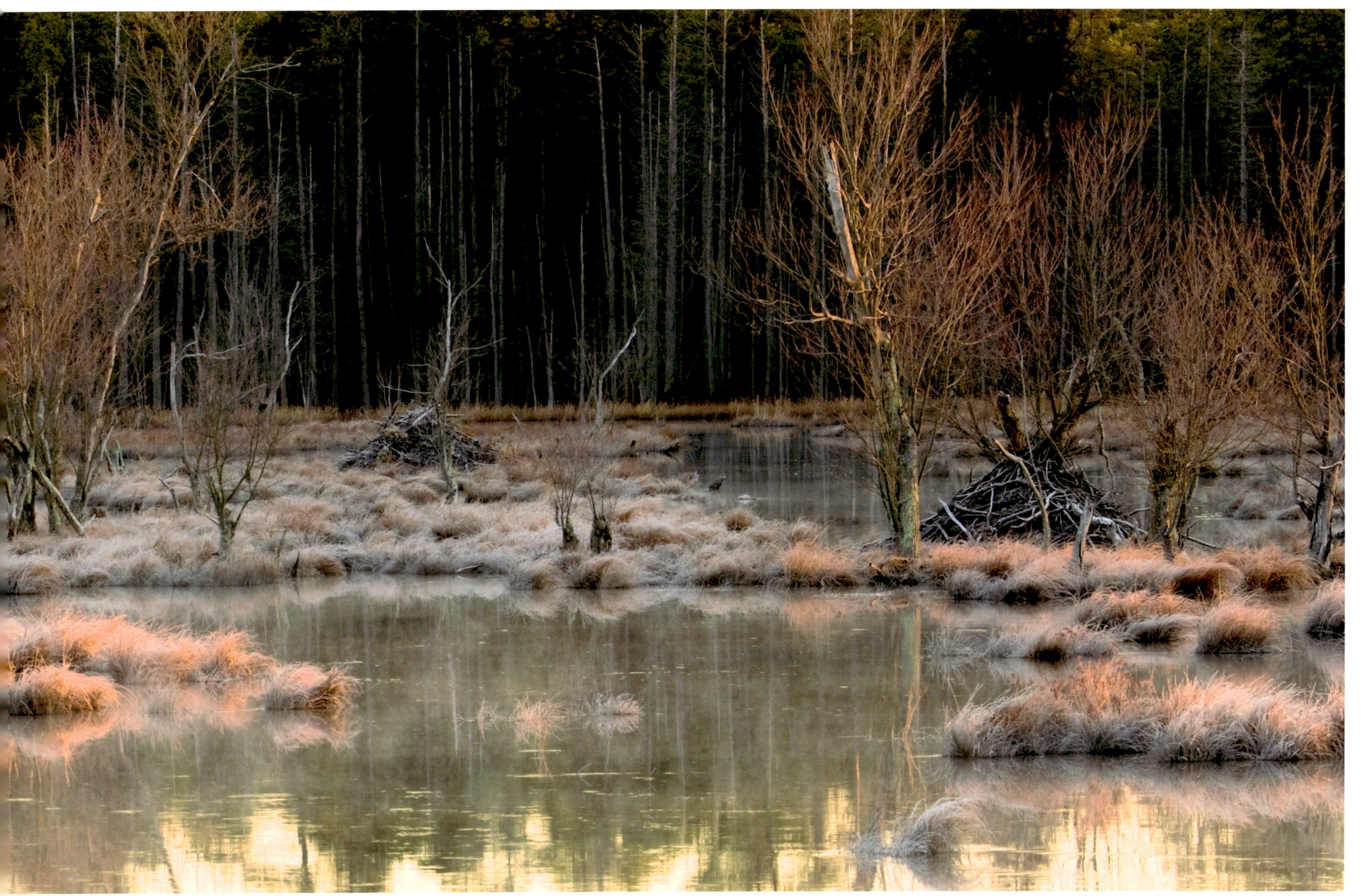

*A voyage begins
in exquisite early morning light
bathed with vivid colors*

—Barbara Spector

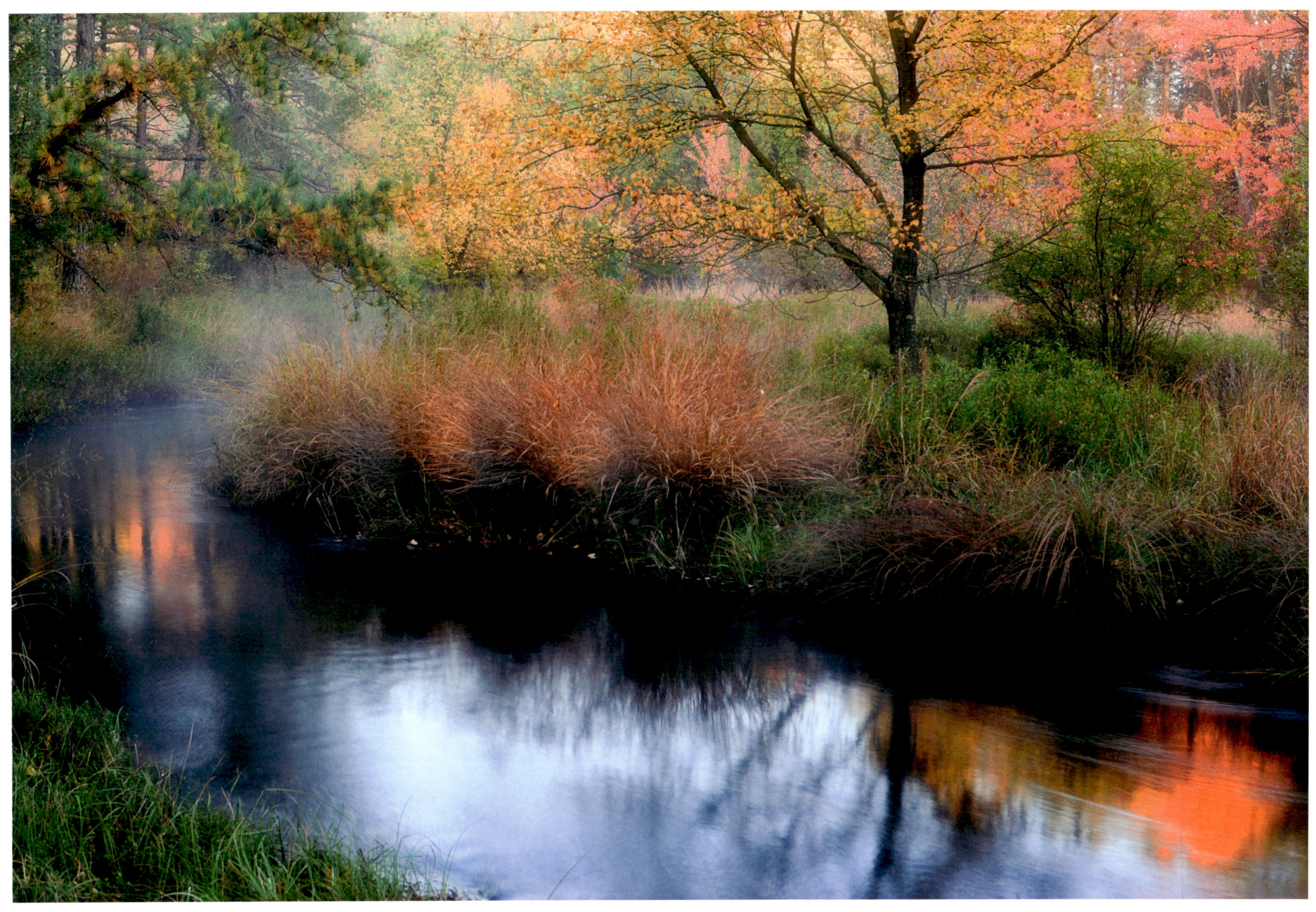

Upper Batsto River, Hampton Furnace

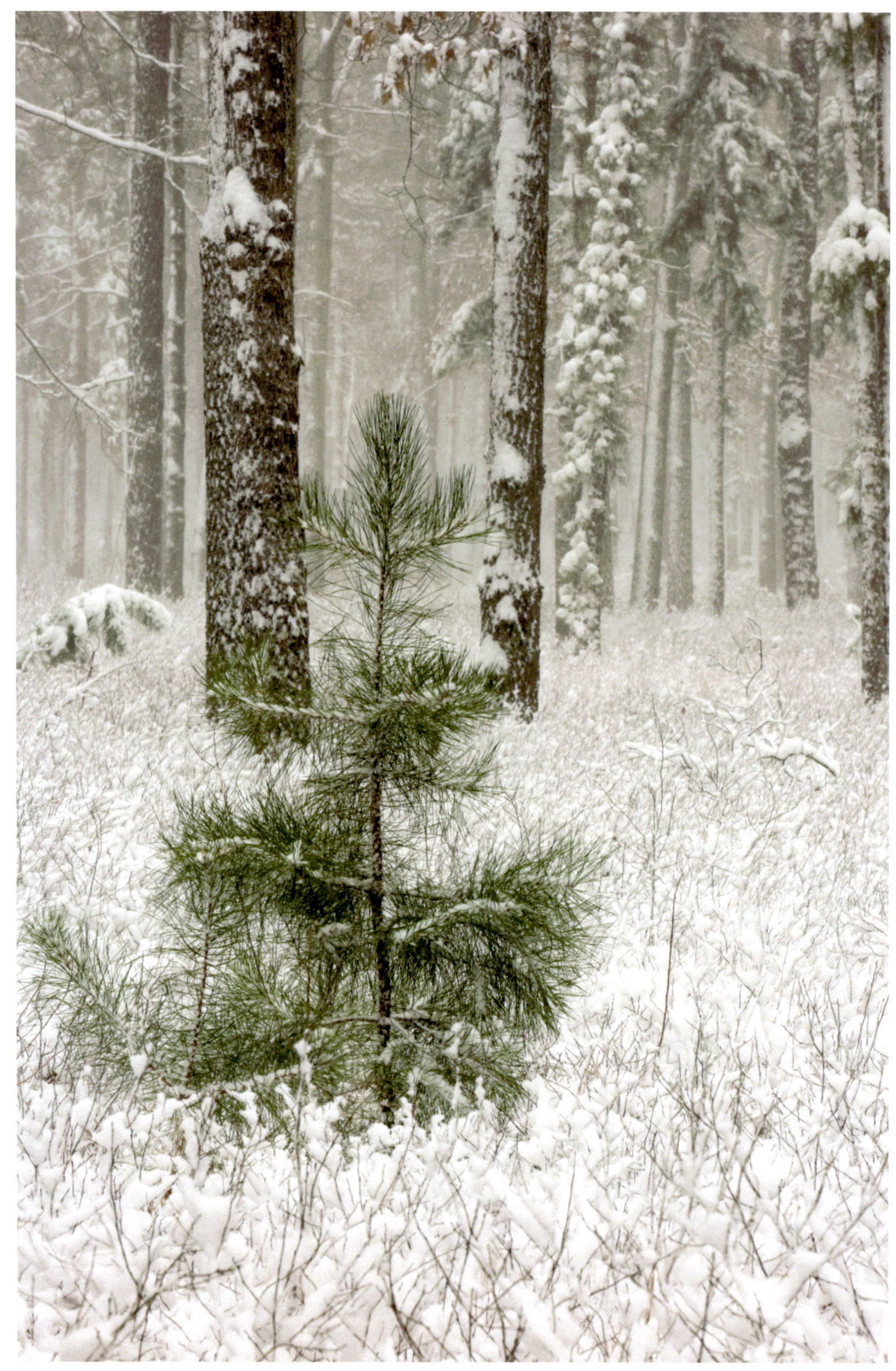

Standing Alone, Wharton State Forest

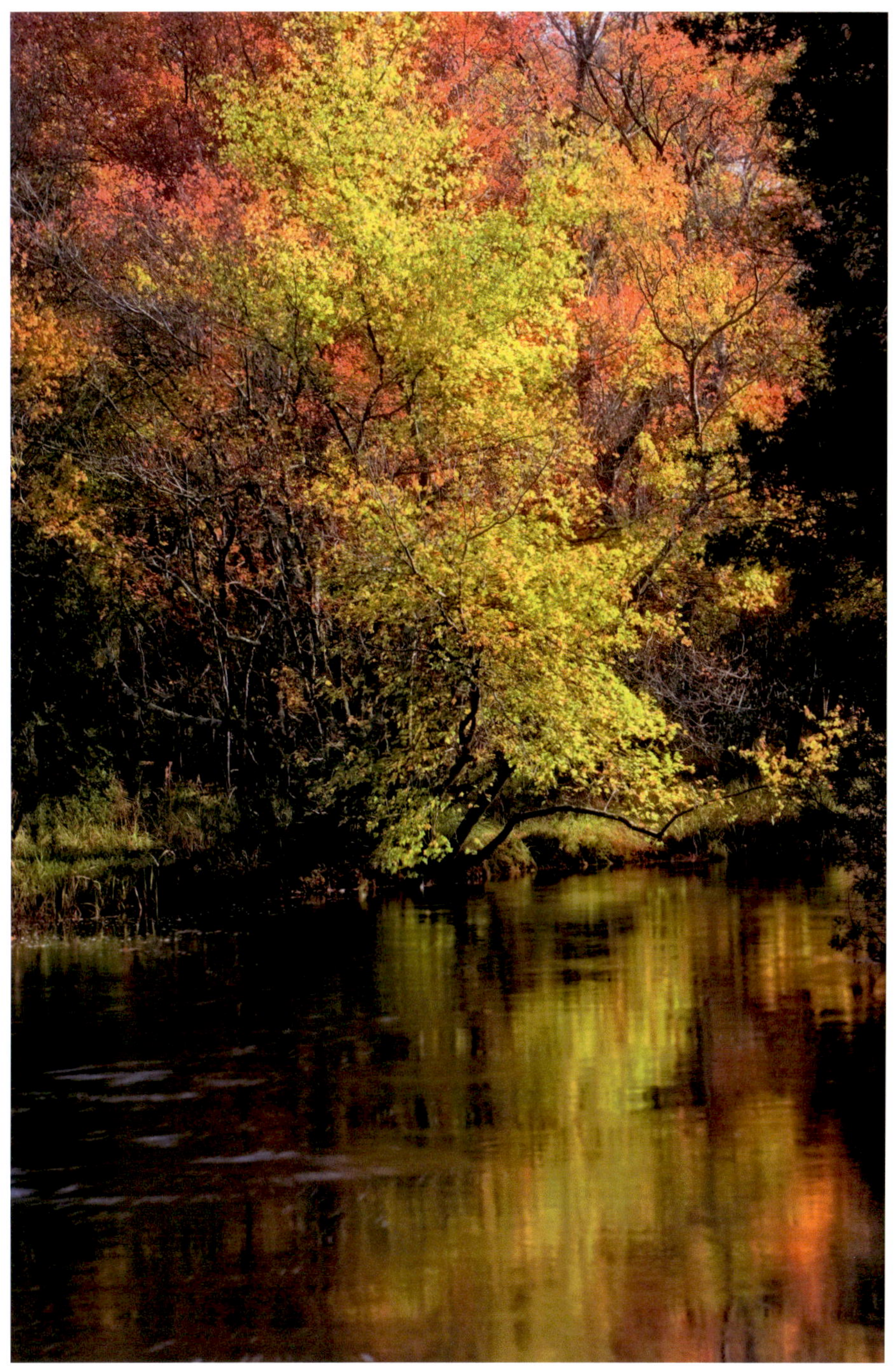

Wading River Reflections, Wharton State Forest

"We must look for a long time before we can see."

—HENRY DAVID THOREAU

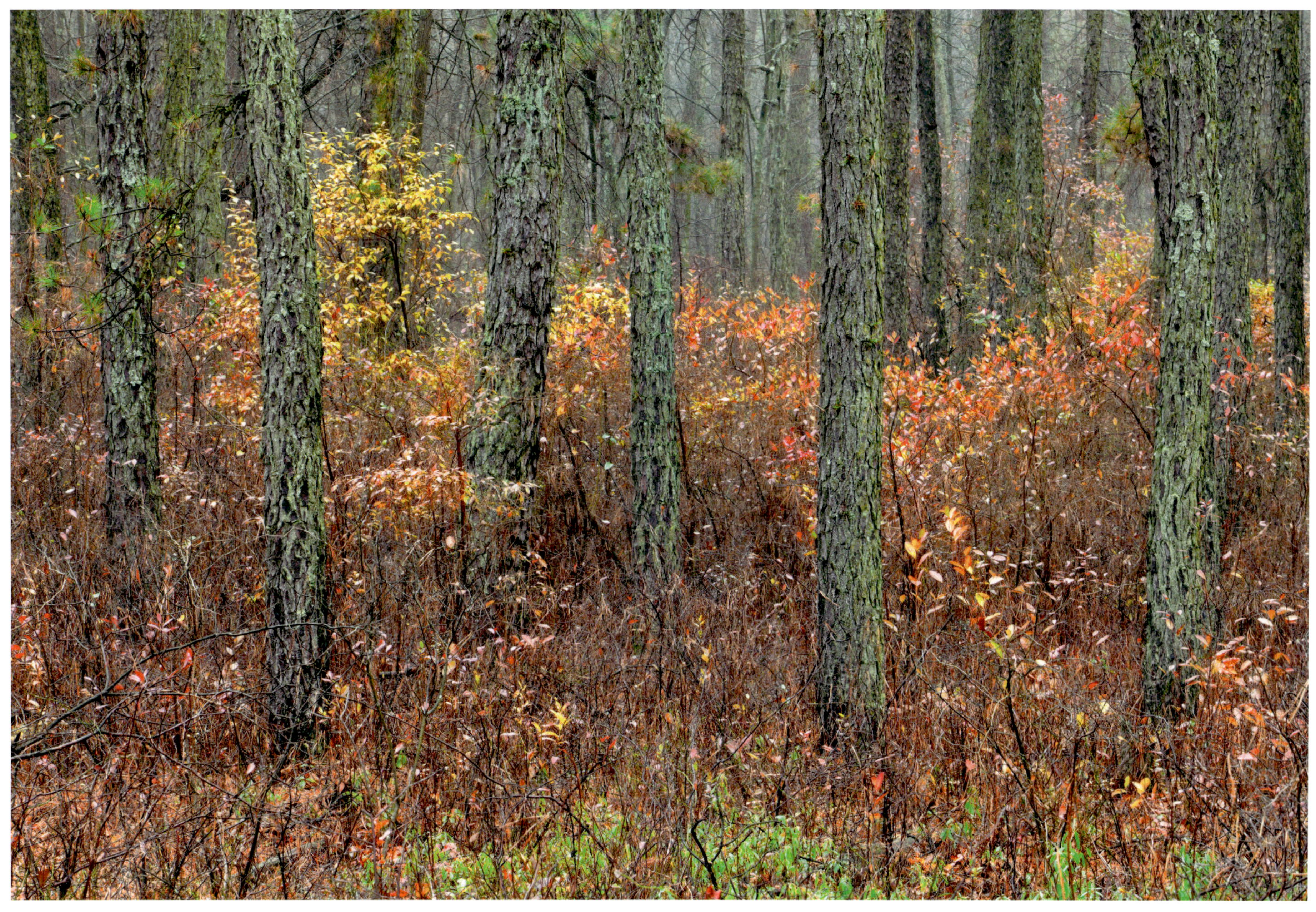

Fall Chaos, Jenkins

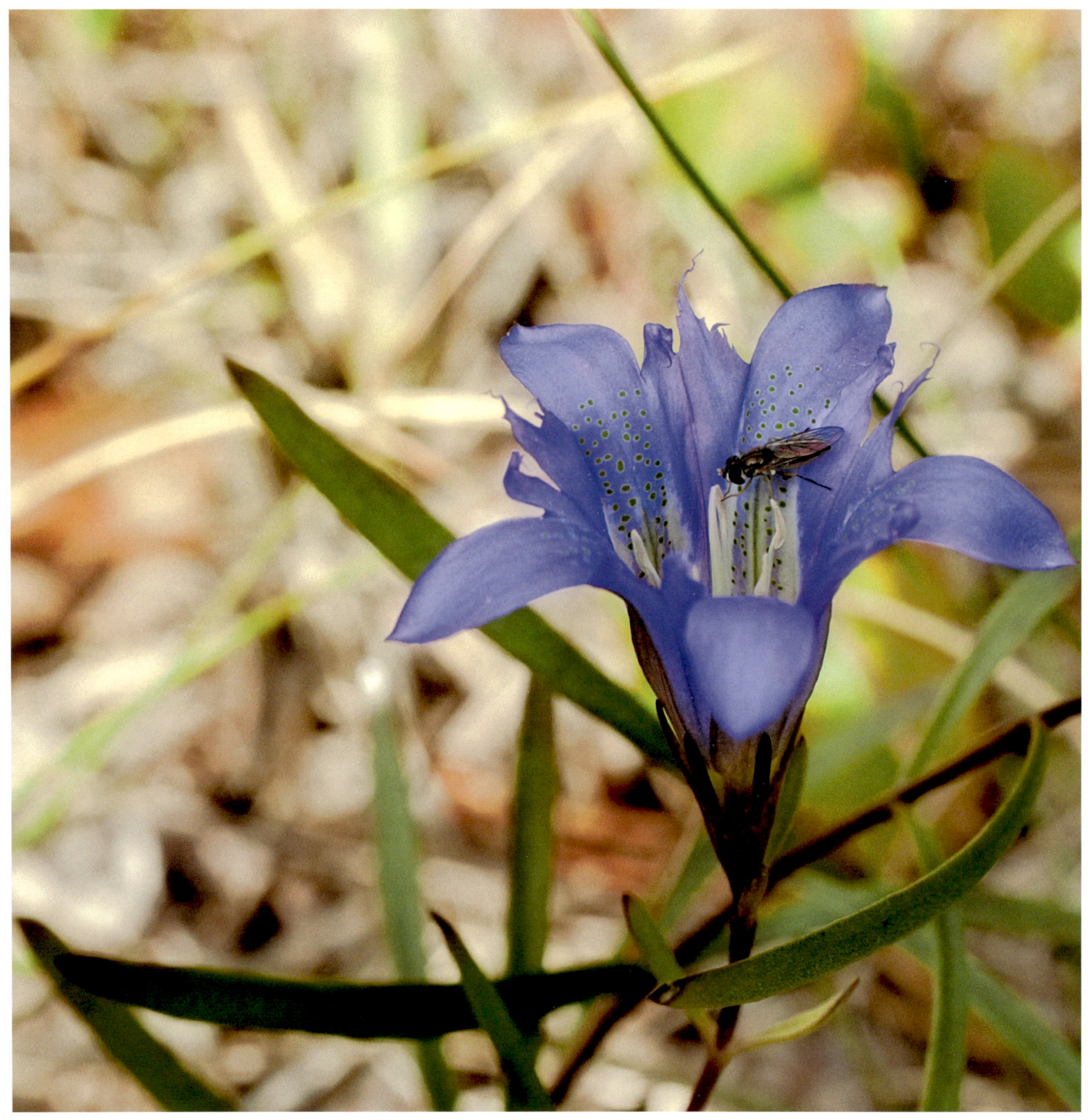

Pine Barren Gentian, Franklin Parker Preserve

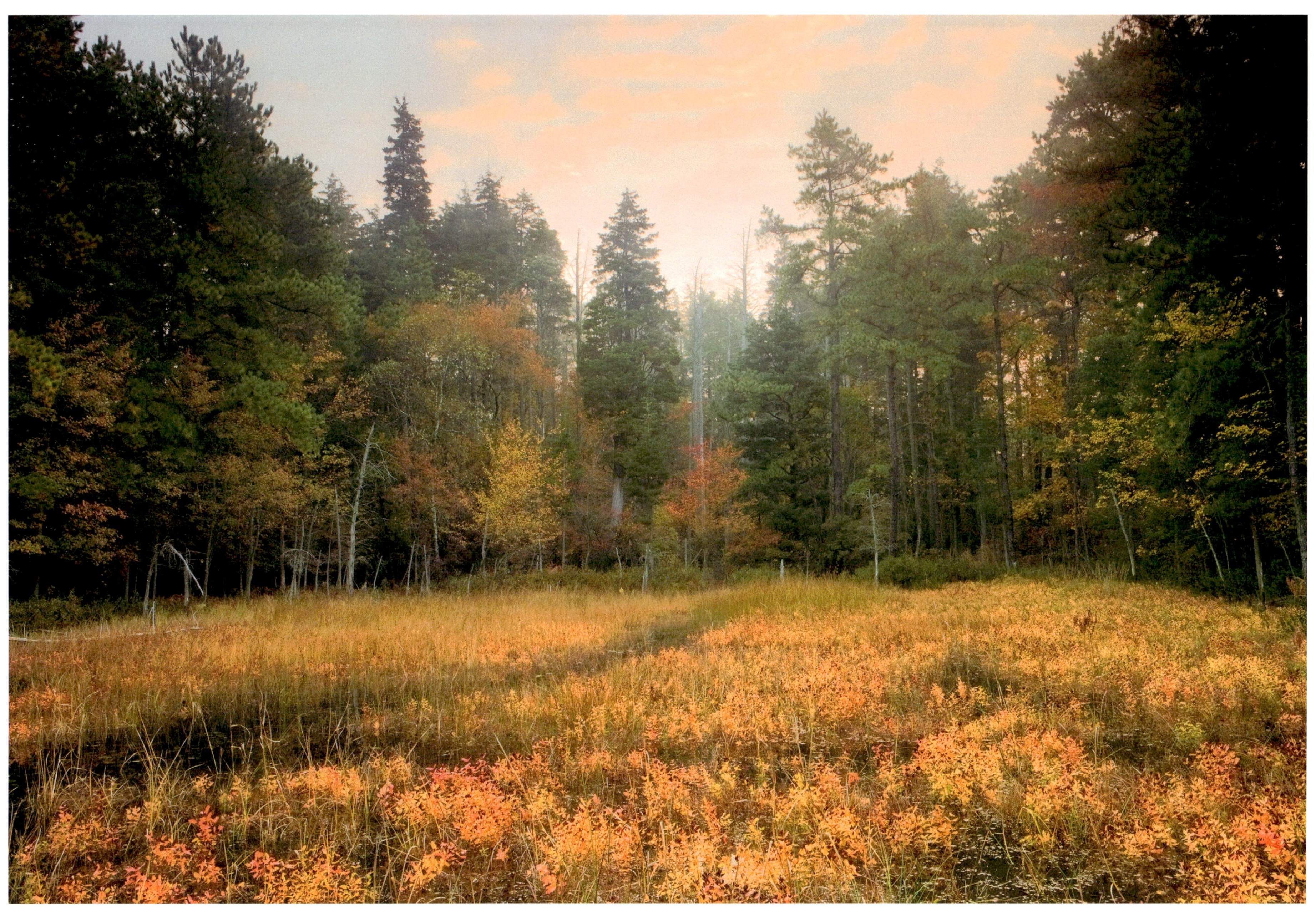

Fall Meadow, Wharton State Forest

A new day arises
frothy foam blankets river bed
flora shines with dew

—Barbara Spector

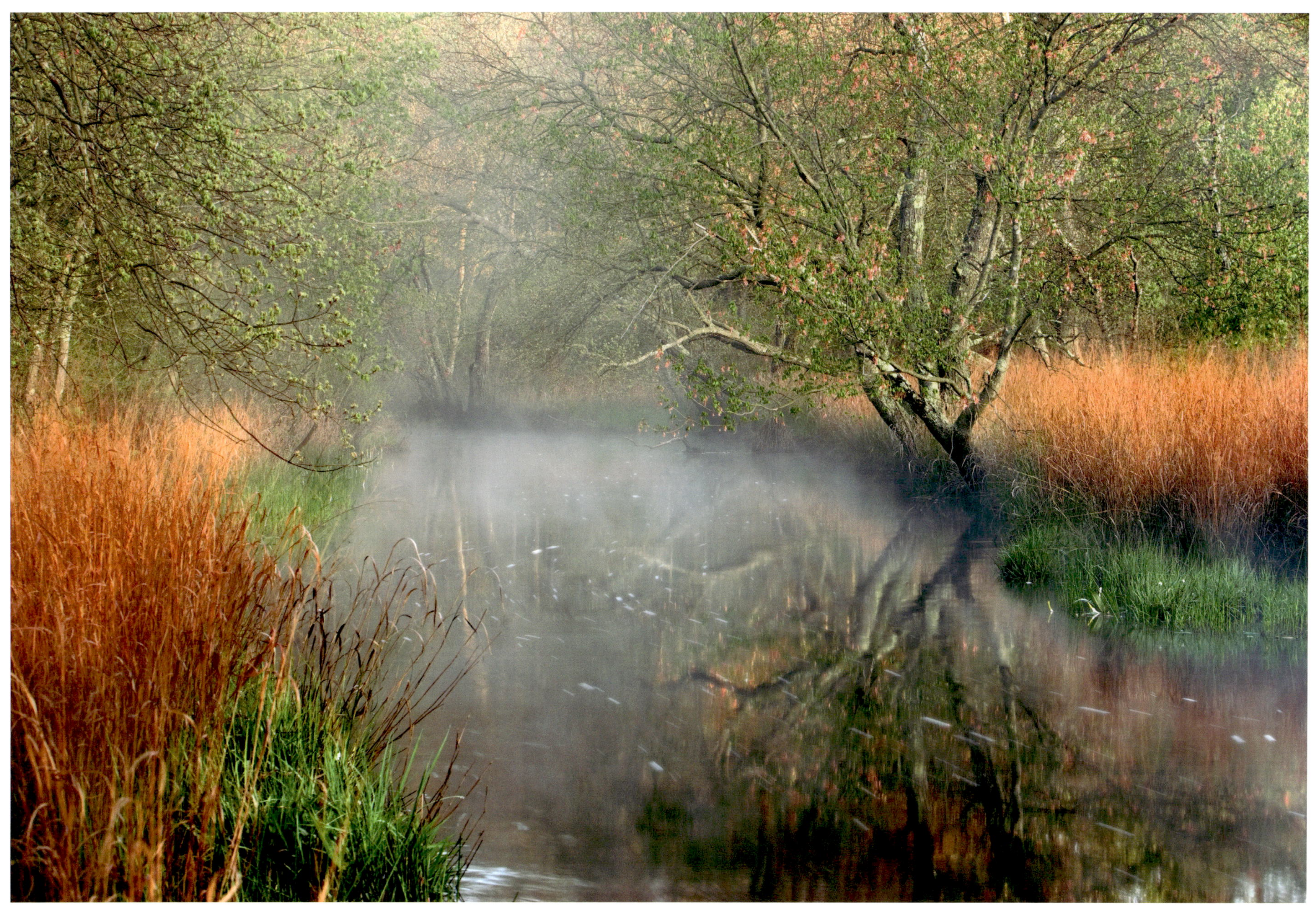

Morning Mist, along the Mullica River

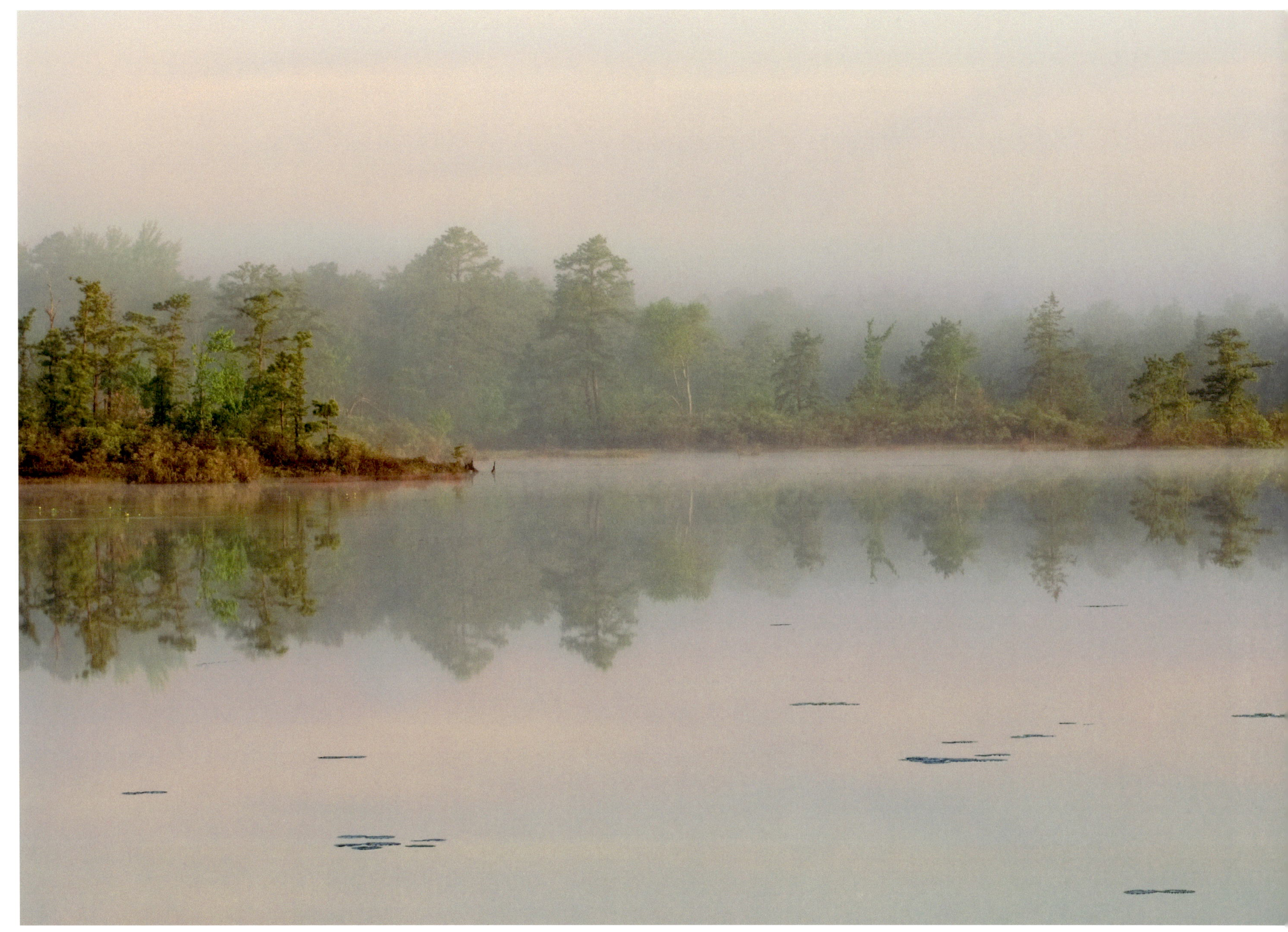

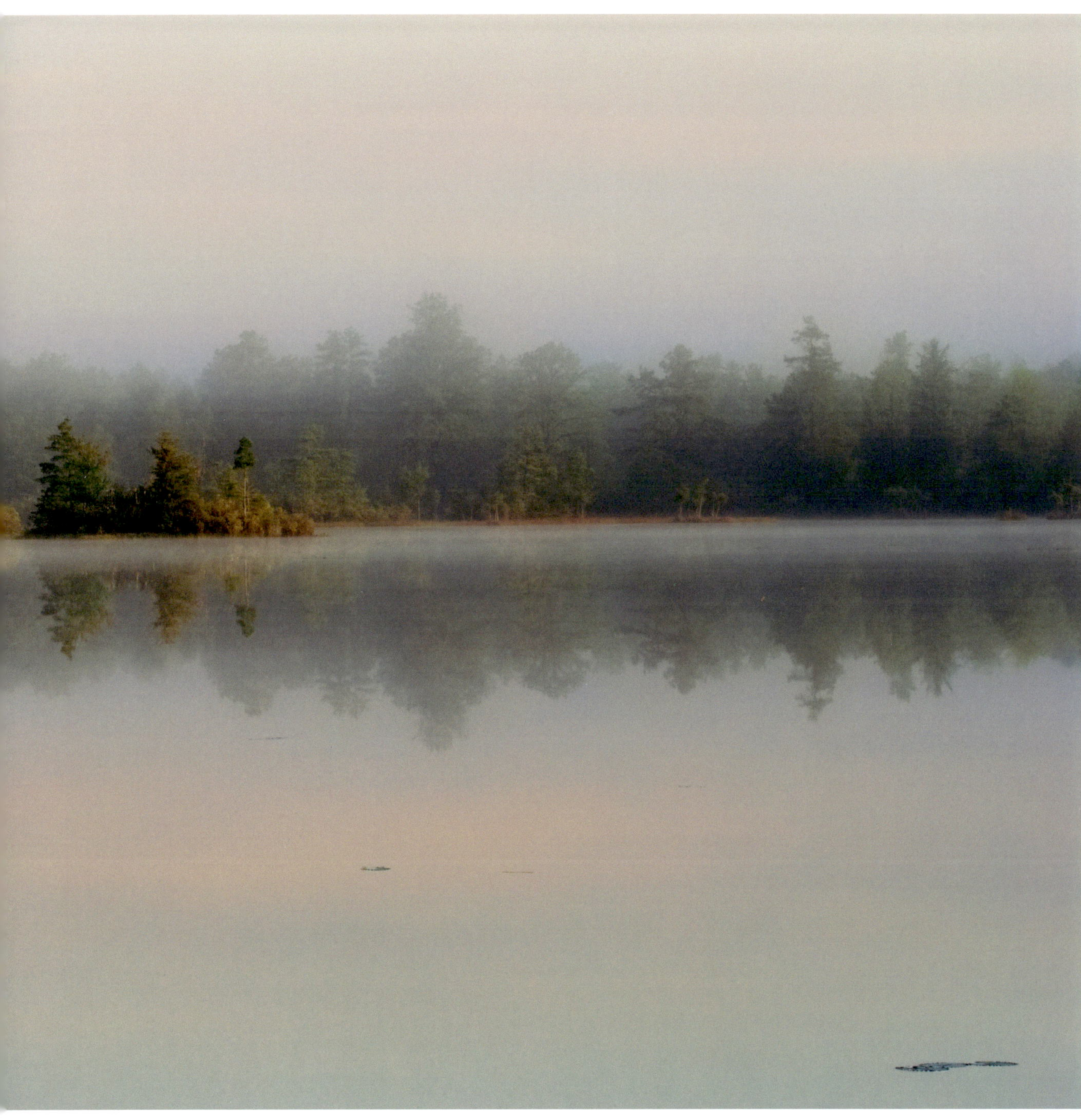

Quietude, West Jersey Cranberry Meadows

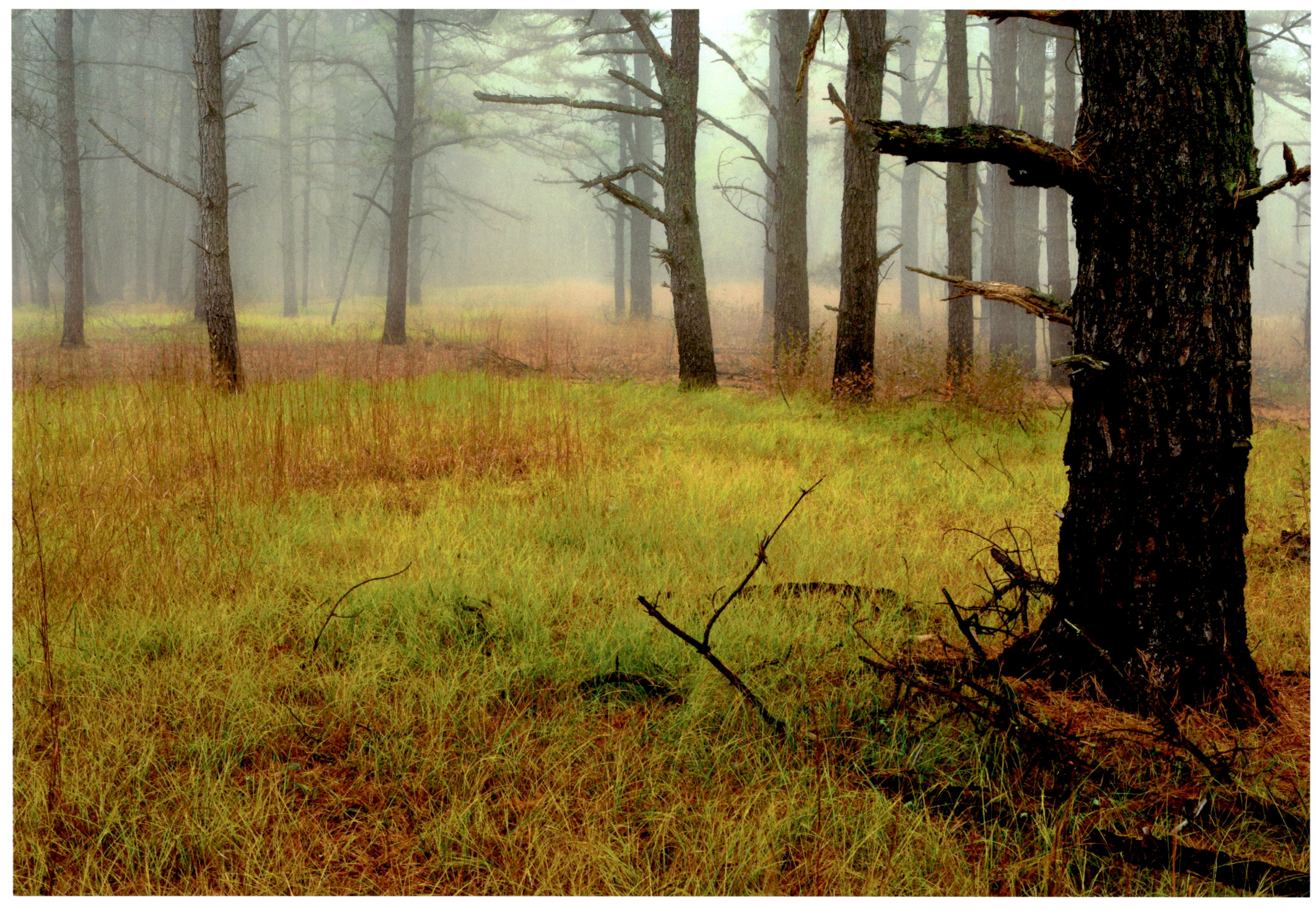

Chartreuse Grove, Hampton Furnace

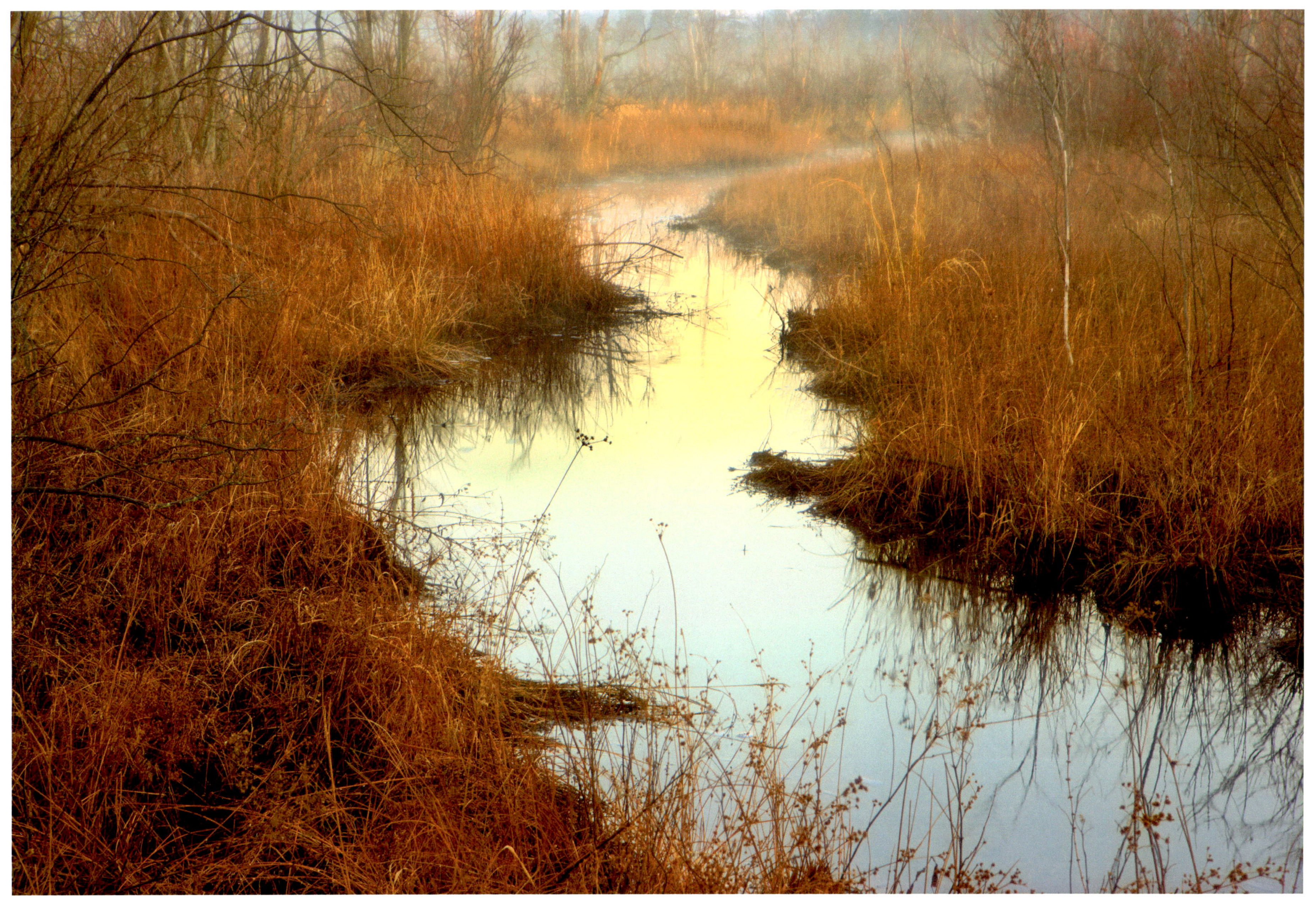

Sleeper Branch, Dutchtown, Shamong

"*A photograph is not an accident—it is a concept.*"

—ANSEL ADAMS

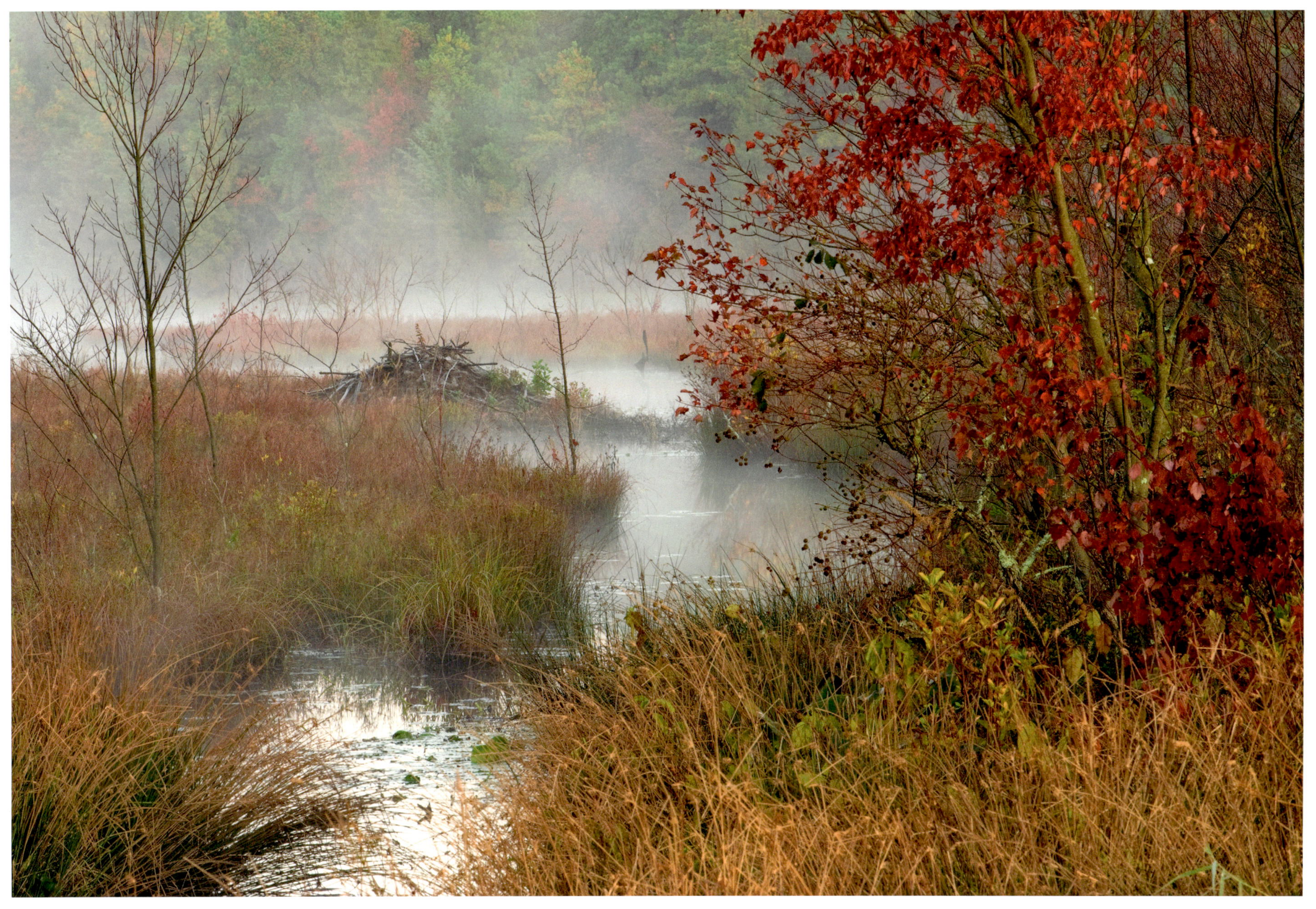

Red Maple, Brendan T. Byrne State Forest

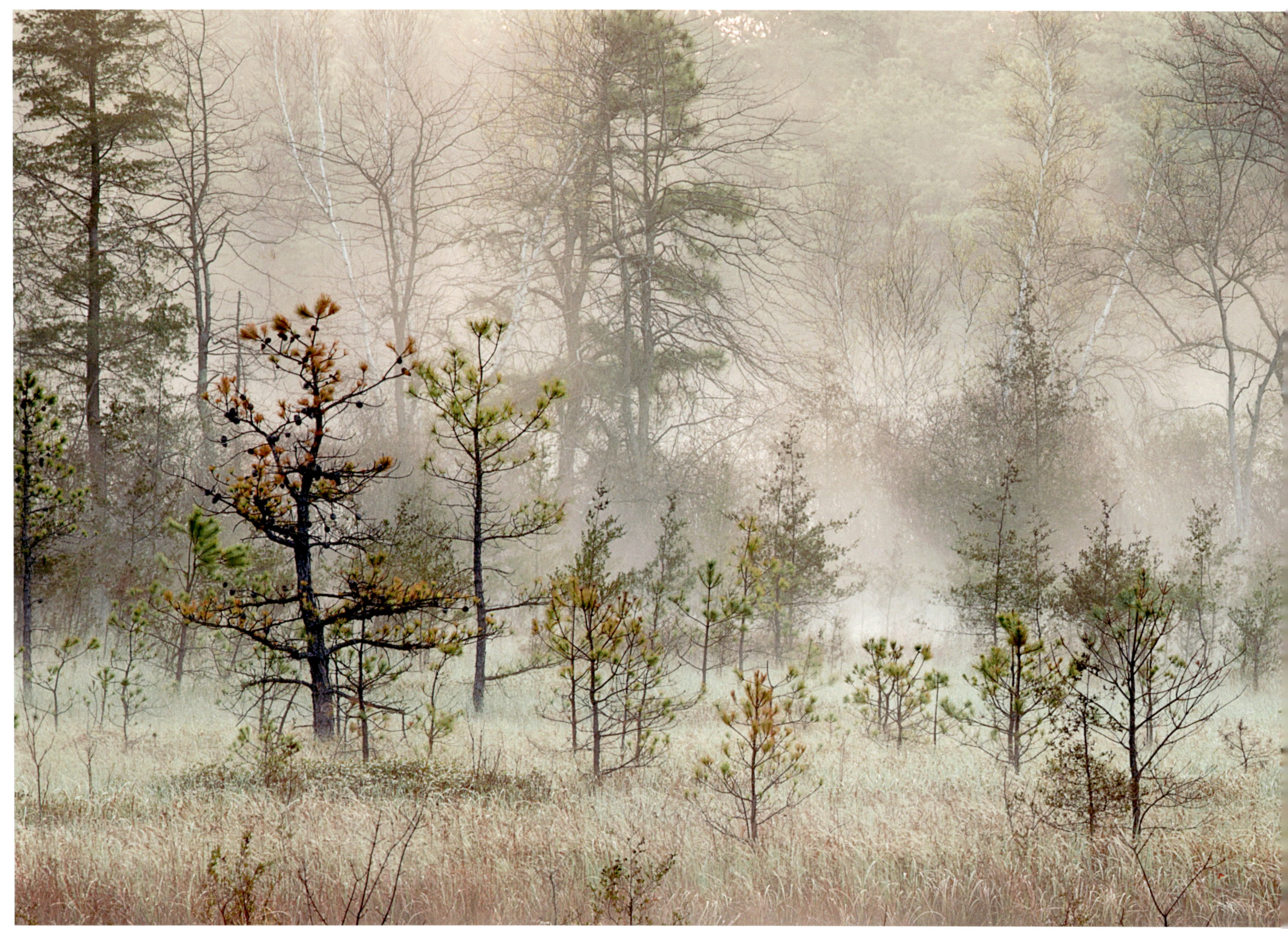

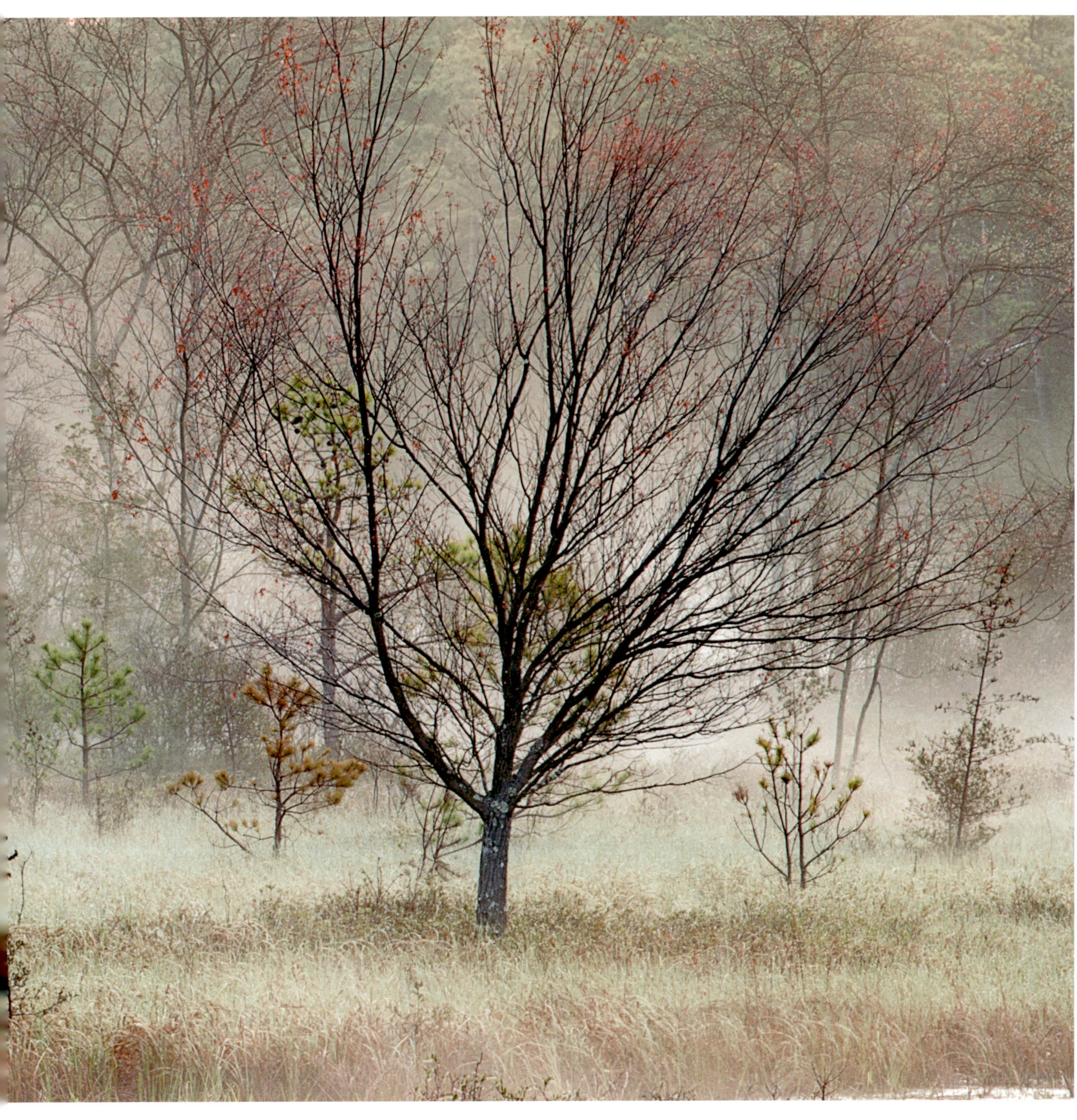

Friendship Mist, Friendship Bogs, Wharton State Forest

*Pineland prophets
crimson-topped trees
reflecting other seasons*

—Ralph Dahle

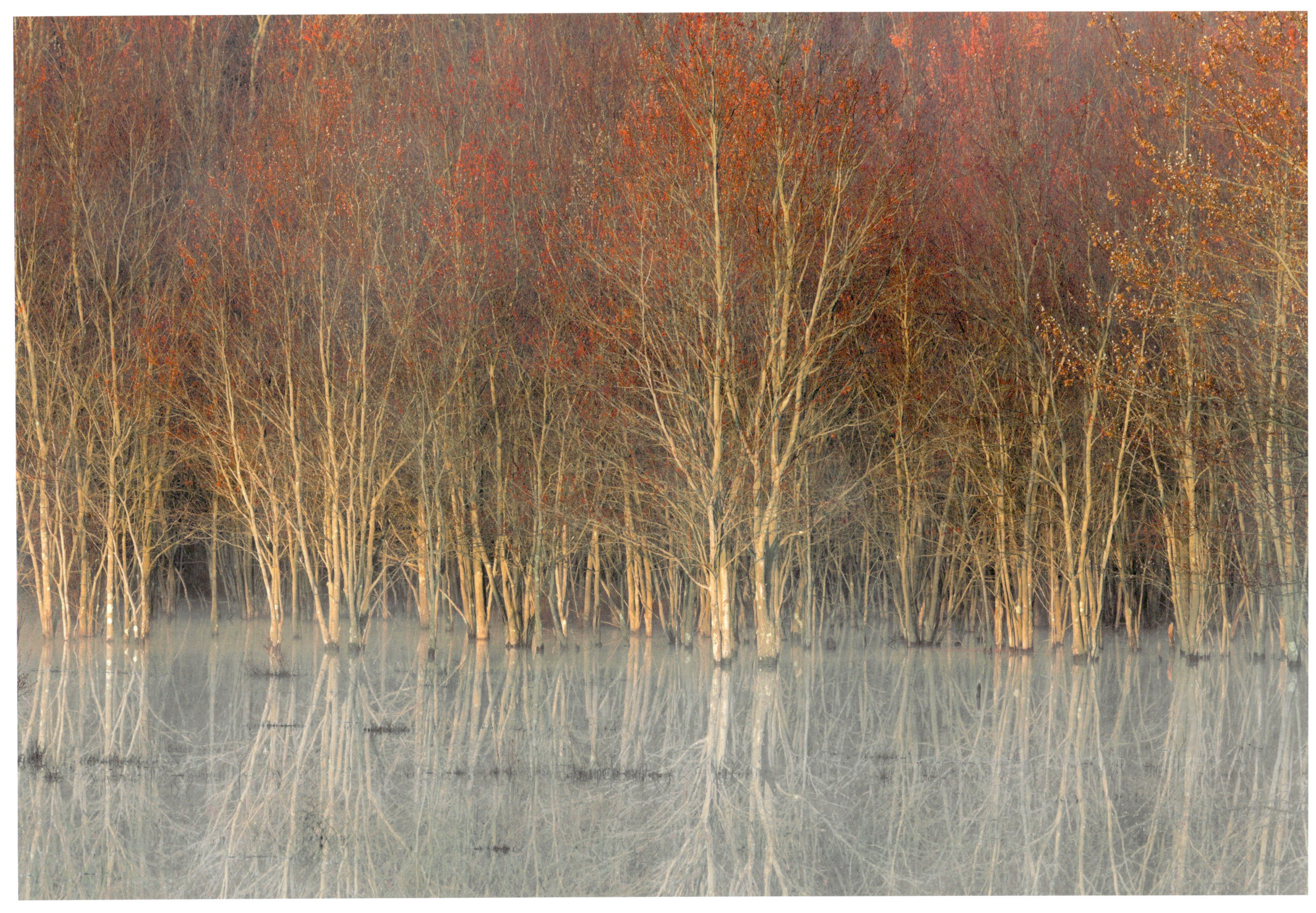

Flooded Maples, West Jersey Cranberry Meadows

Fall moon and pine
a shuddering stop
at dawn

—RALPH DAHLE

Crescent Moon, near Penn State Forest

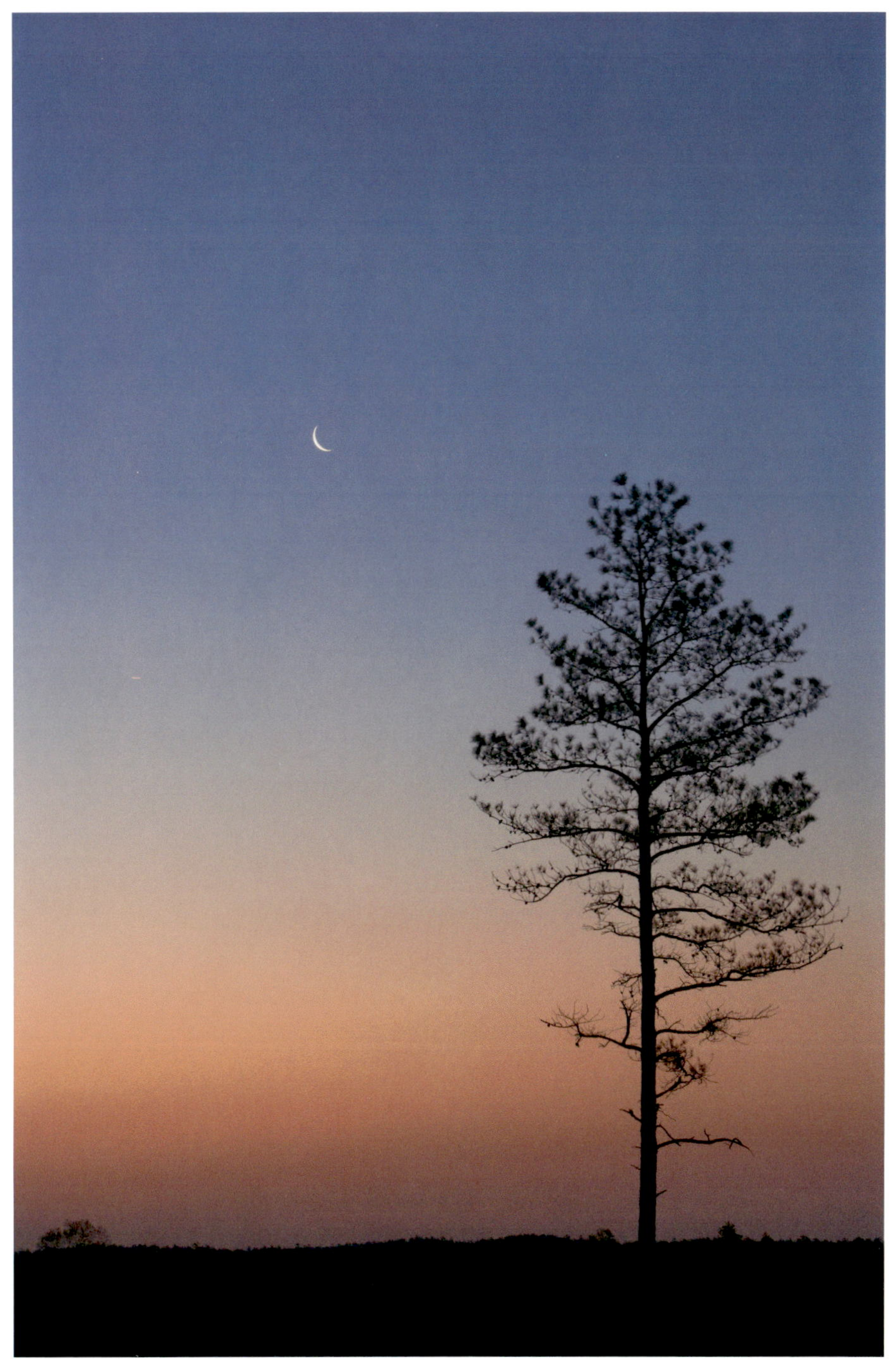

Conifers stand tall
reaching for first light of day
ready for morning

—Barbara Spector

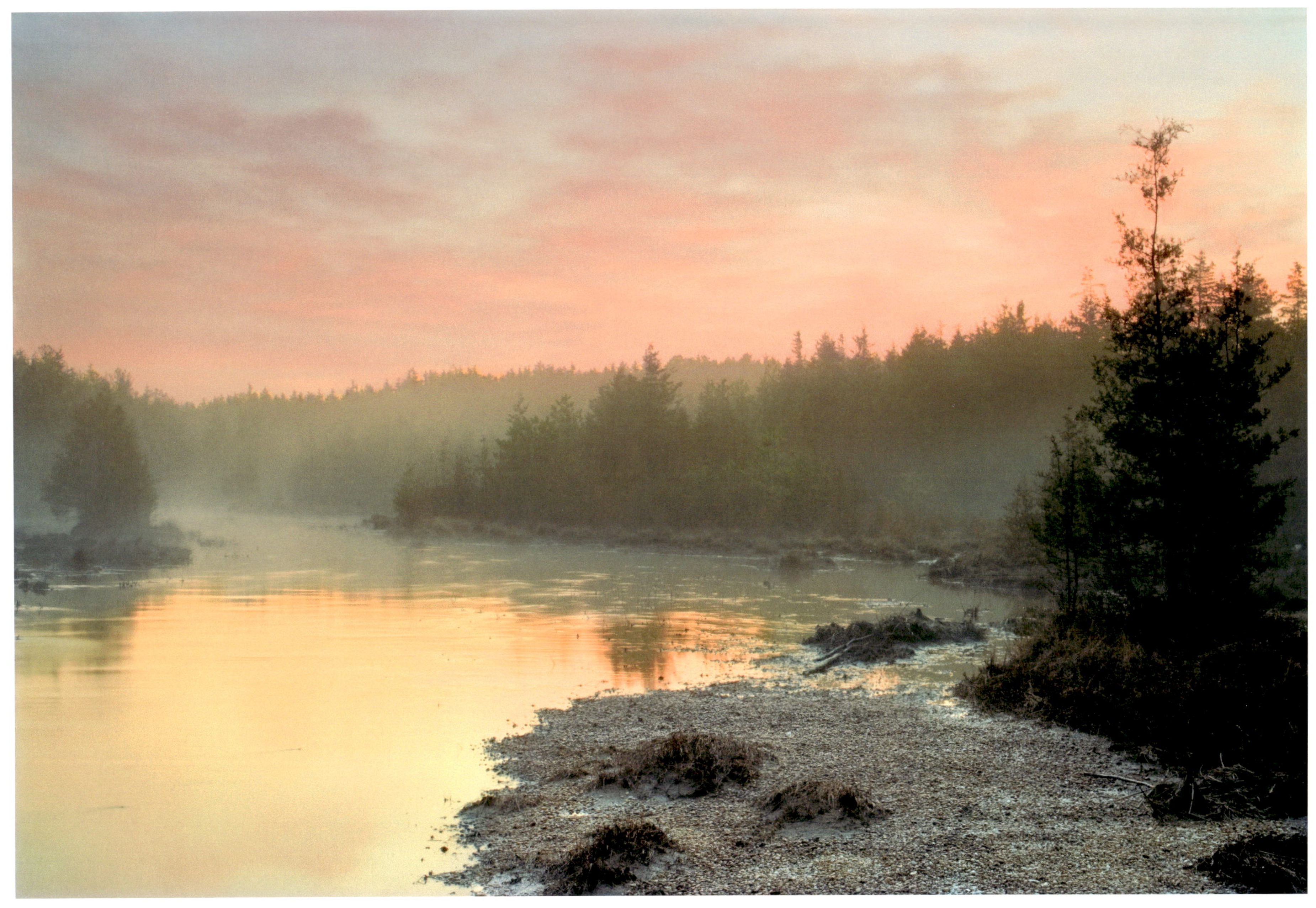

Martha Pond, Oswego River

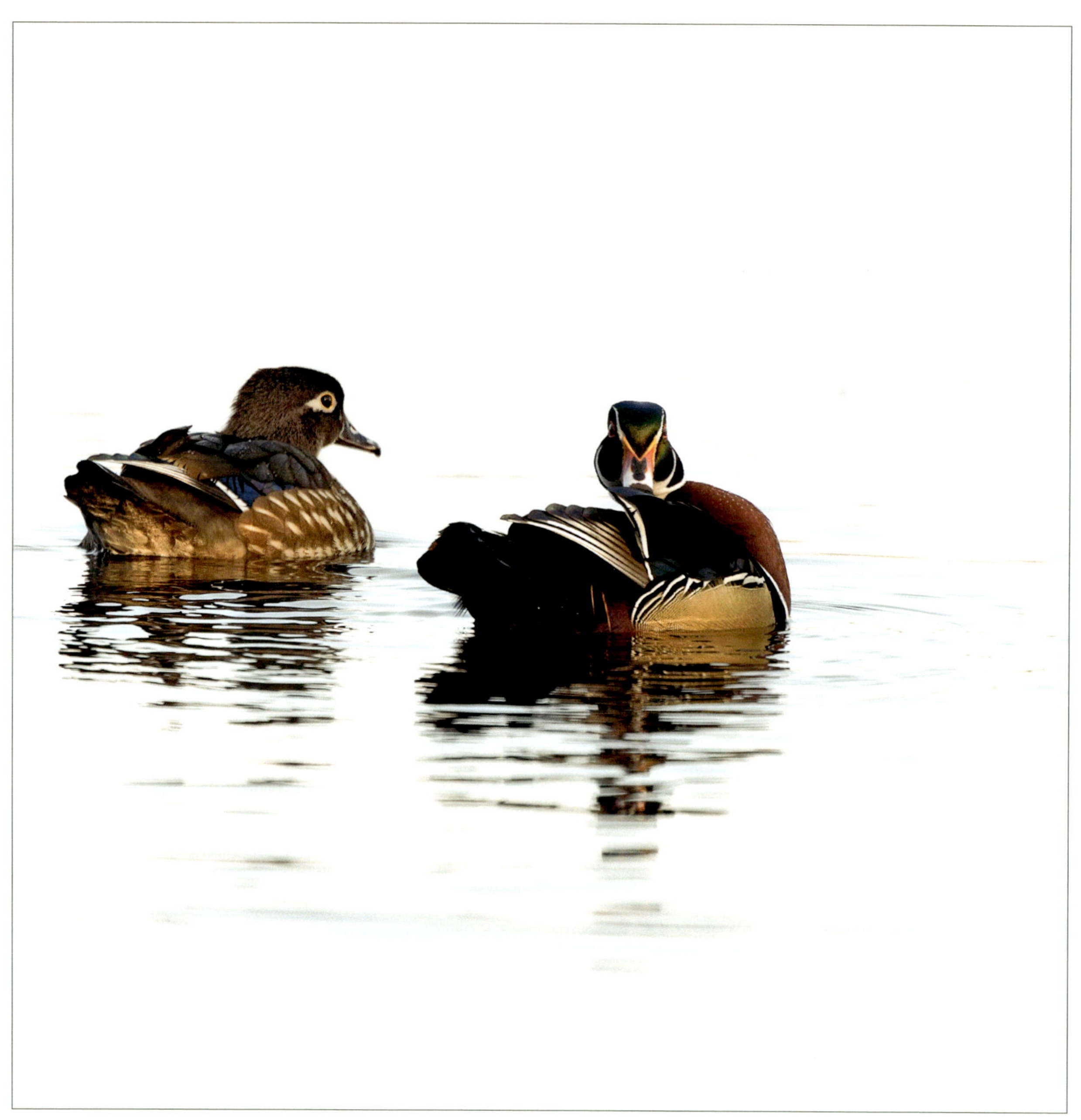

Preener and Hen, along the Mullica River waterway

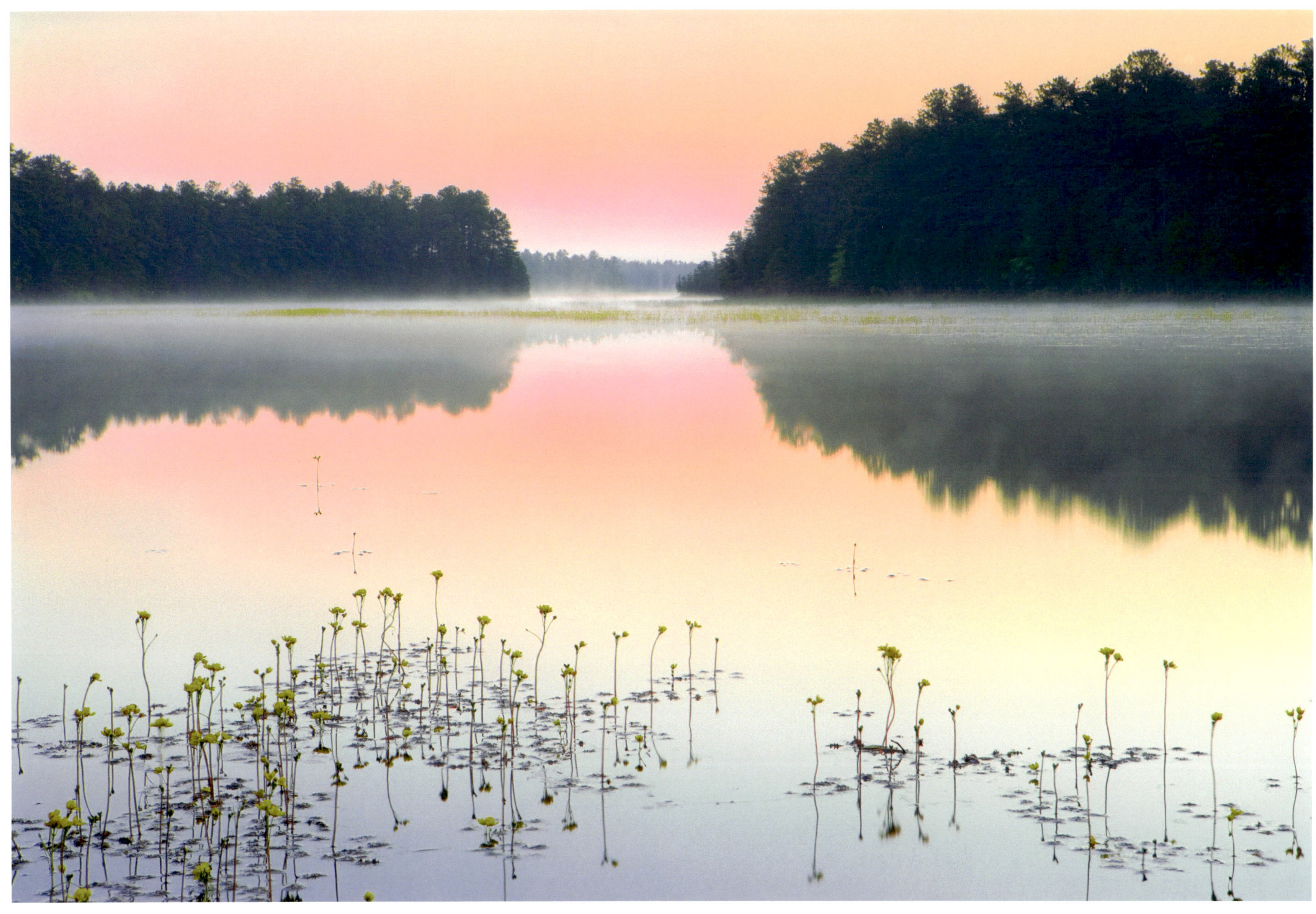

Blooming Bladderwort, Harrisville Pond

"Treat the earth well: it was not given to you by your parents, it was loaned to you by your children. We do not inherit the earth from our ancestors, we borrow it from our children."

—Ancient Indian Proverb

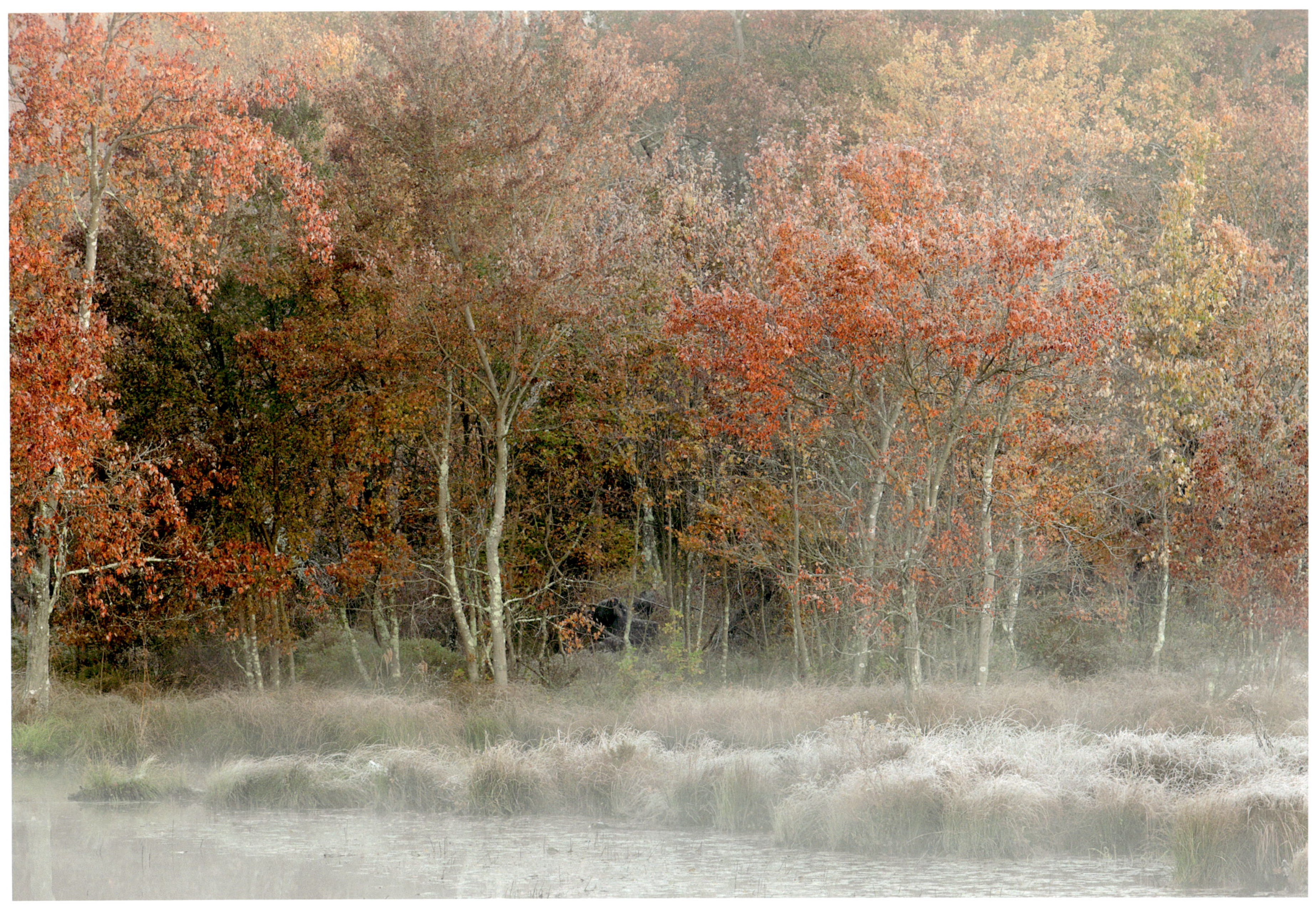

Mullica Maples, Mullica River, Wharton State Forest

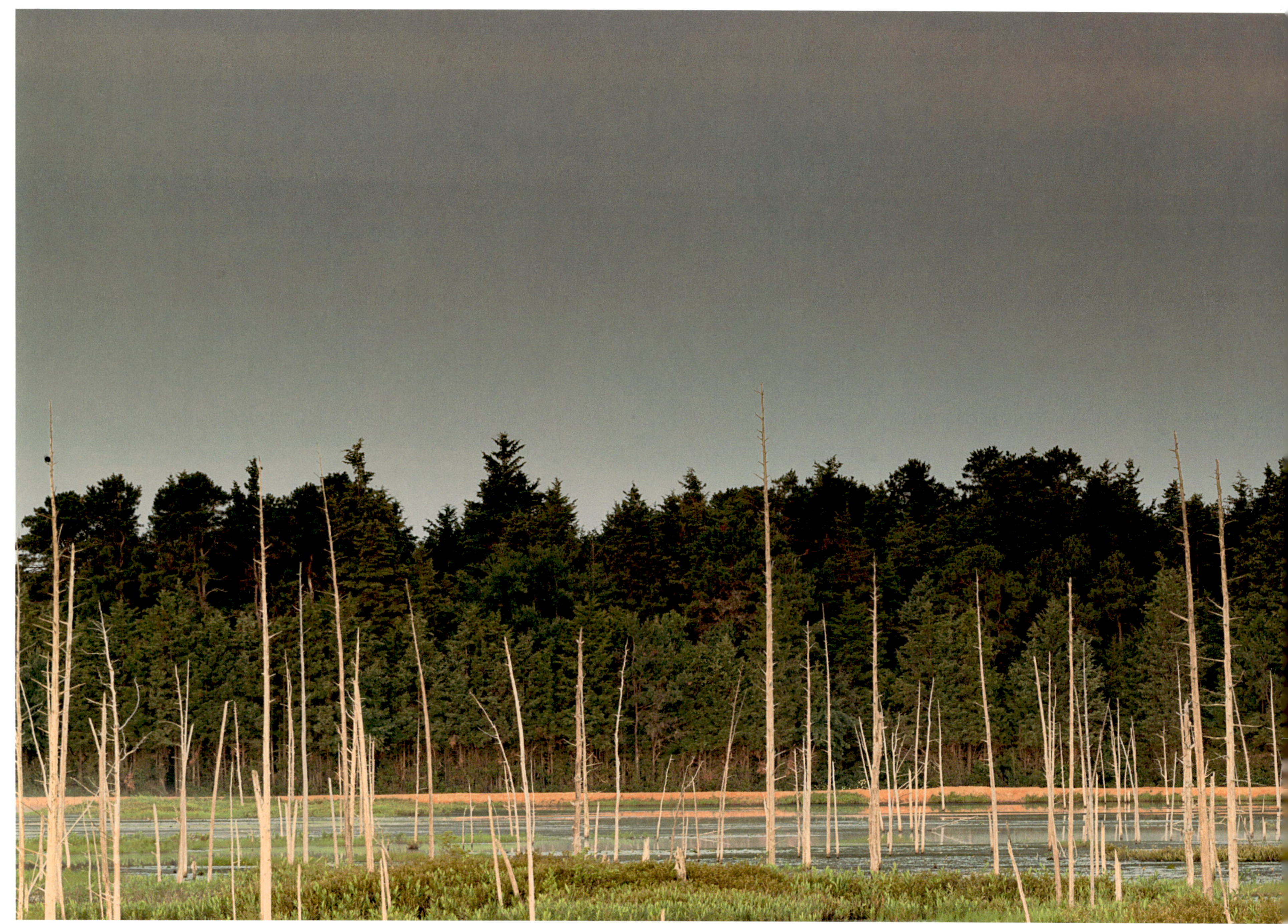

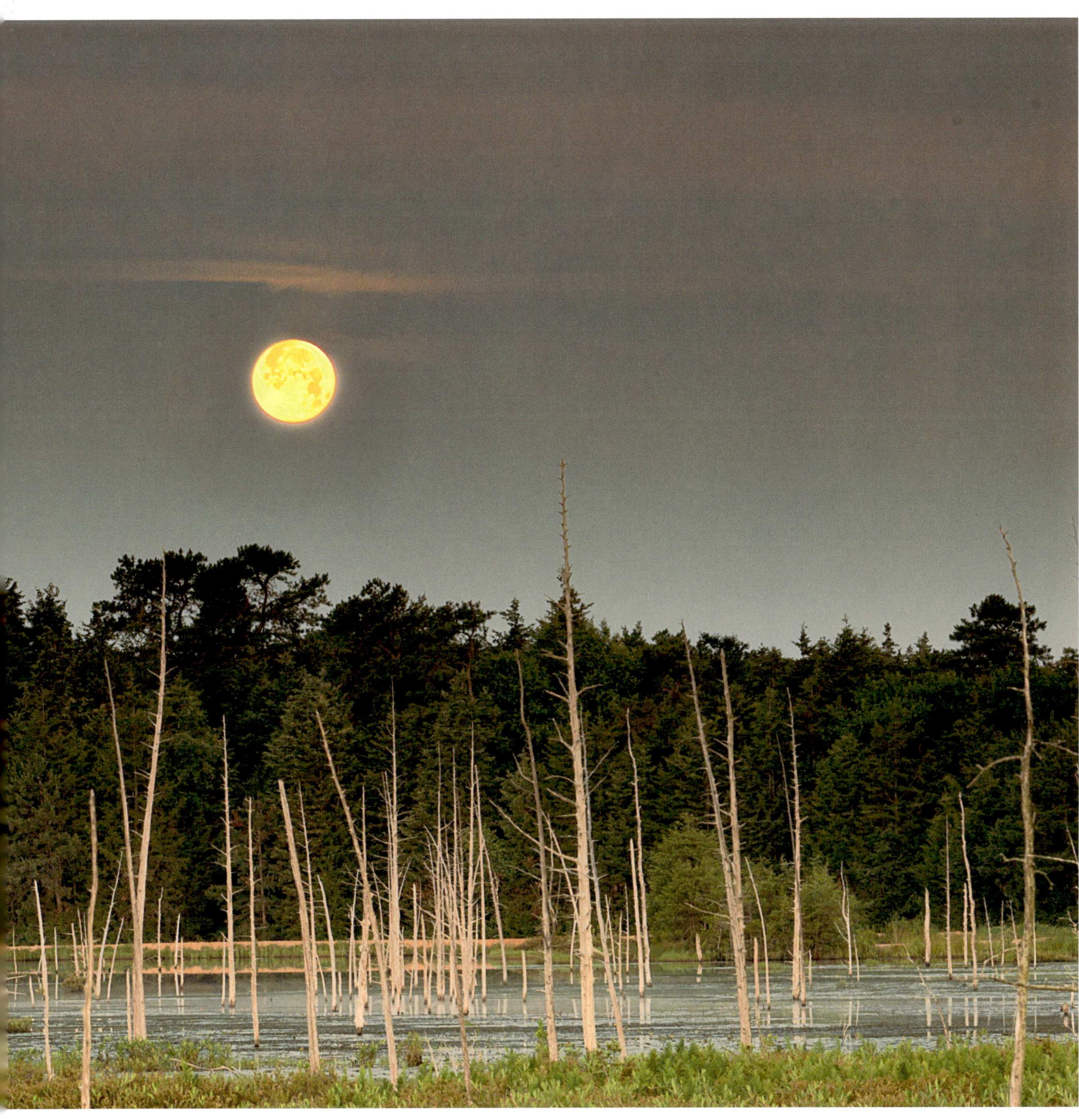

Super Moon over Franklin Parker Preserve, Woodland Township

The Jewel of the Pinelands

Emerald trees sparkle
intoxicated by sunlight.
Smoky topaz waters
flow swiftly downstream.
Ruby red cranberries
garnish riverbanks.
Diamond-studded light
flickers across river paths.
Warm golden rays
stream through forest land.
Amethyst fiddlehead ferns
dance along unspoiled banks.
Opaline beaches welcome
weary water travelers
dazzled by gems on Oswego River.

—Barbara Spector

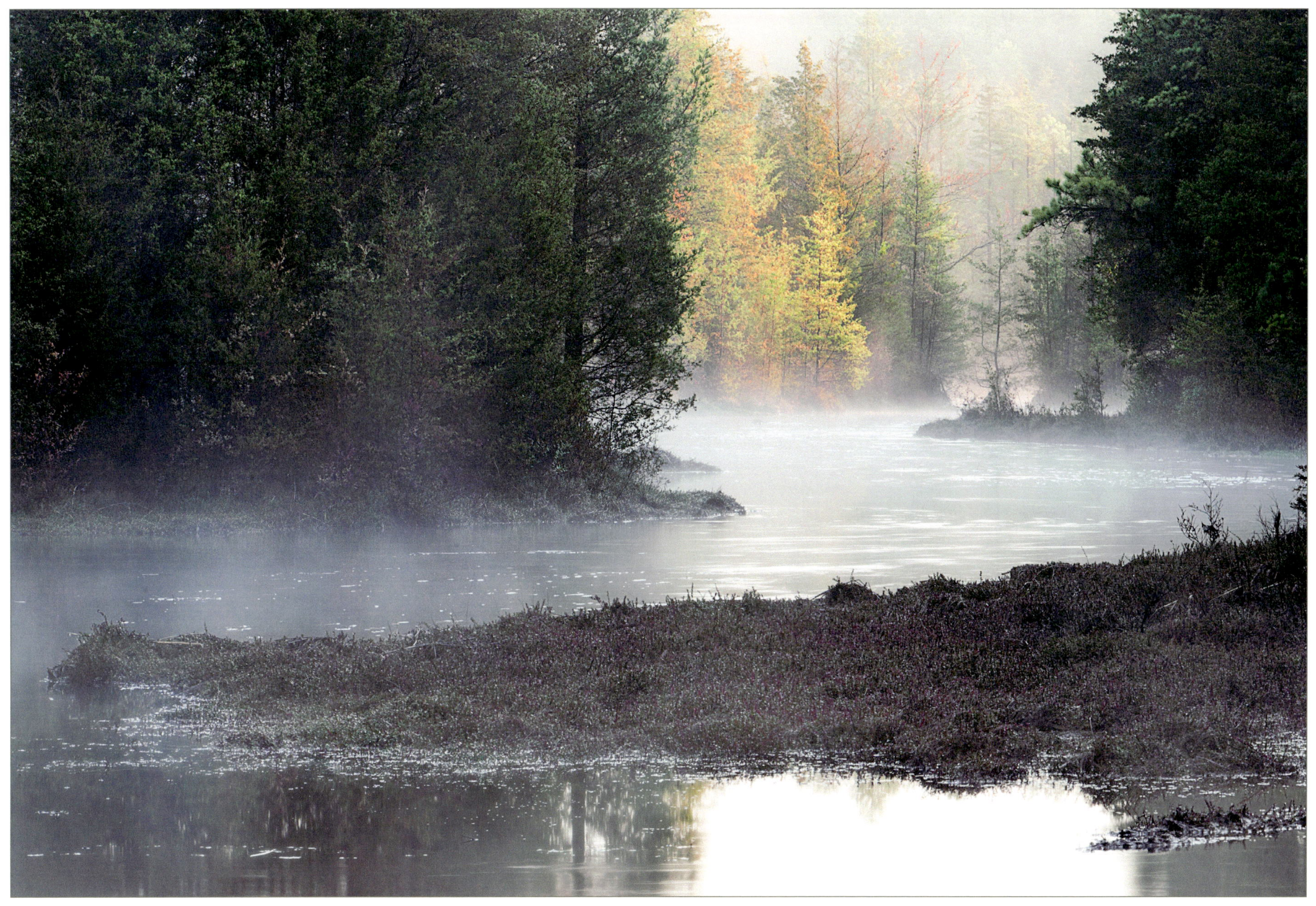

Oswego Spring, Oswego River

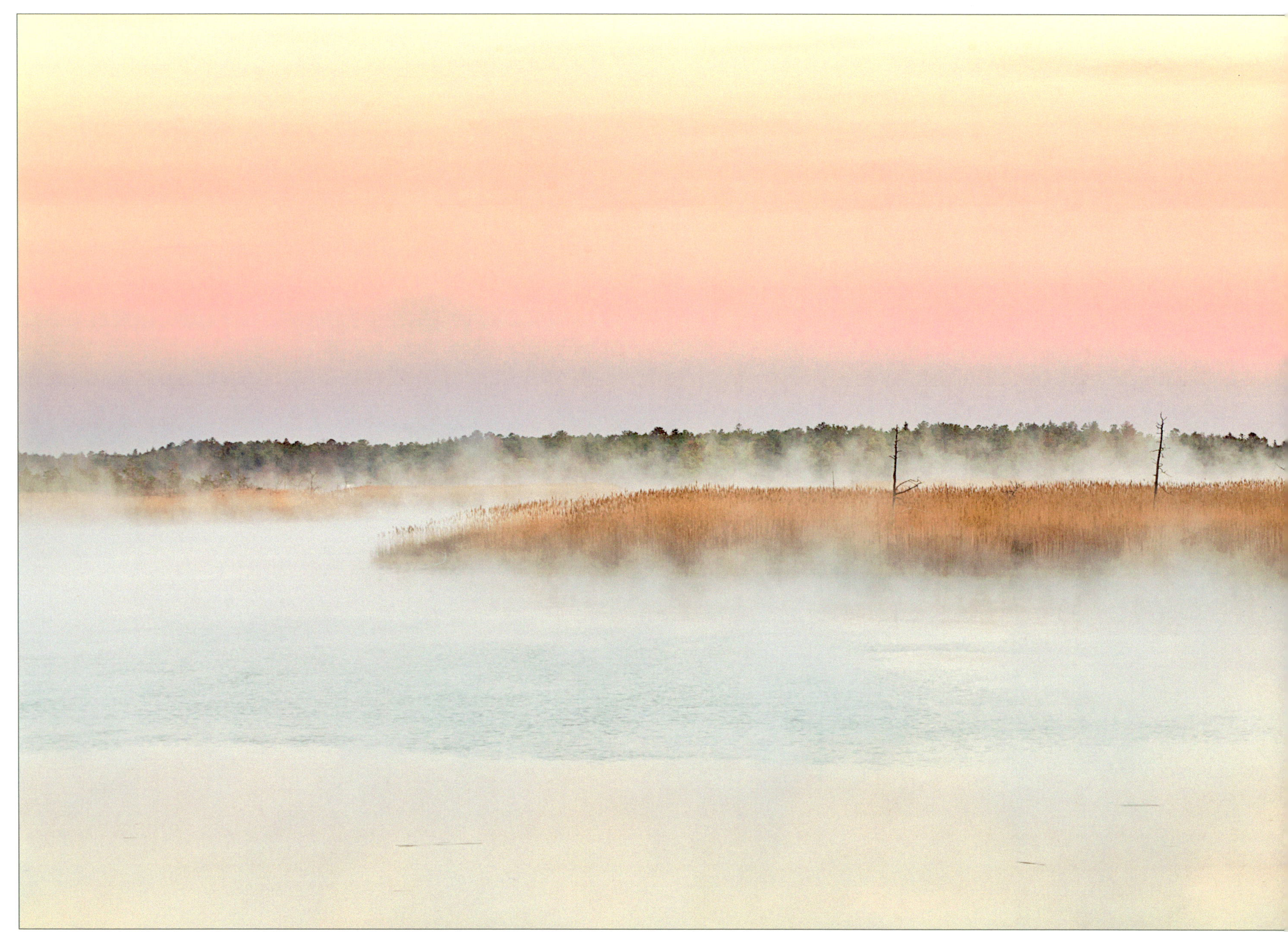

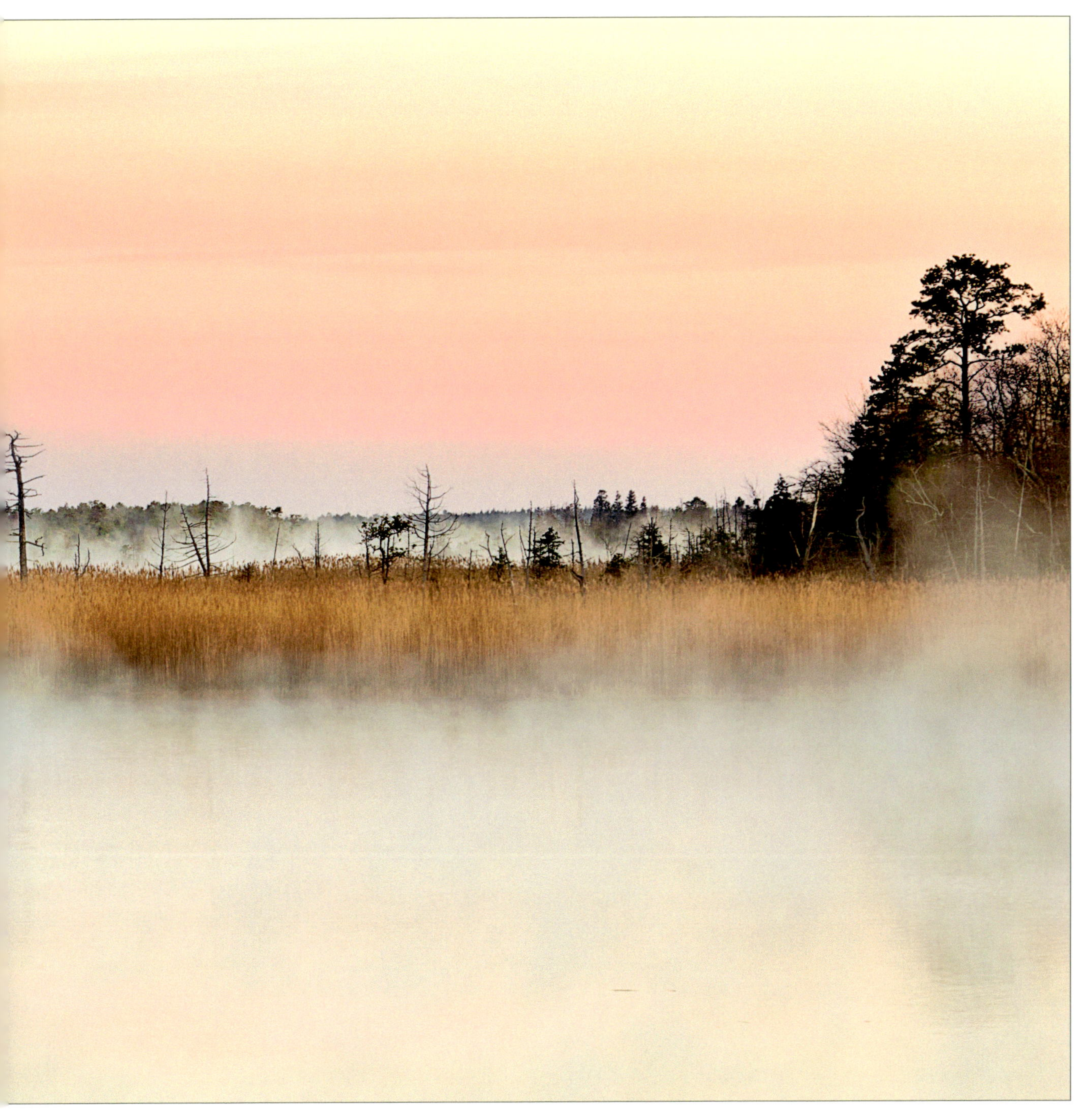

Wading River Point, Wading River

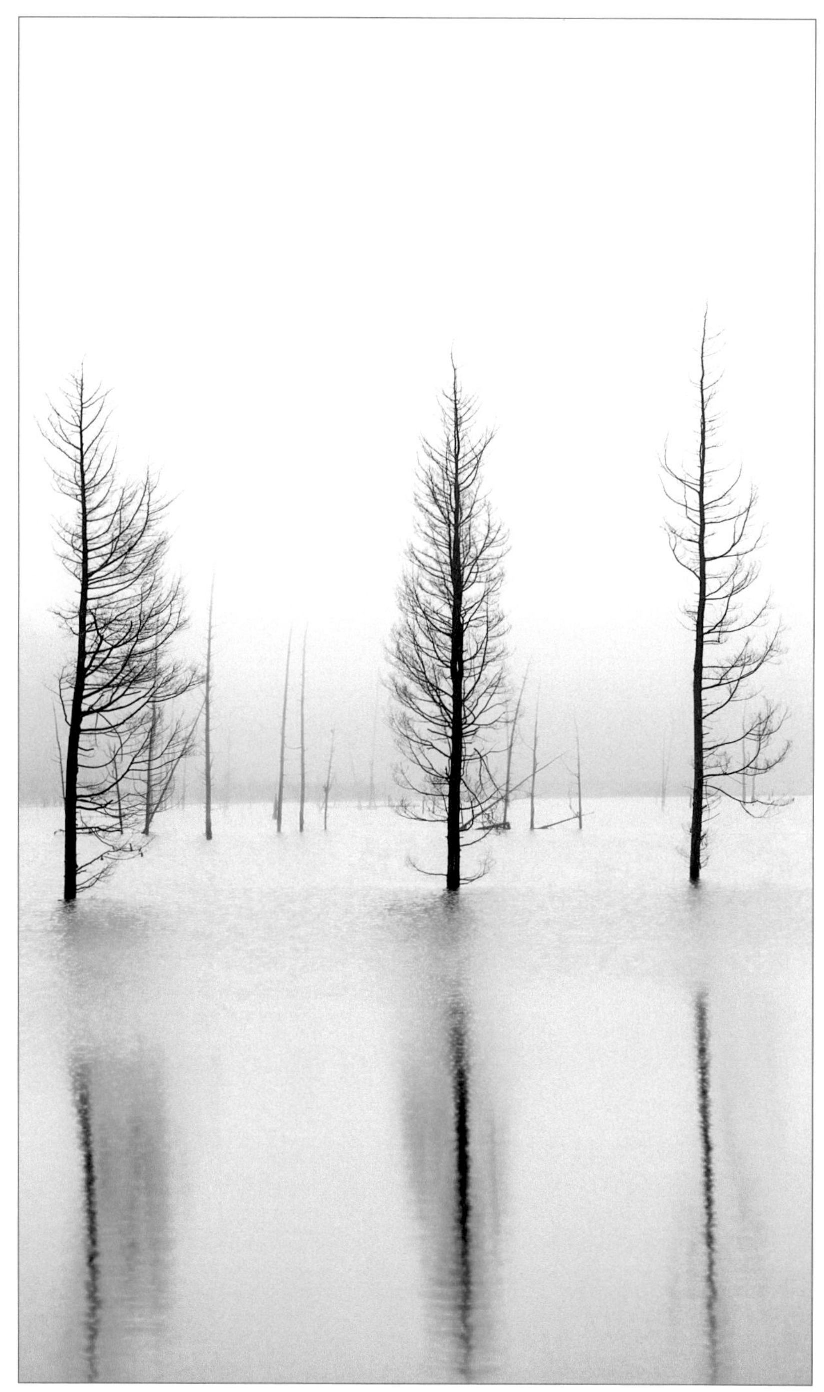

Tres Trees, Franklin Parker Preserve

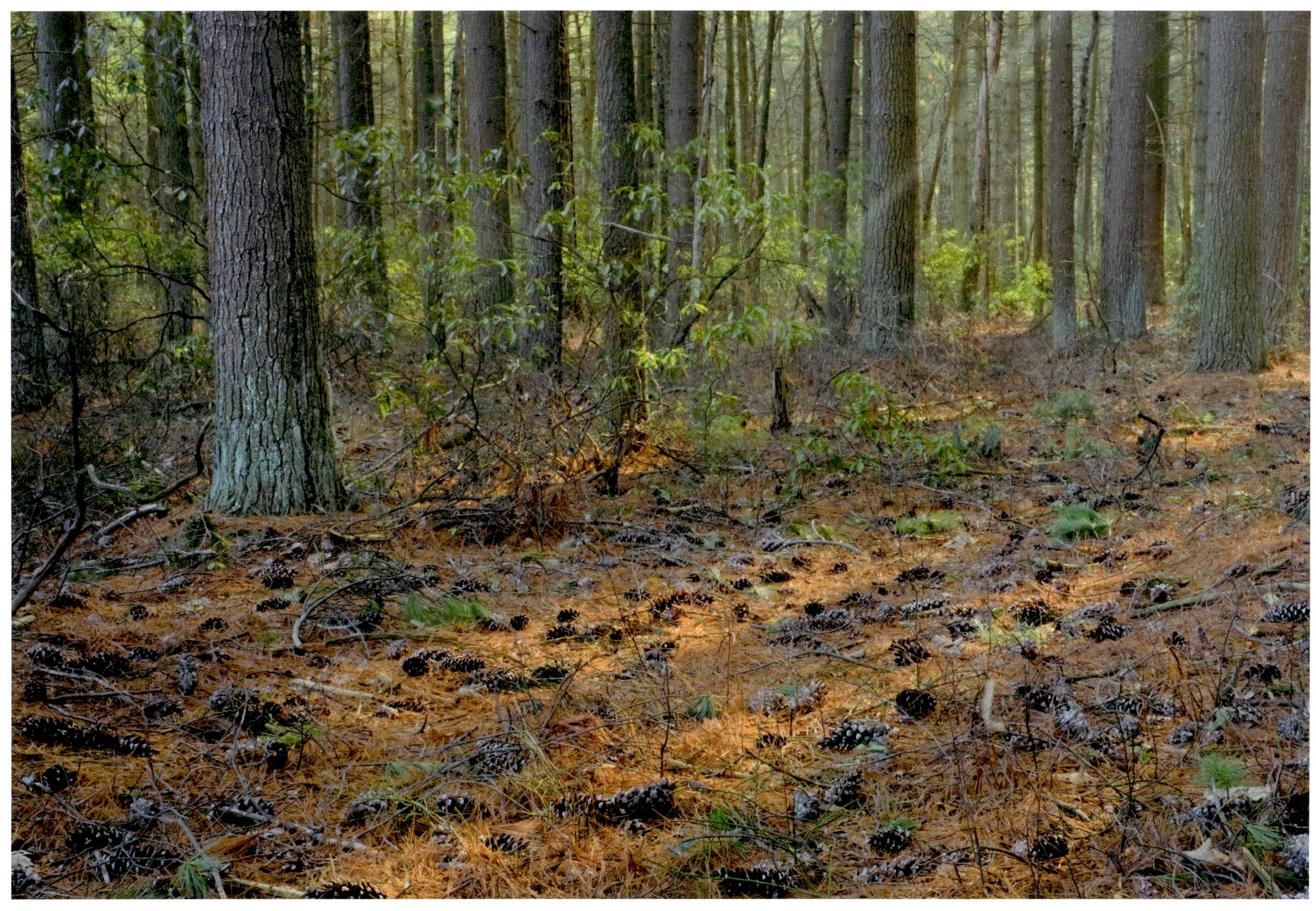

Forest Floor, Brendan T. Byrne State Forest

"The clearest way into the Universe is through a forest wilderness."

—John Muir

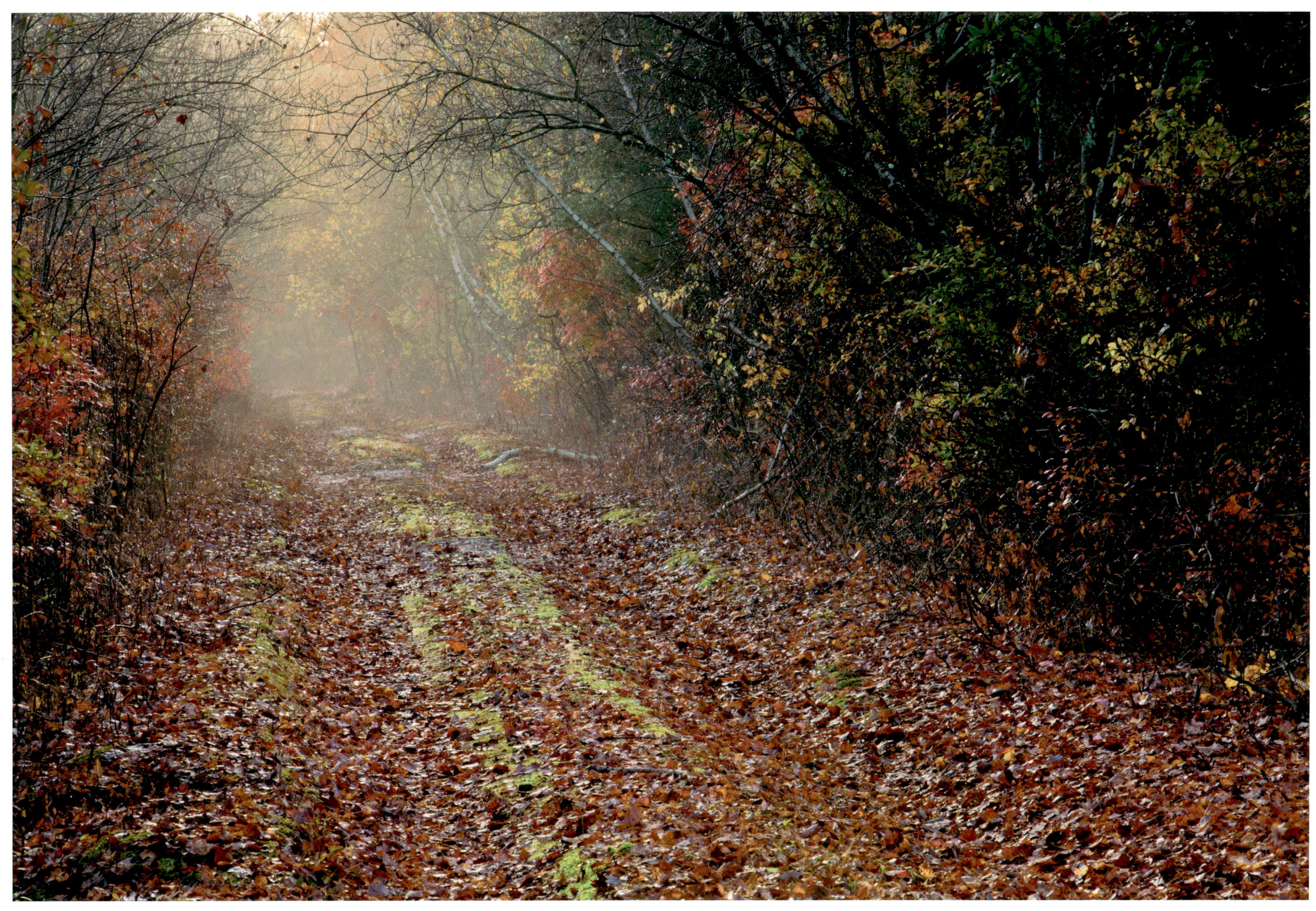

Fall Tunnel, West Jersey Cranberry Meadows

Reflecting the hues
of a cold dawn, the river
runs on to the sea

—Ralph Dahle

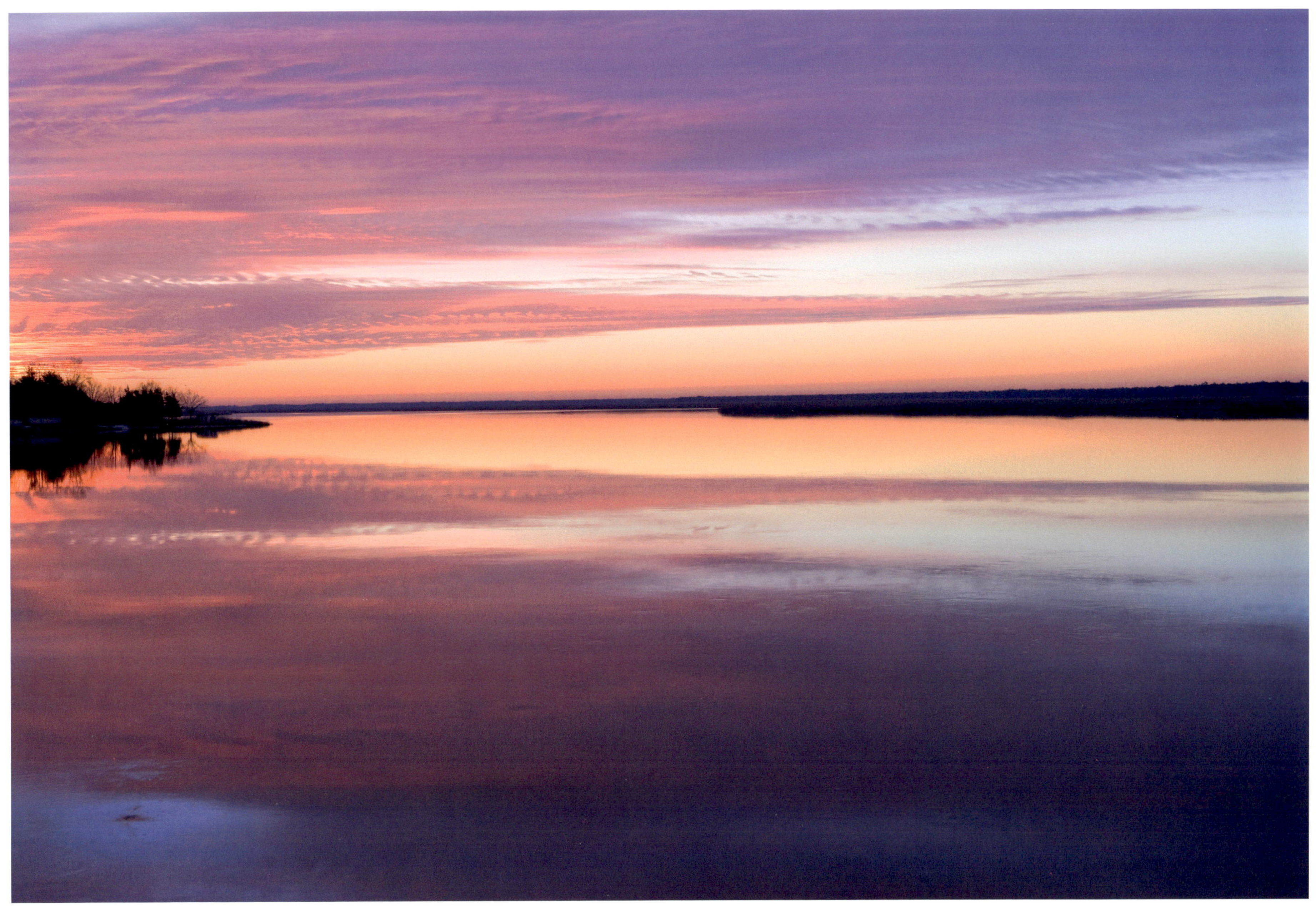

Mullica River at Lower Bank, Lower Bank

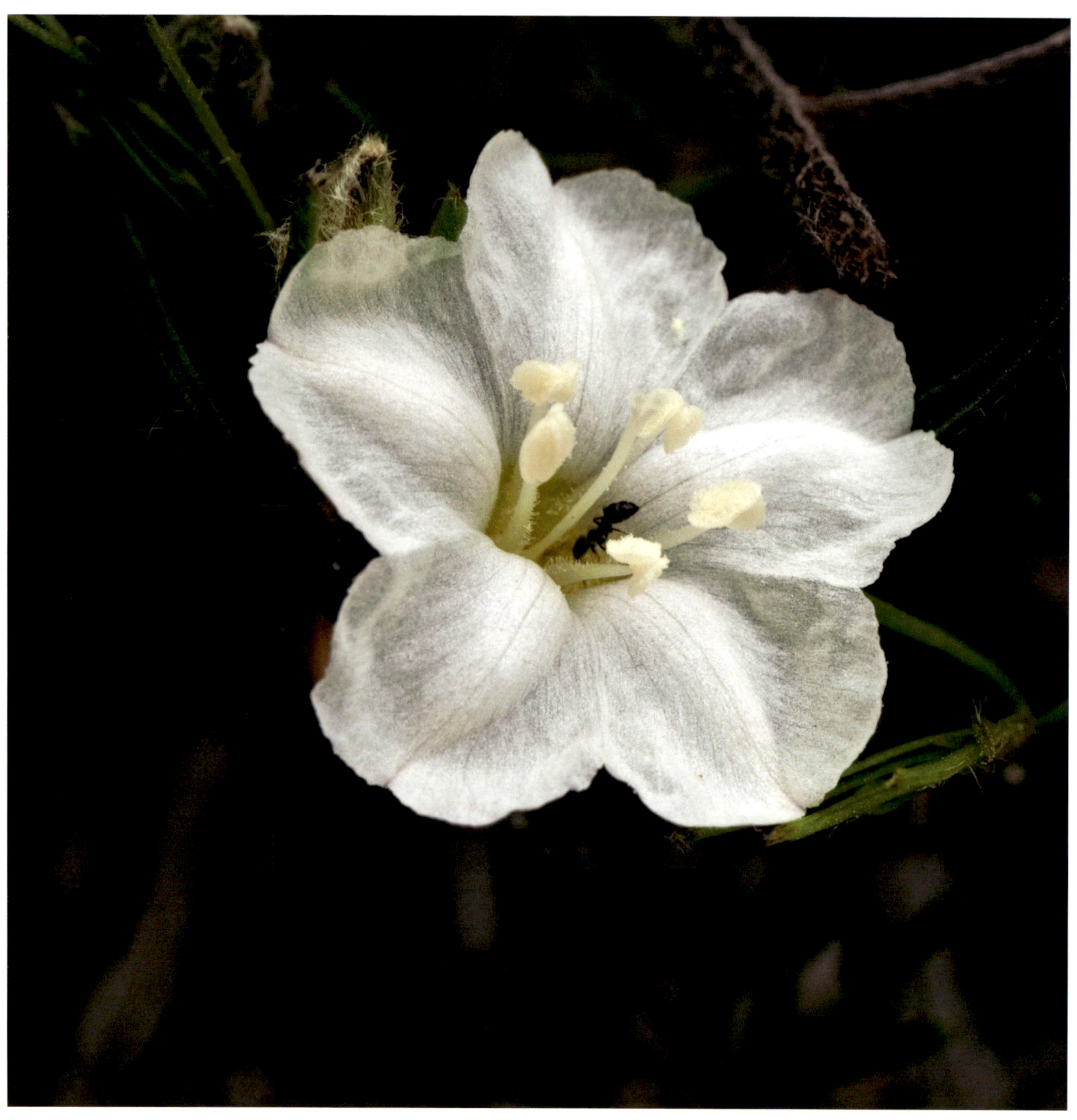

Pickering's Morning Glory, Wharton State Forest

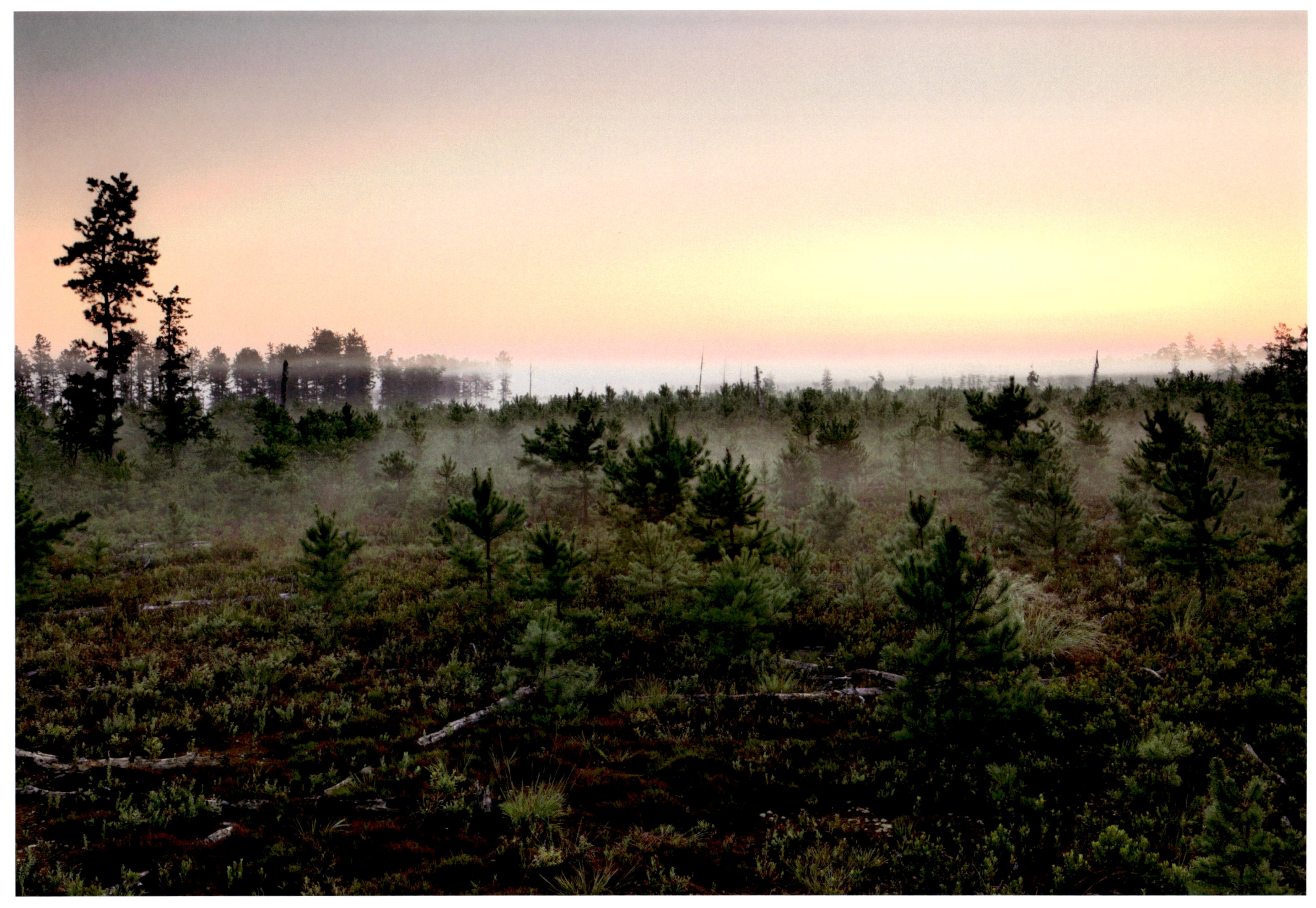

Summer Morning, near "¼ Mile", Hampton Furnace

"It is horrifying that we have to fight our own government to save the environment."

—Ansel Adams

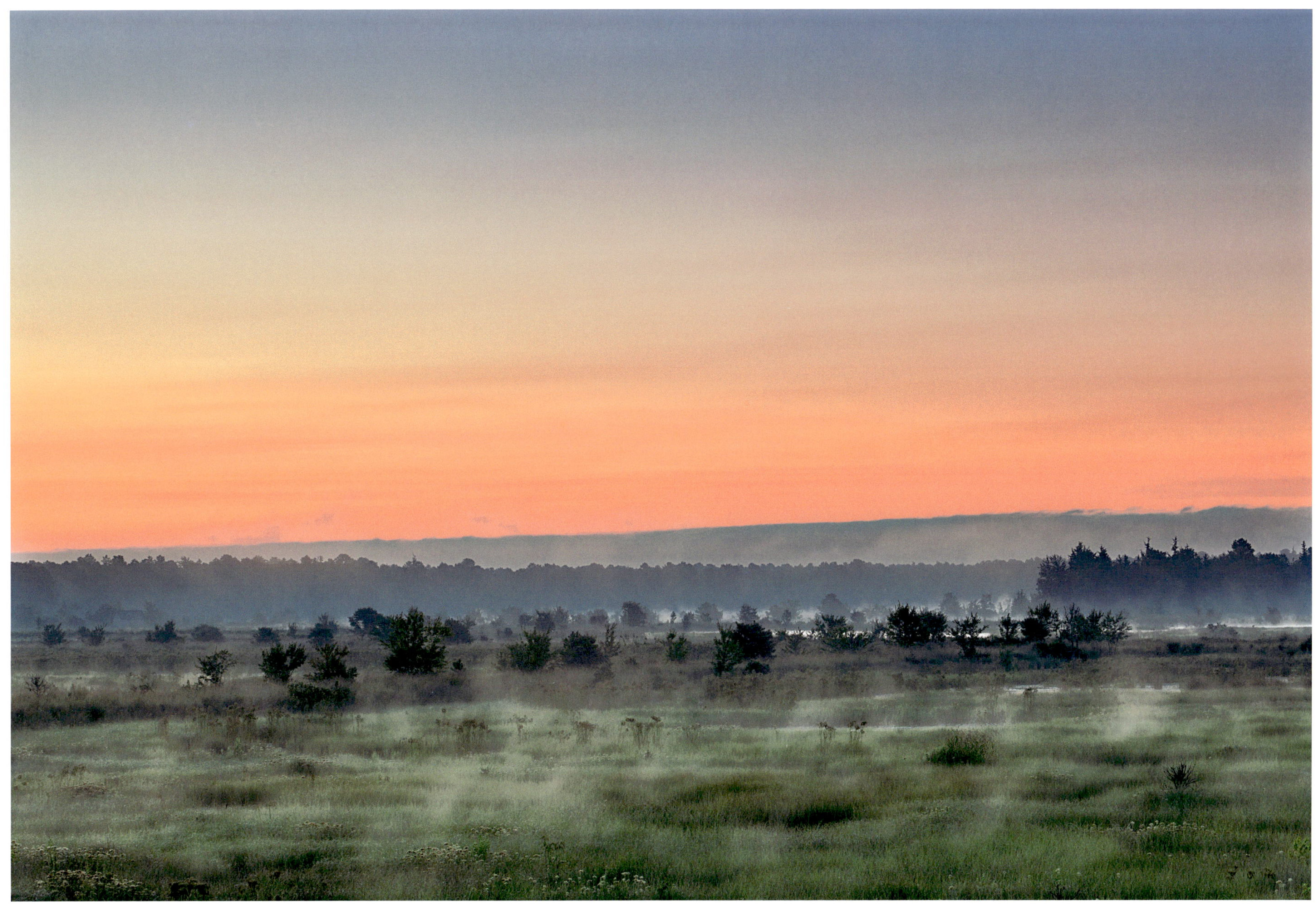
Summer Sunrise, Franklin Parker Preserve

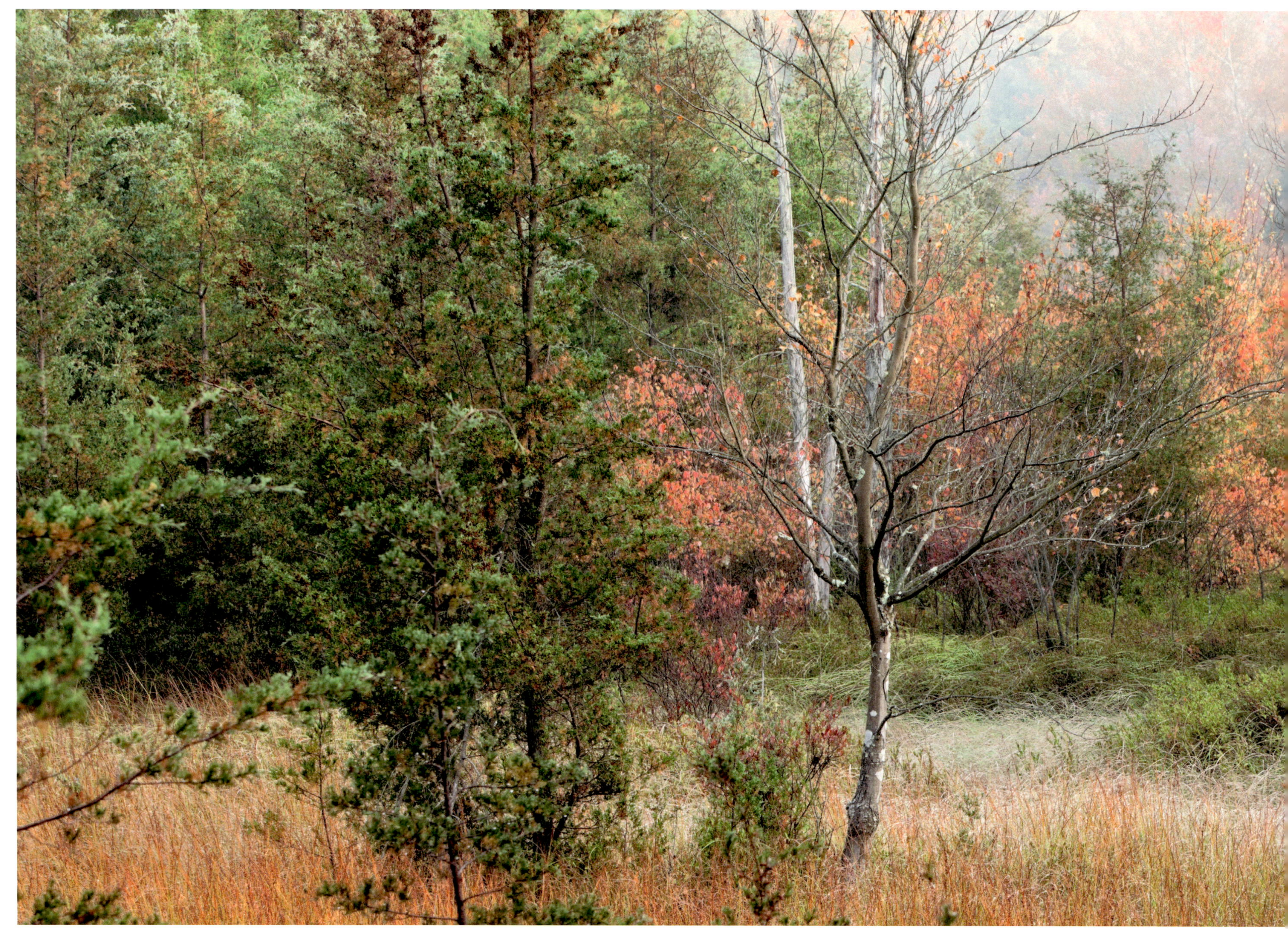

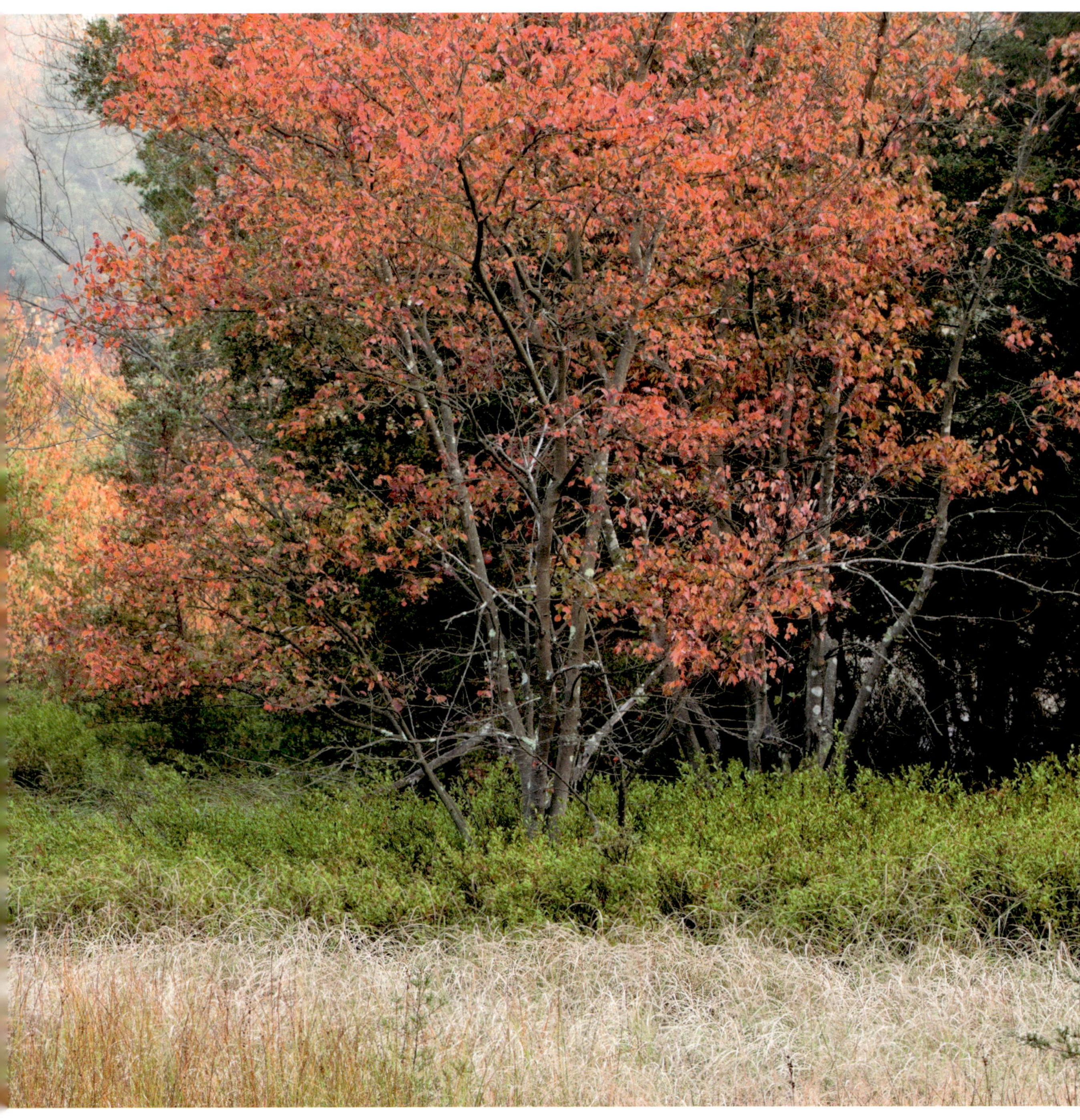

Pinelands Fall, along the Wading River

*"I like this place and could willingly
waste my time in it."*

—William Shakespeare

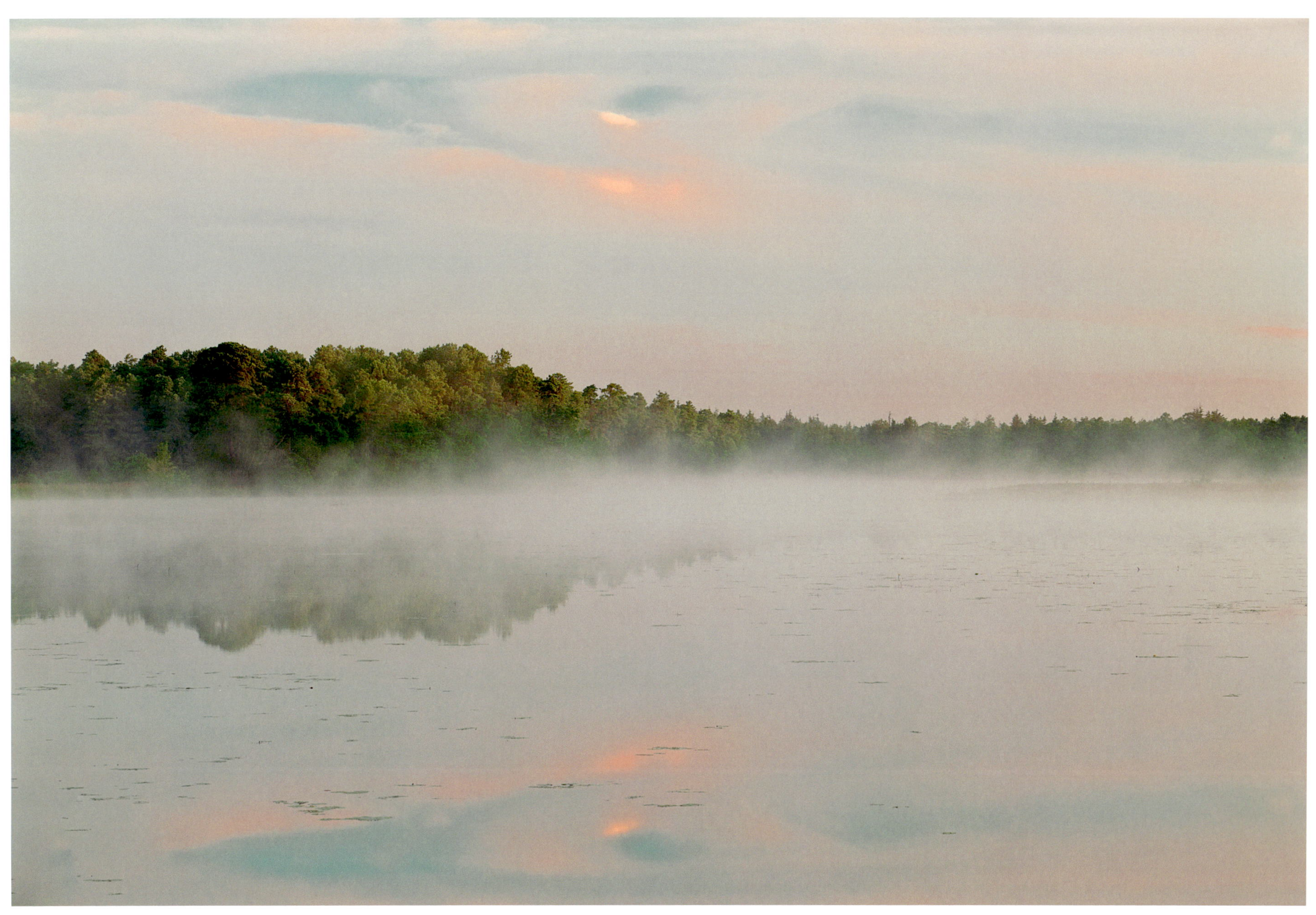

Wading River Reservoir, Franklin Parker Preserve

Sun lights horizon
pink purple clouds fill huge sky
daybreak fades out moon sliver

—Barbara Spector

Mullica Bend Sunrise, Wharton State Forest

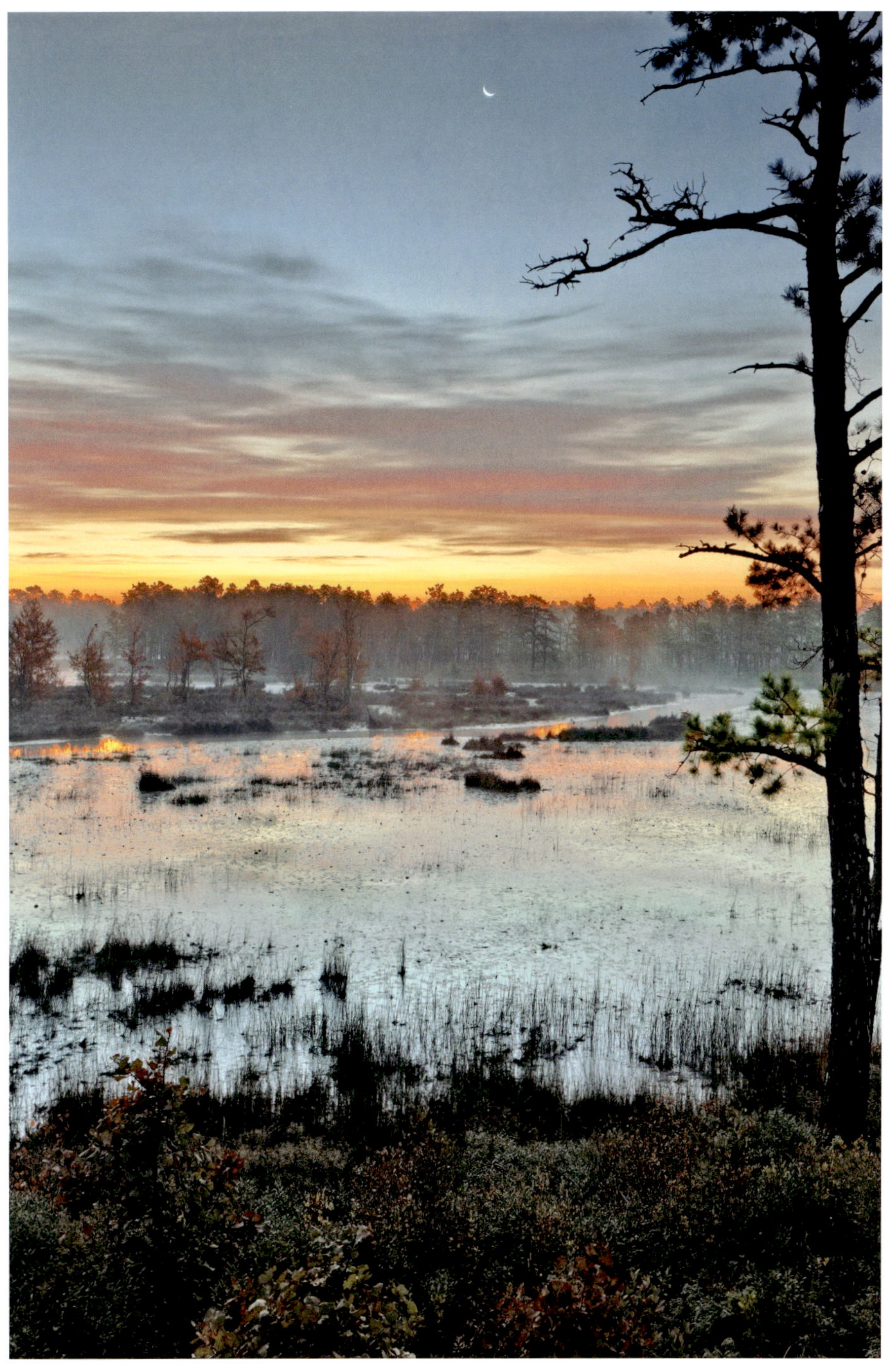

Pastel morning
stark trees on a distant shore
Pineland paradox

—Ralph Dahle

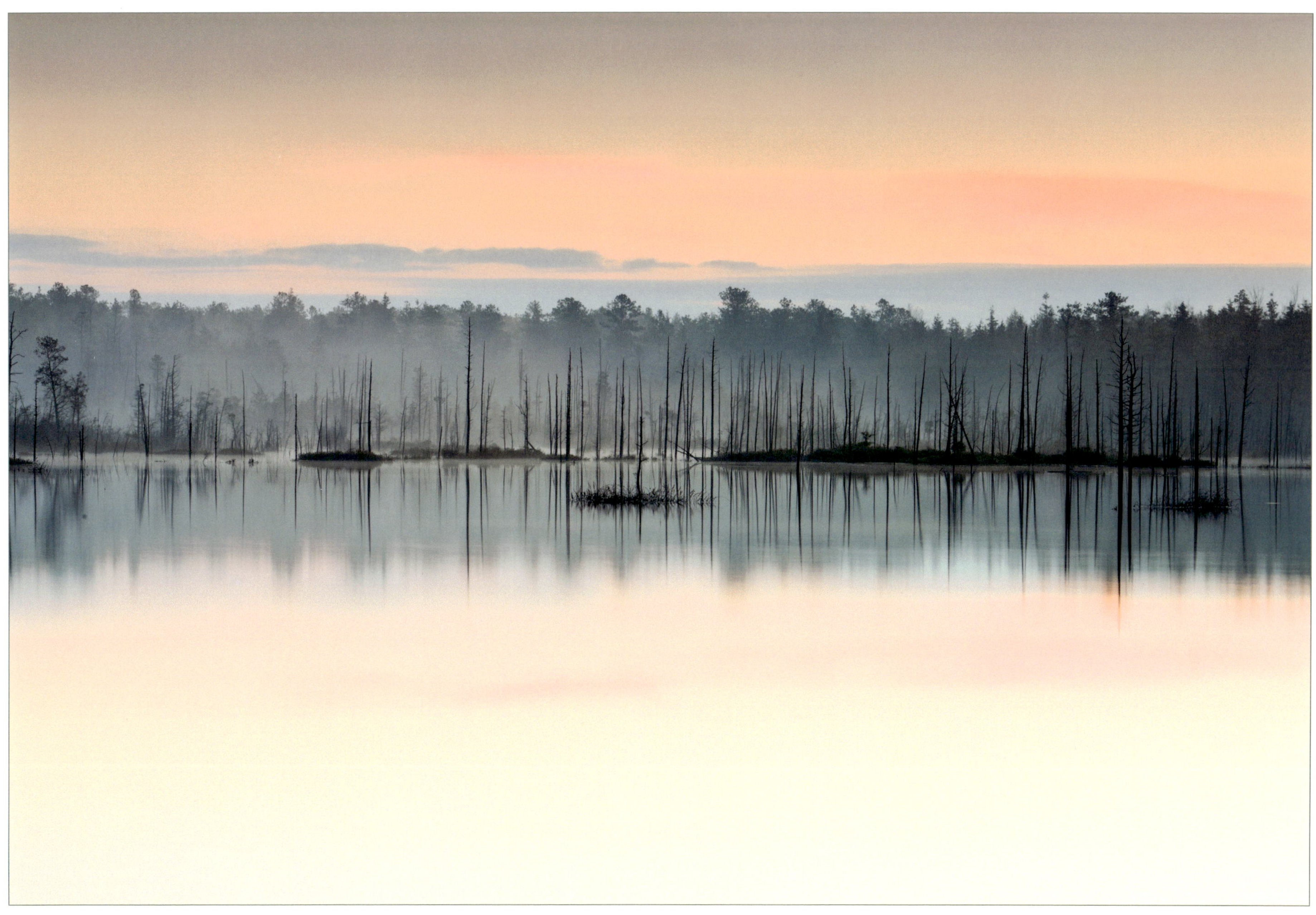

Morning is Coming, Franklin Parker Preserve

"*Man must go back to nature for information.*"

—THOMAS PAINE

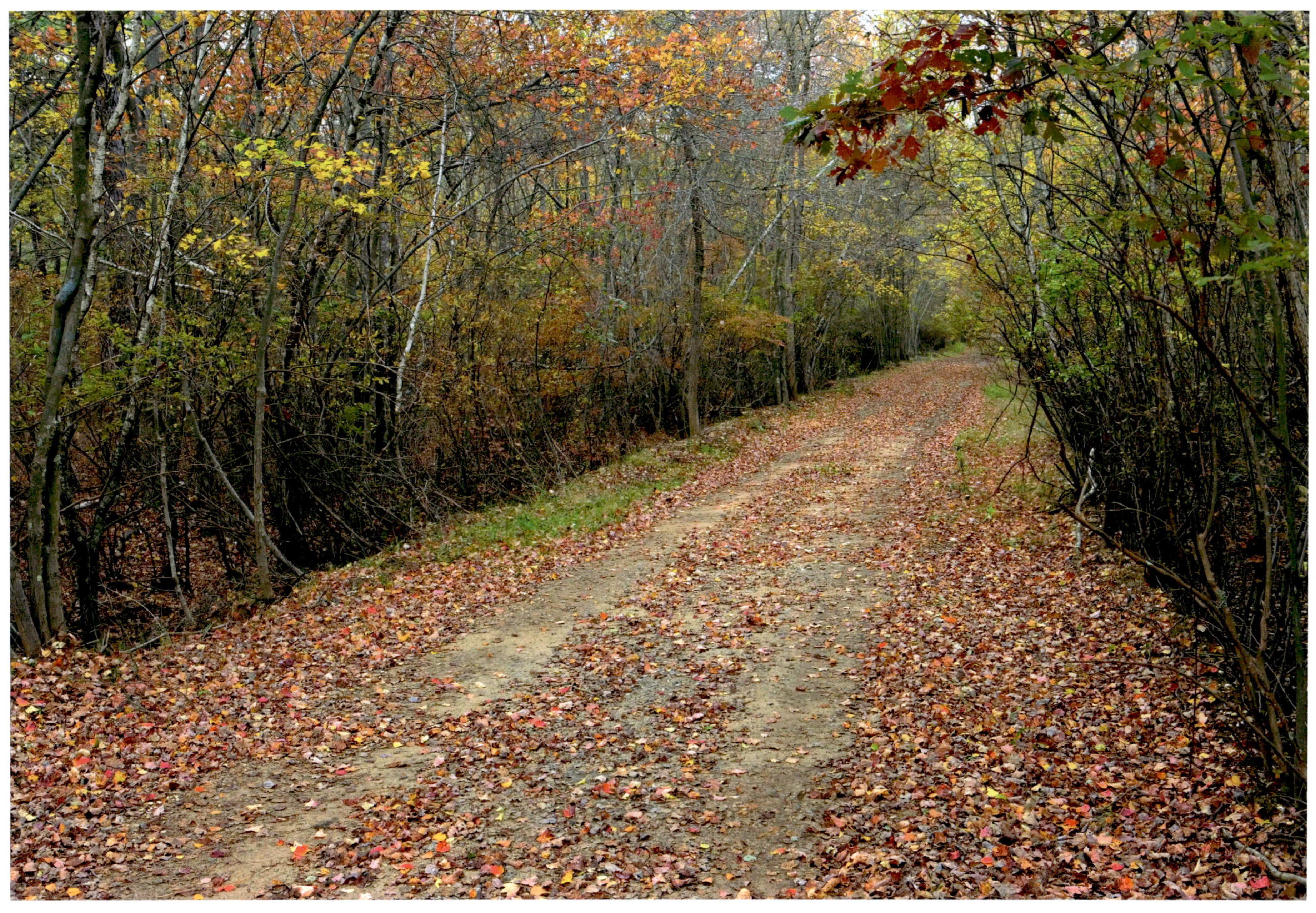

Fallen Leaf Road, Woodland Township

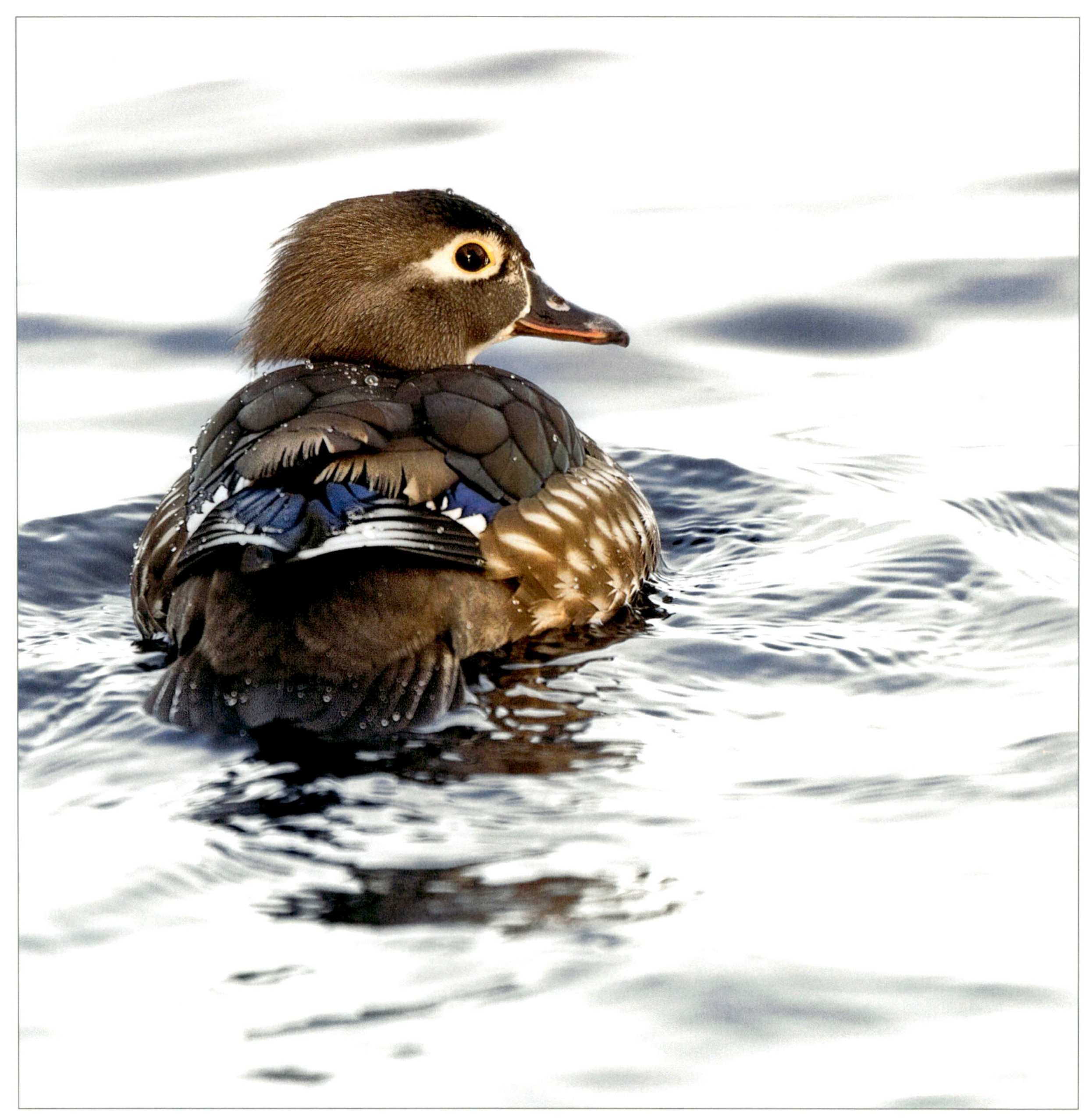

The Female, along the Mullica River waterway

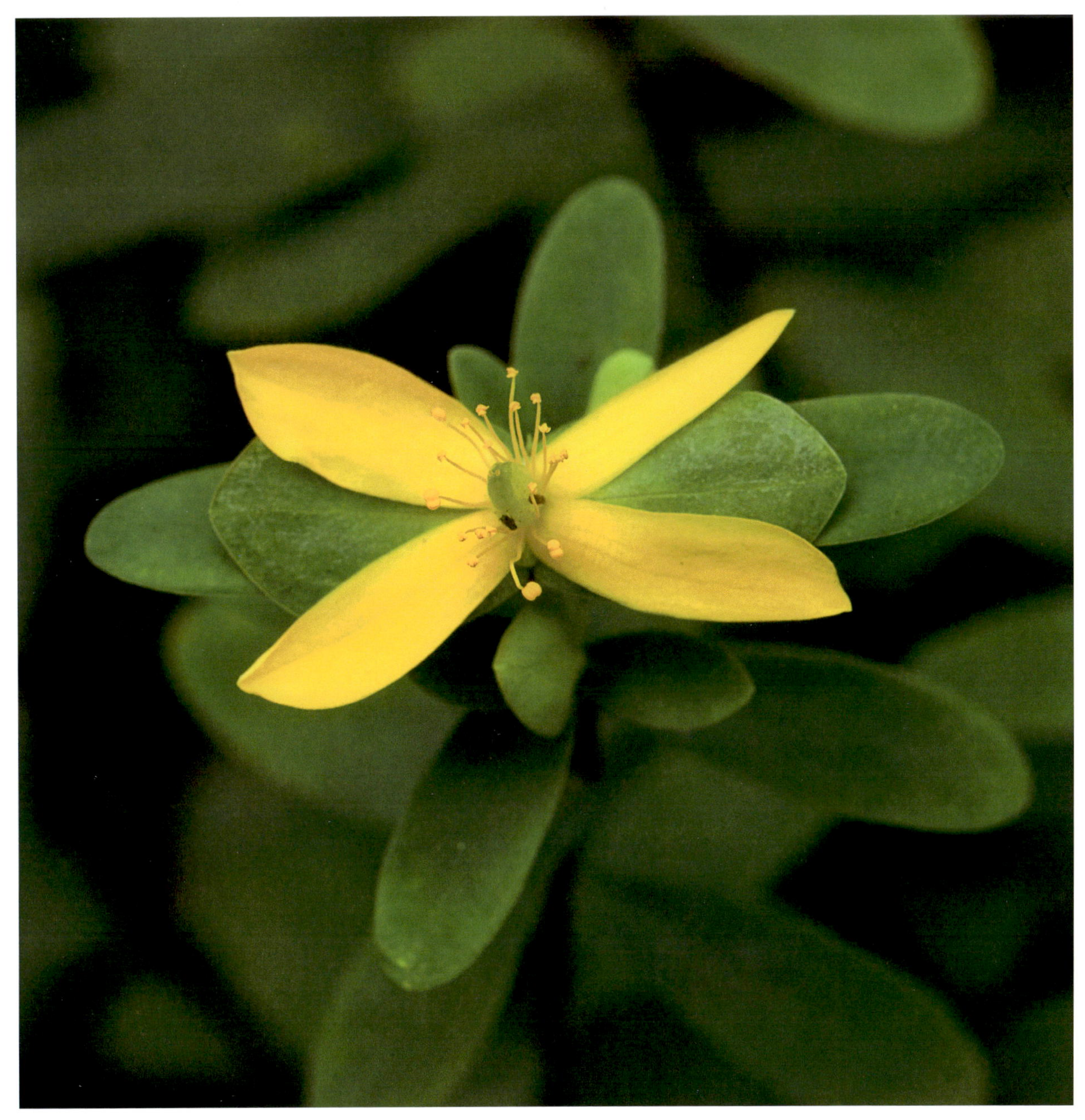

St. Andrews Cross, Wharton State Forest

Follow river lanes downstream
where water reflections of trees emerge
and capture your heart's dream

—Barbara Spector

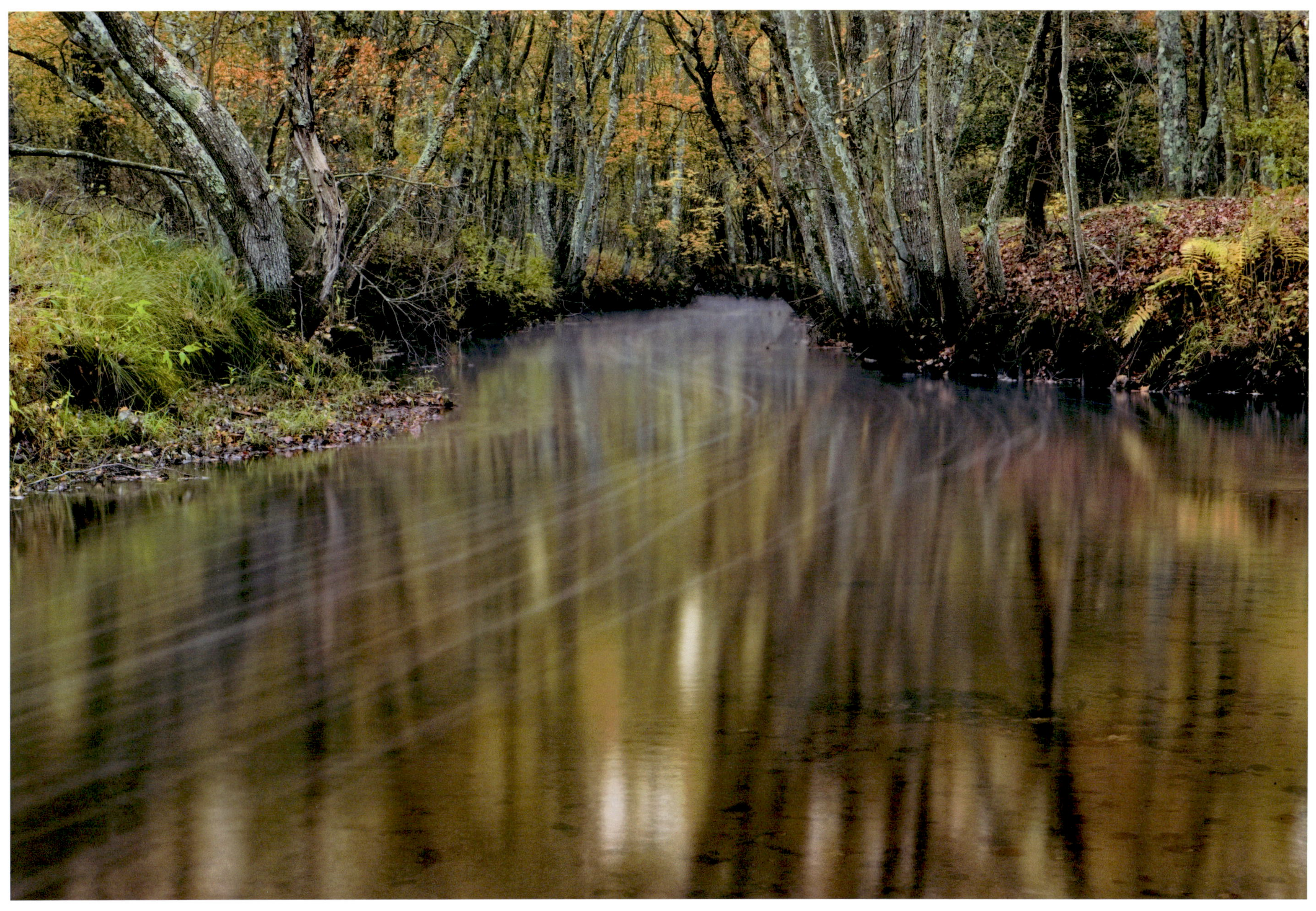

Batsto Tunnel, Hampton Furnace

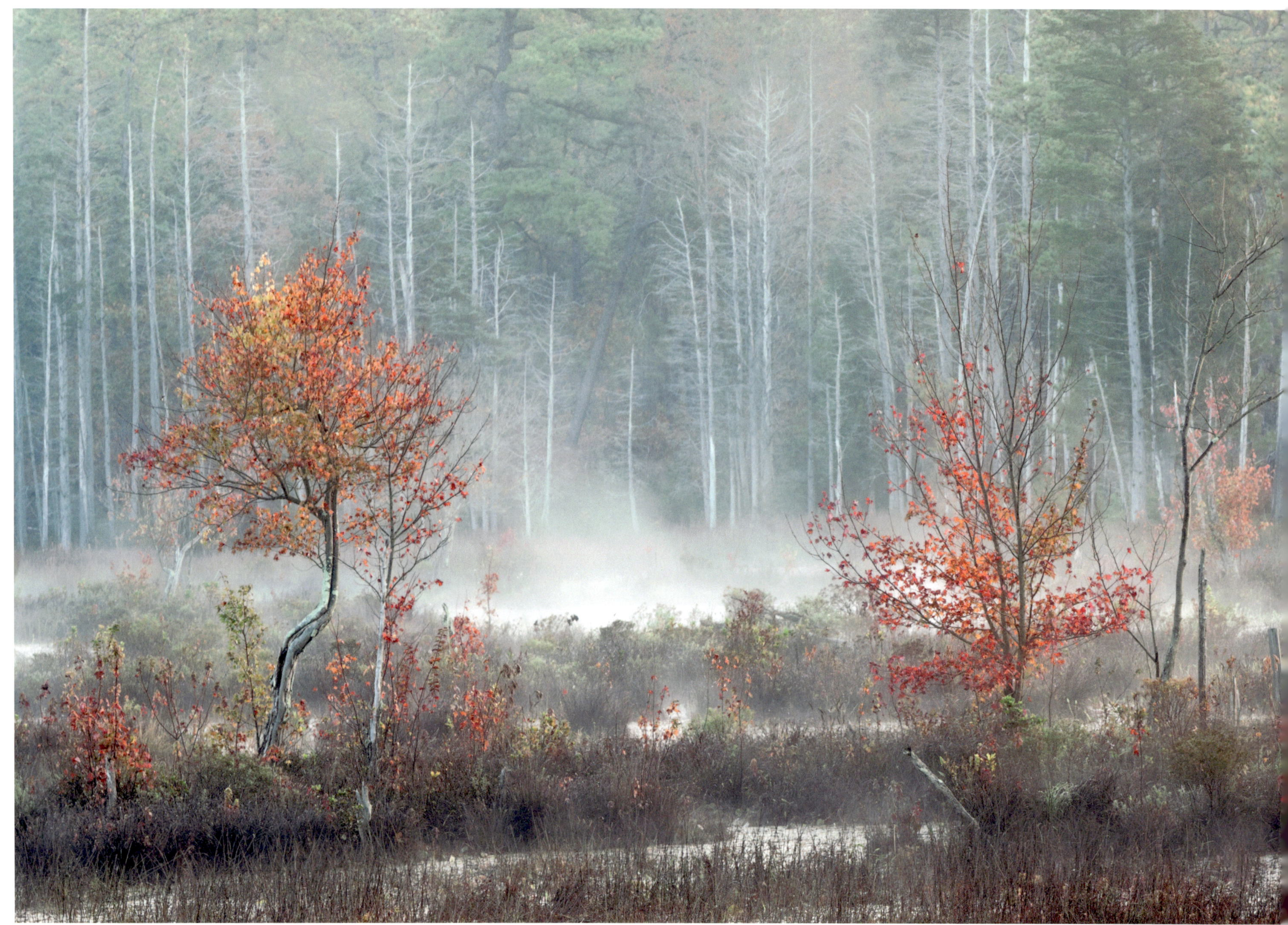

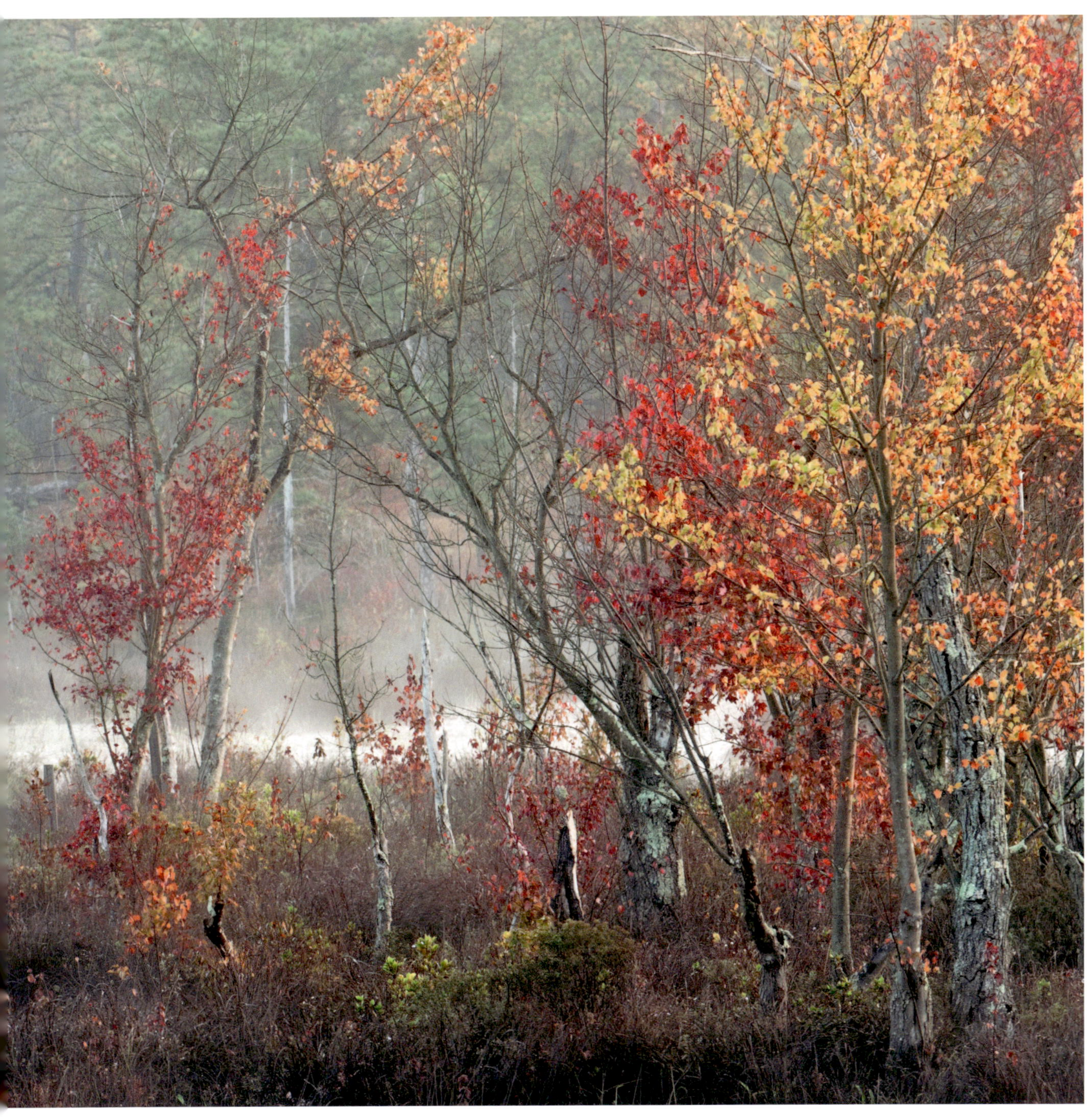

Mullica Bend Maples, Mullica River, Wharton State Forest

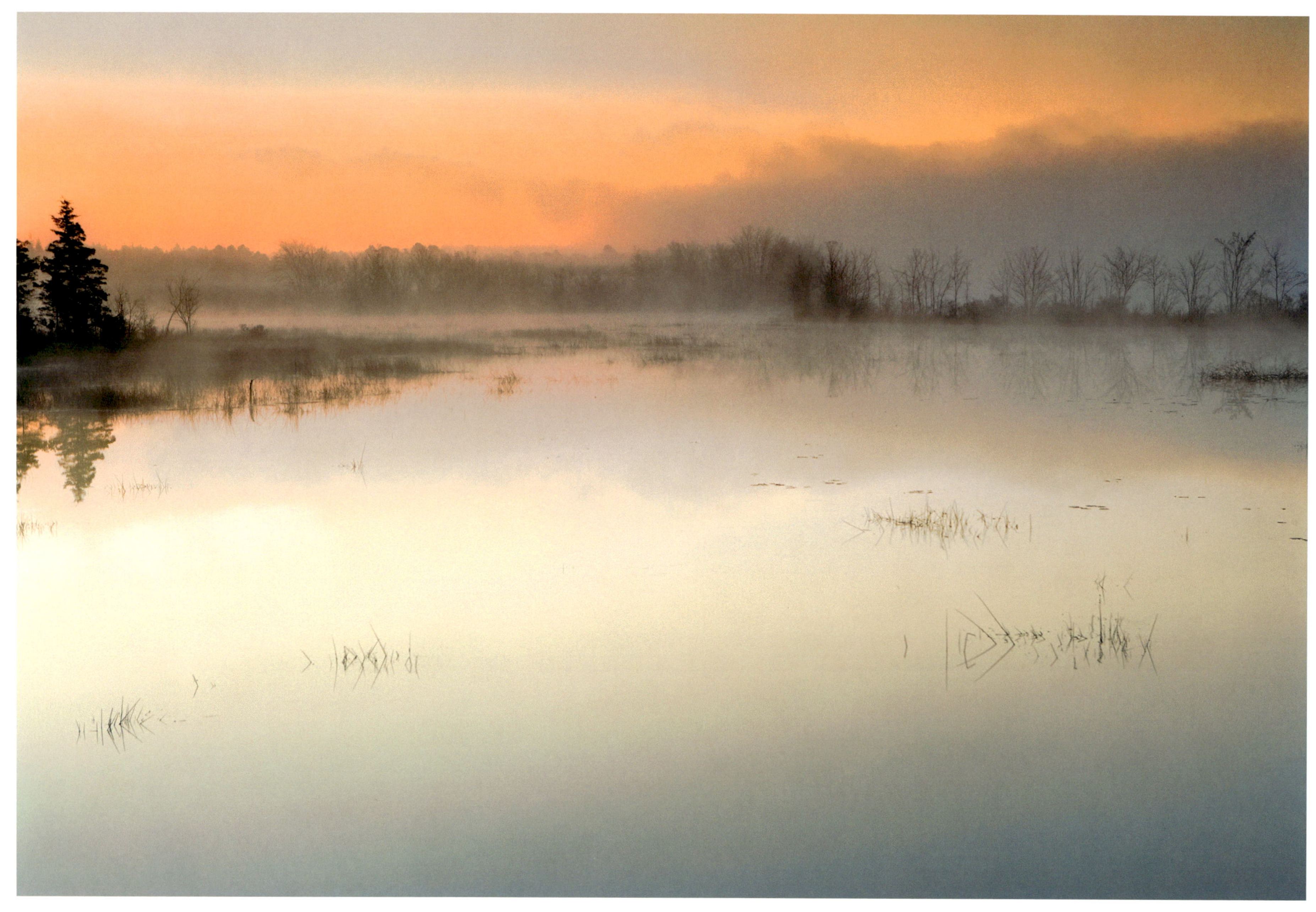

Fire Fog, West Jersey Cranberry Meadows

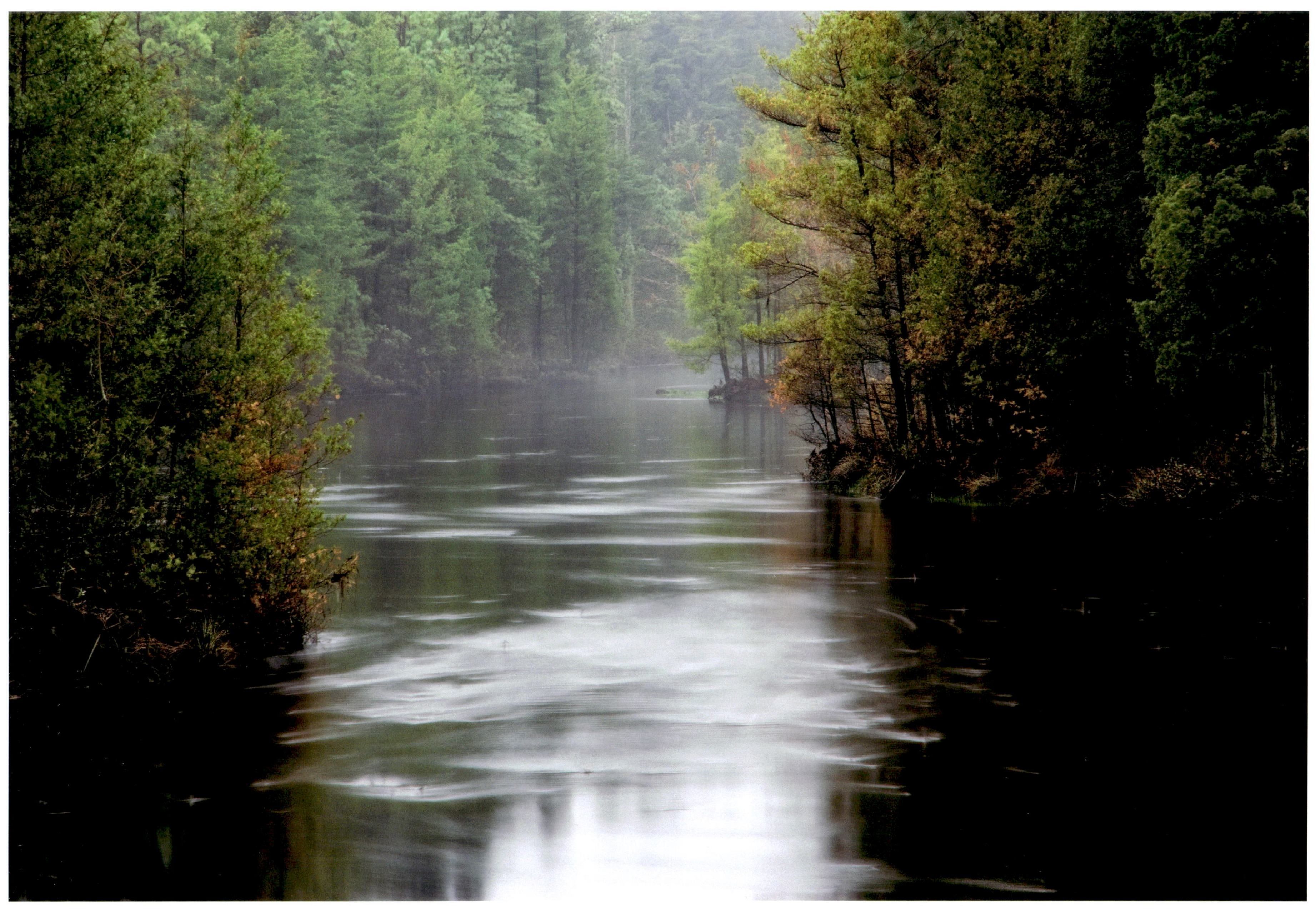

Cedar Canyon, Oswego River

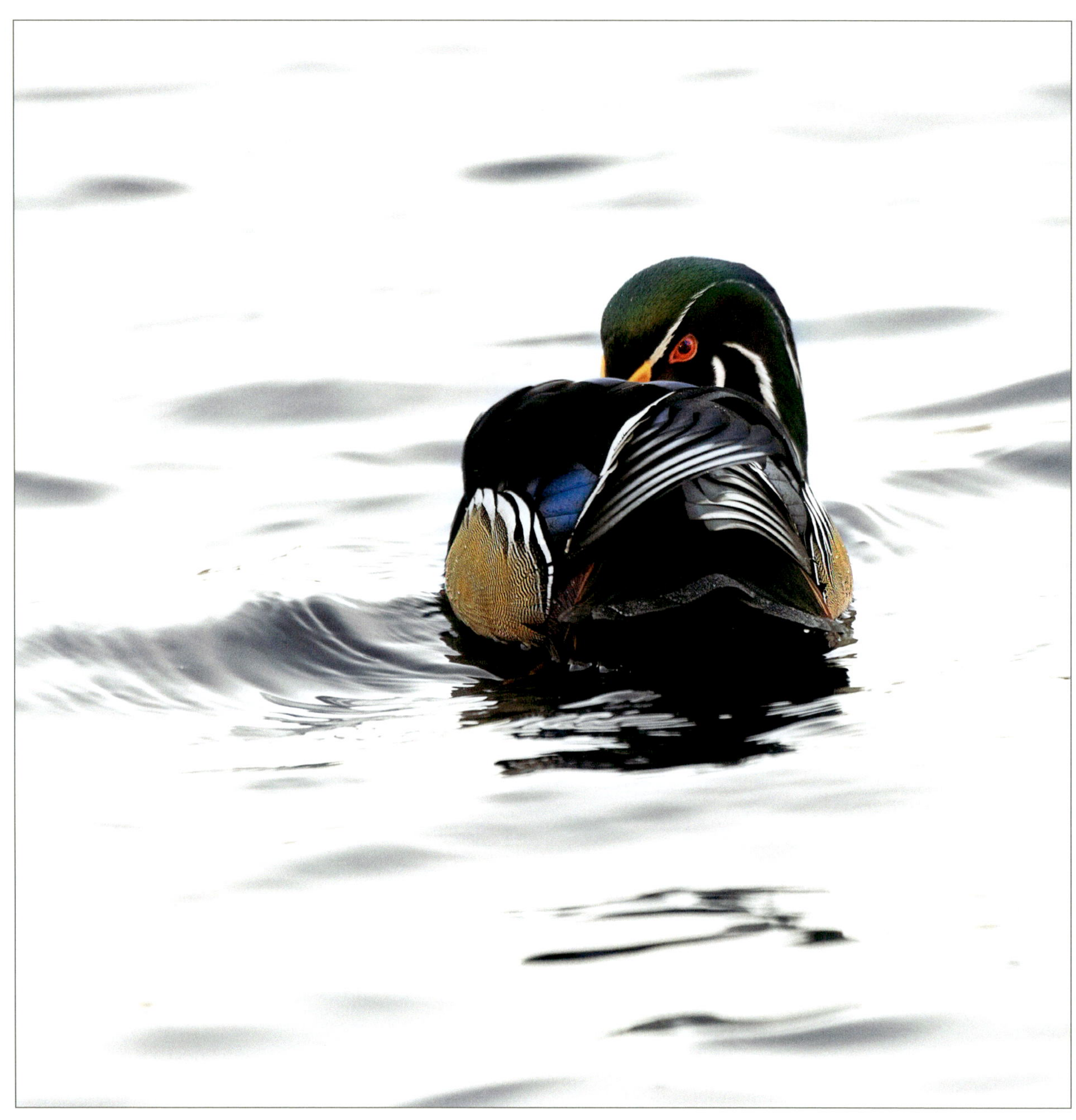

Looking Back, along the Mullica River waterway

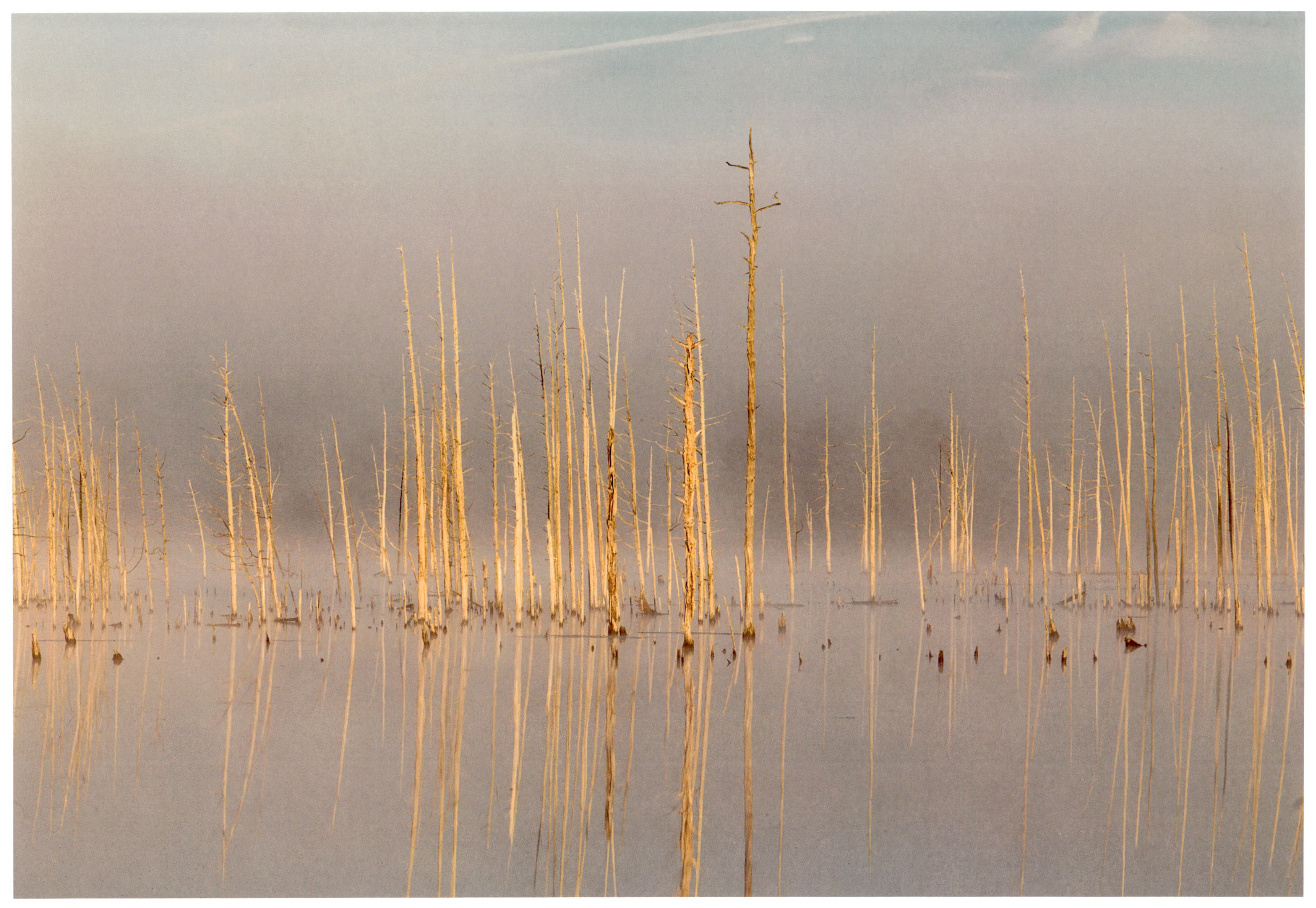

Eagle Reservoir, Franklin Parker Preserve

Pale blue sky beams through
autumn trees
create sparkling river path

—Barbara Spector

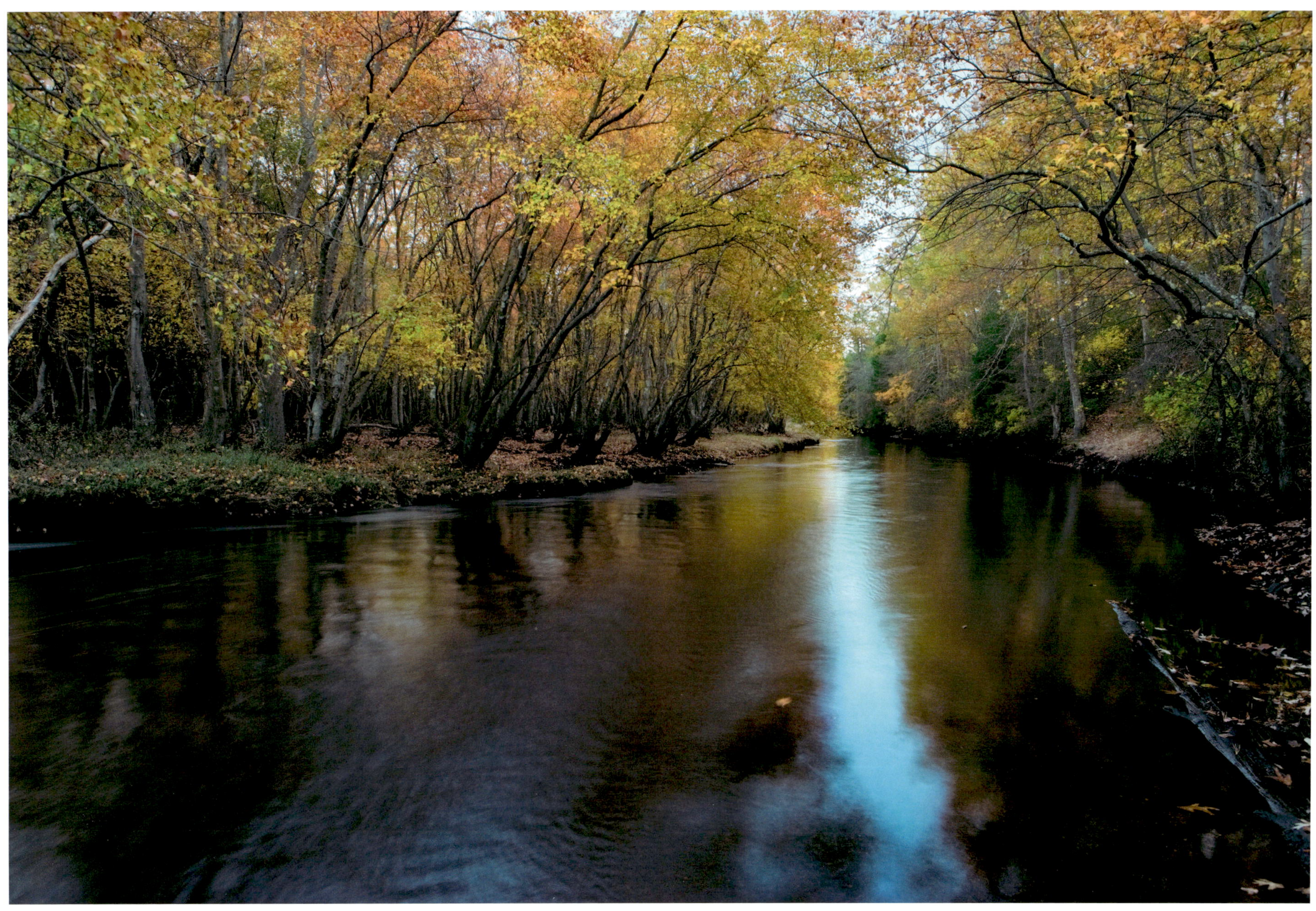

Wading River Fall, Wharton State Forest

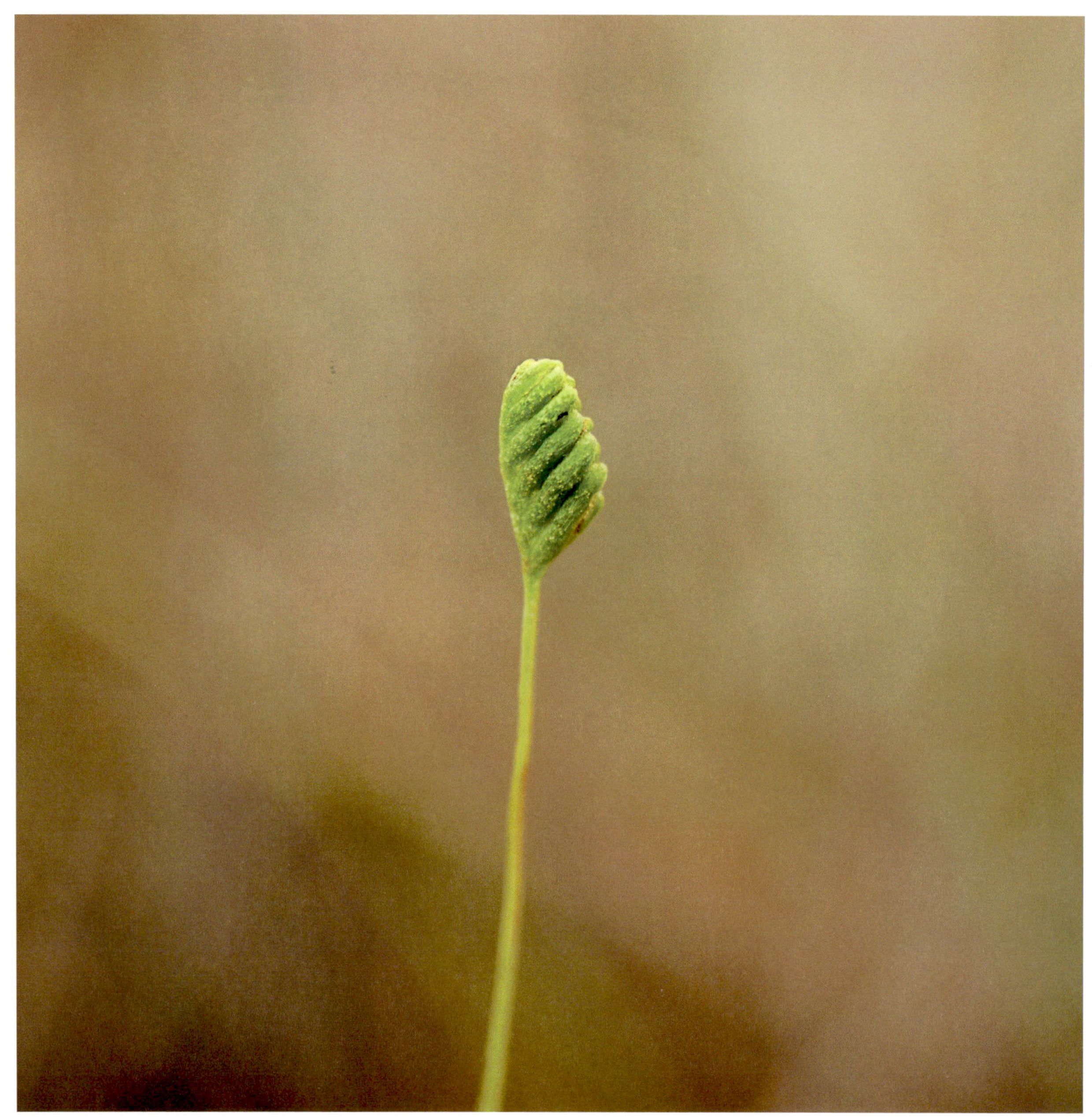

Curly Grass Fern, Wharton State Forest

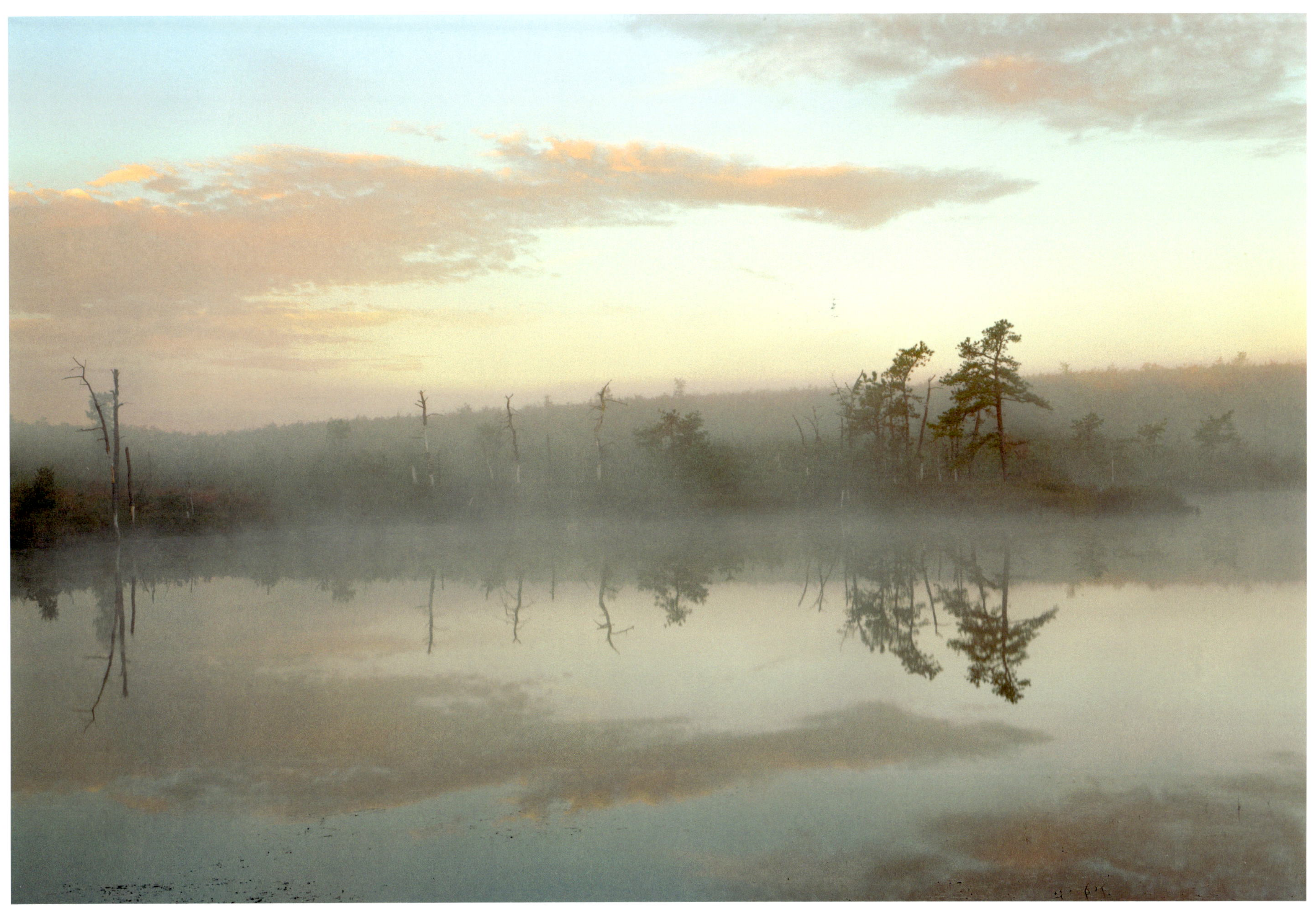

Clearing Fog, Watering Place Pond, The East Plains

*Full moon waxes high
looking down at misty ground
where winter trees are found.*

—Barbara Spector

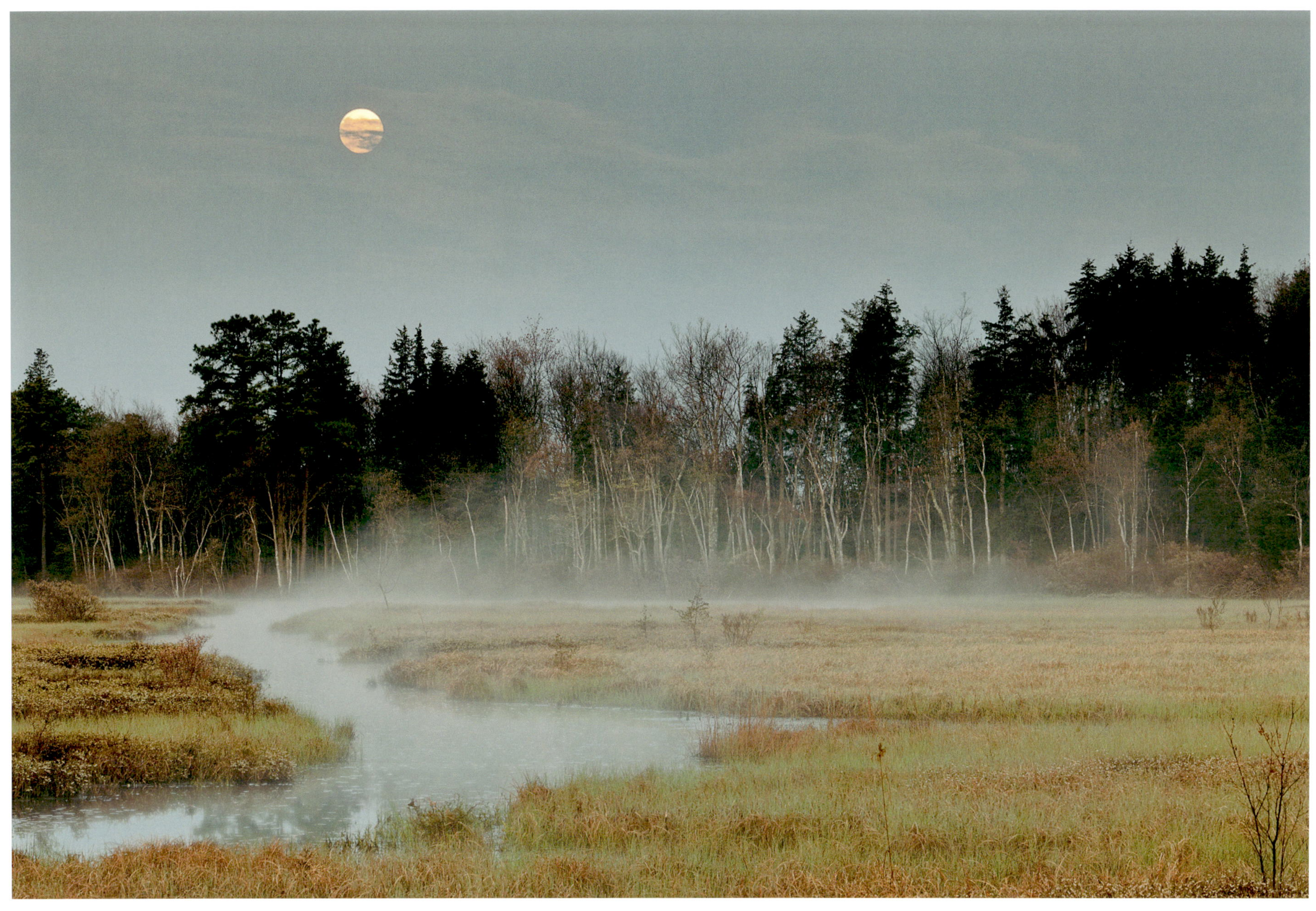

Friendship Moon, Friendship Bogs, Wharton State Forest

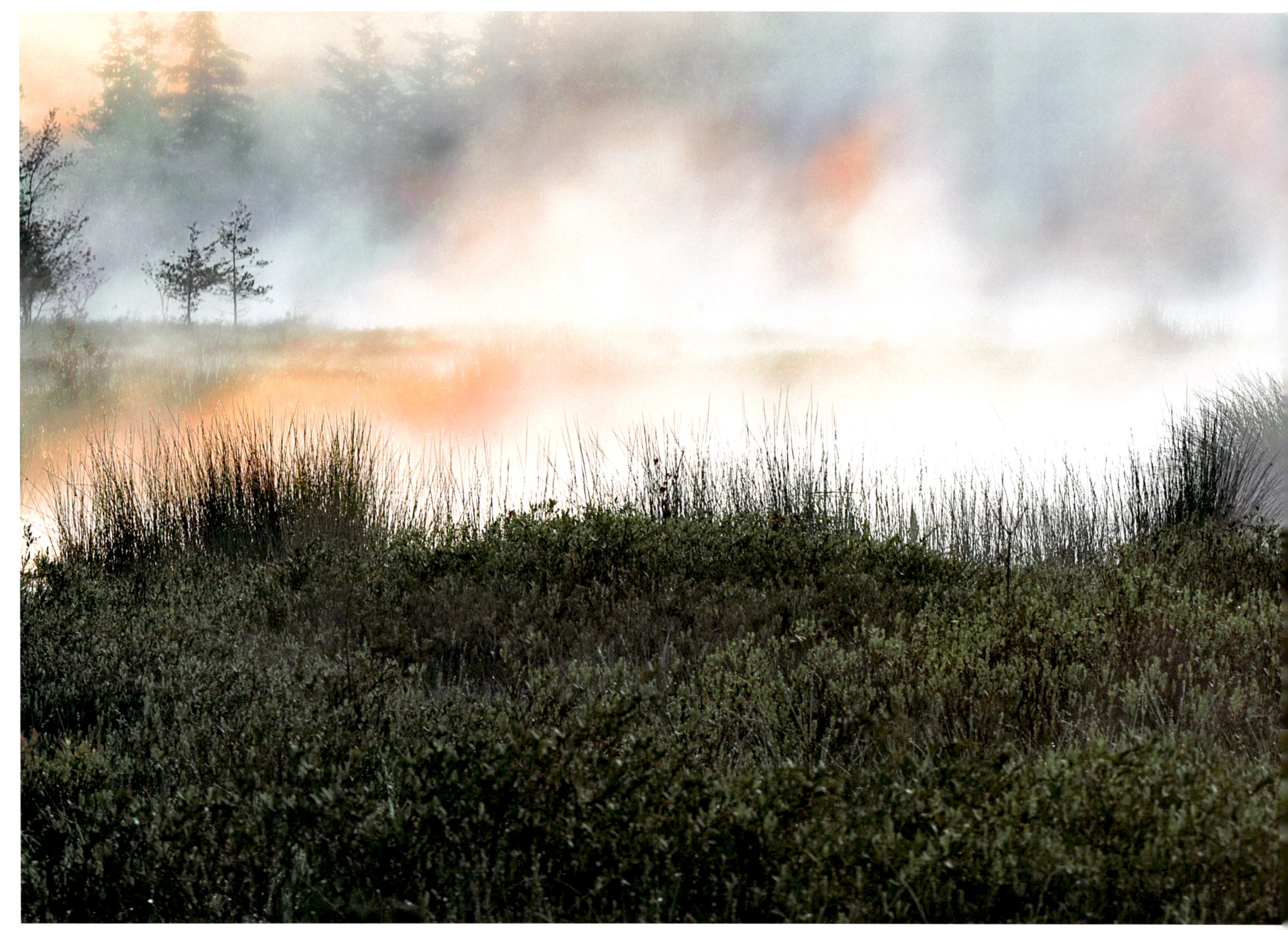

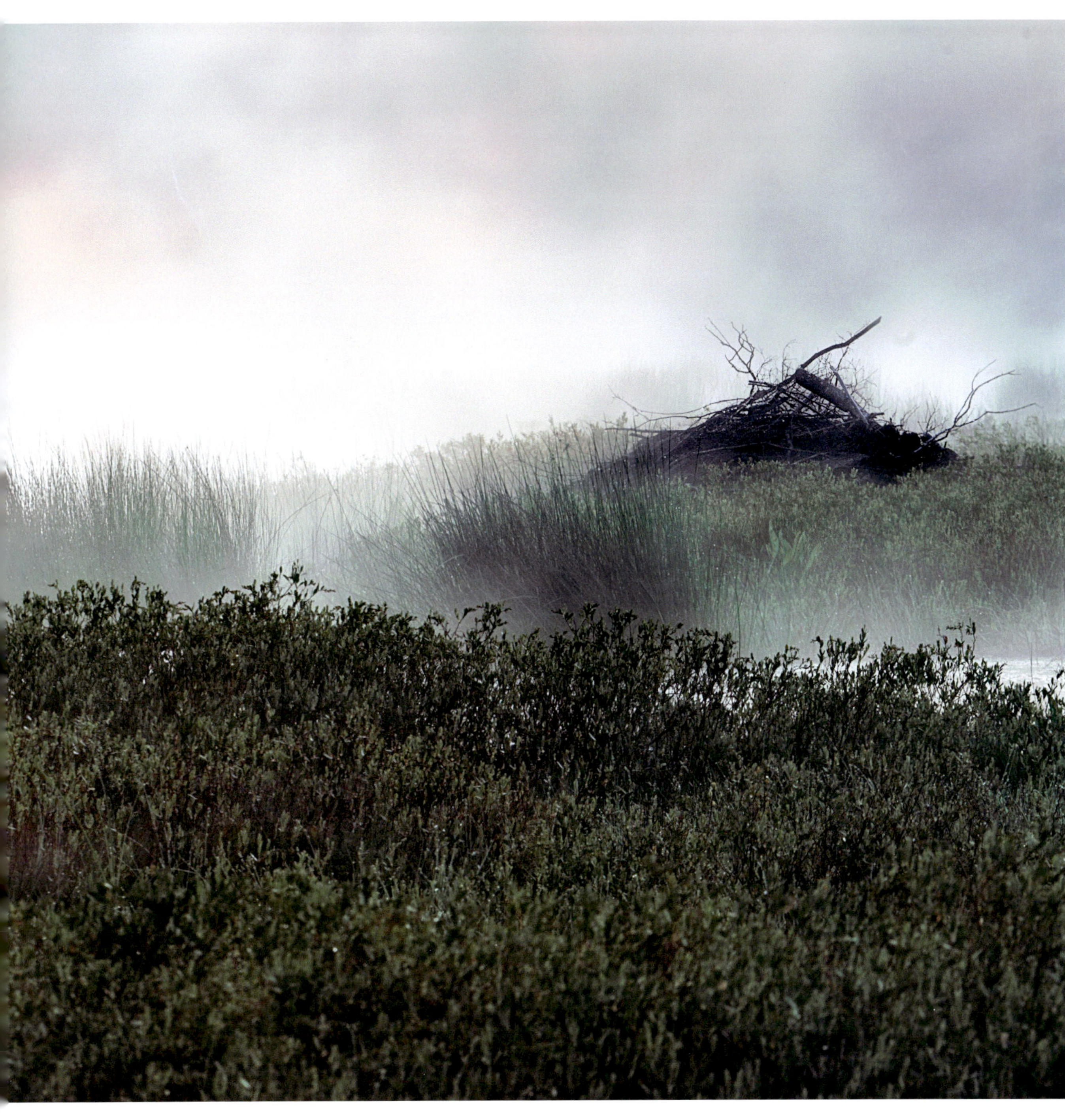

Morning on the Meadows, Chatsworth

"There is something infinitely healing in the repeated refrains of nature—the assurance that dawn comes after night, and spring after winter."

—RACHEL CARSON

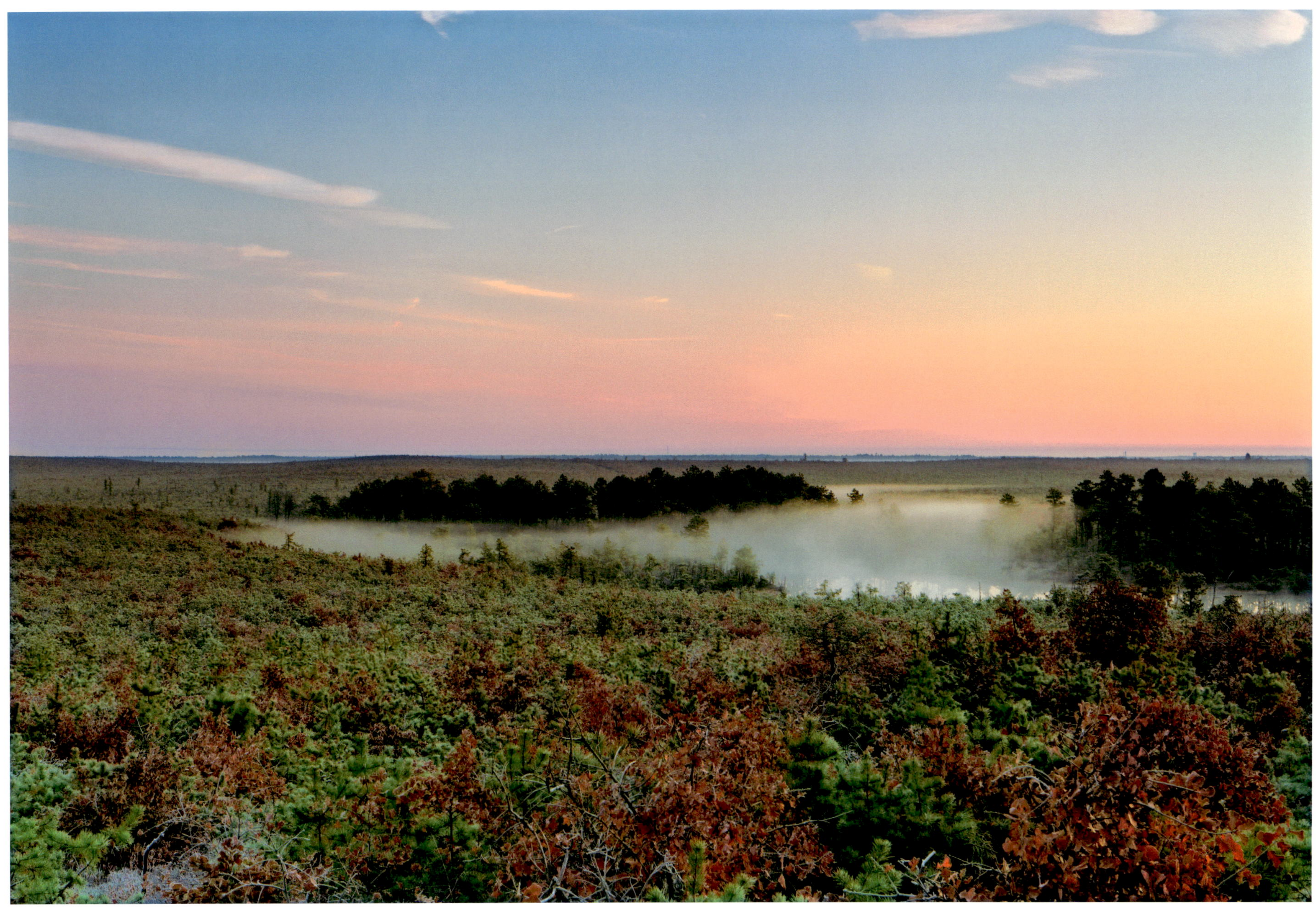

East Plains Sunrise, The East Plains

"Look deep into nature, and then you will understand everything better."

—Albert Einstein

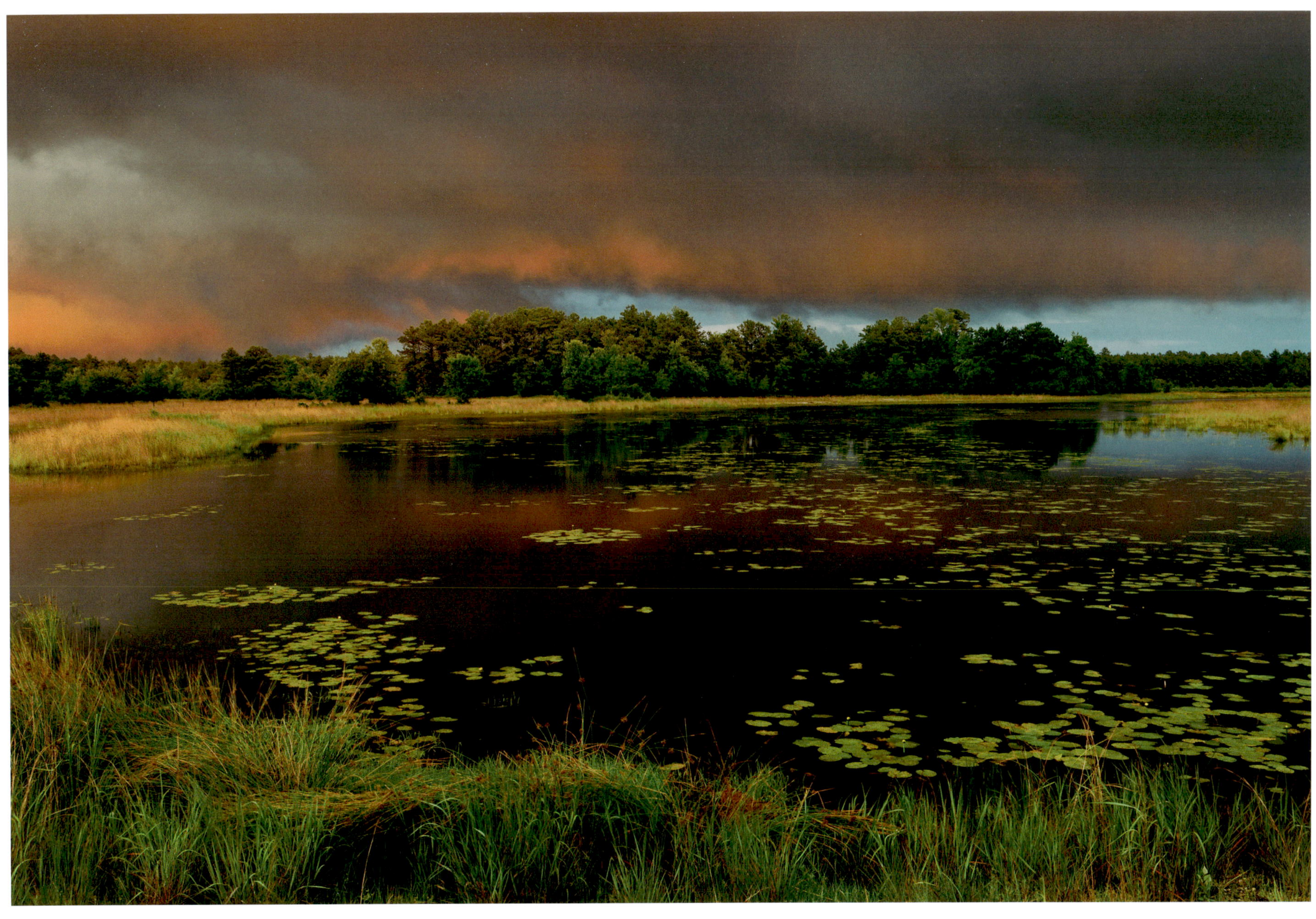

Clearing Storm, Franklin Parker Preserve

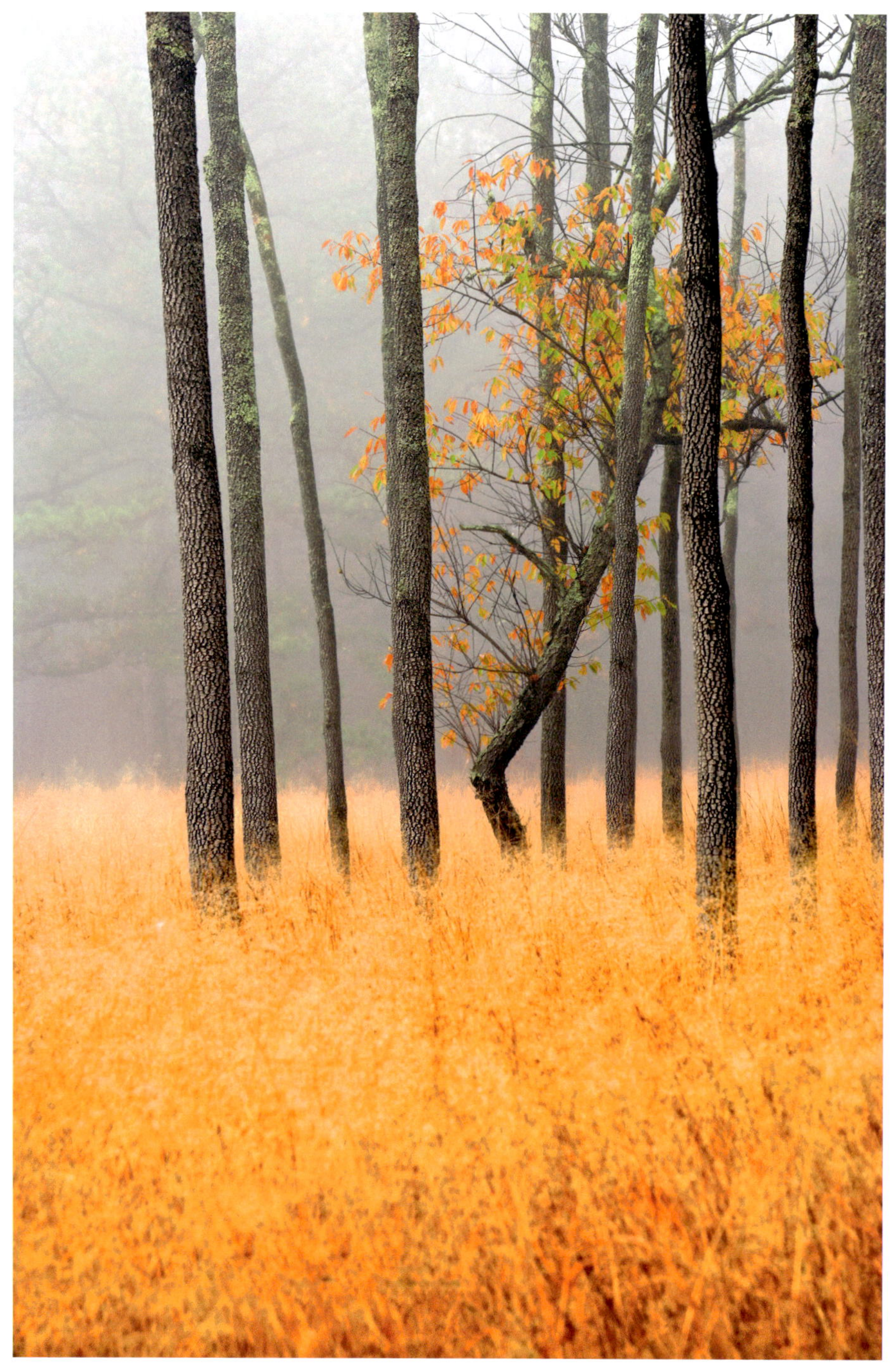

The Grove, Hampton Furnace

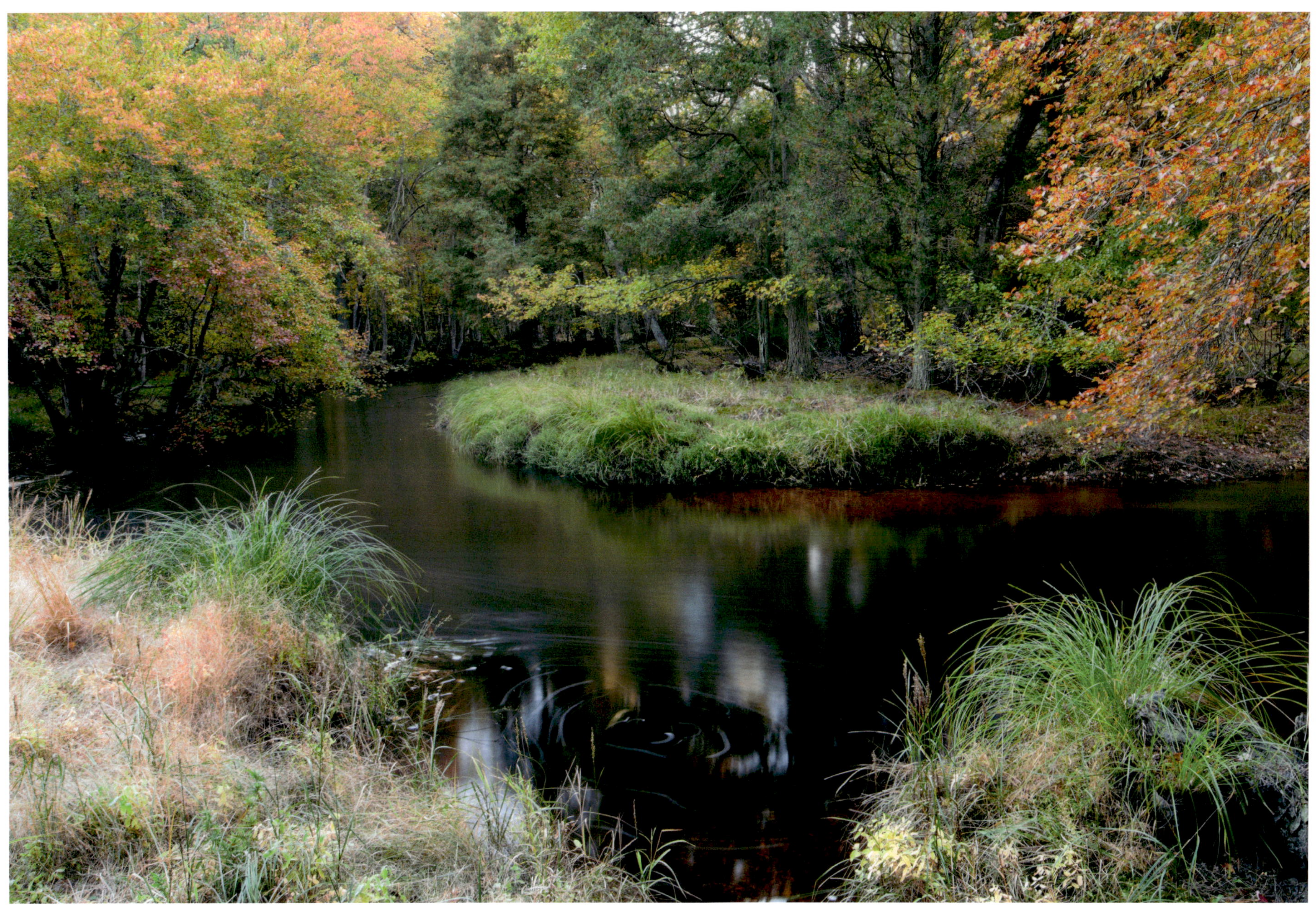

Gentle Wading, Wading River, Wharton State Forest

New Jersey morning
Spring's bewildering beauty
in river rich mist

—RALPH DAHLE

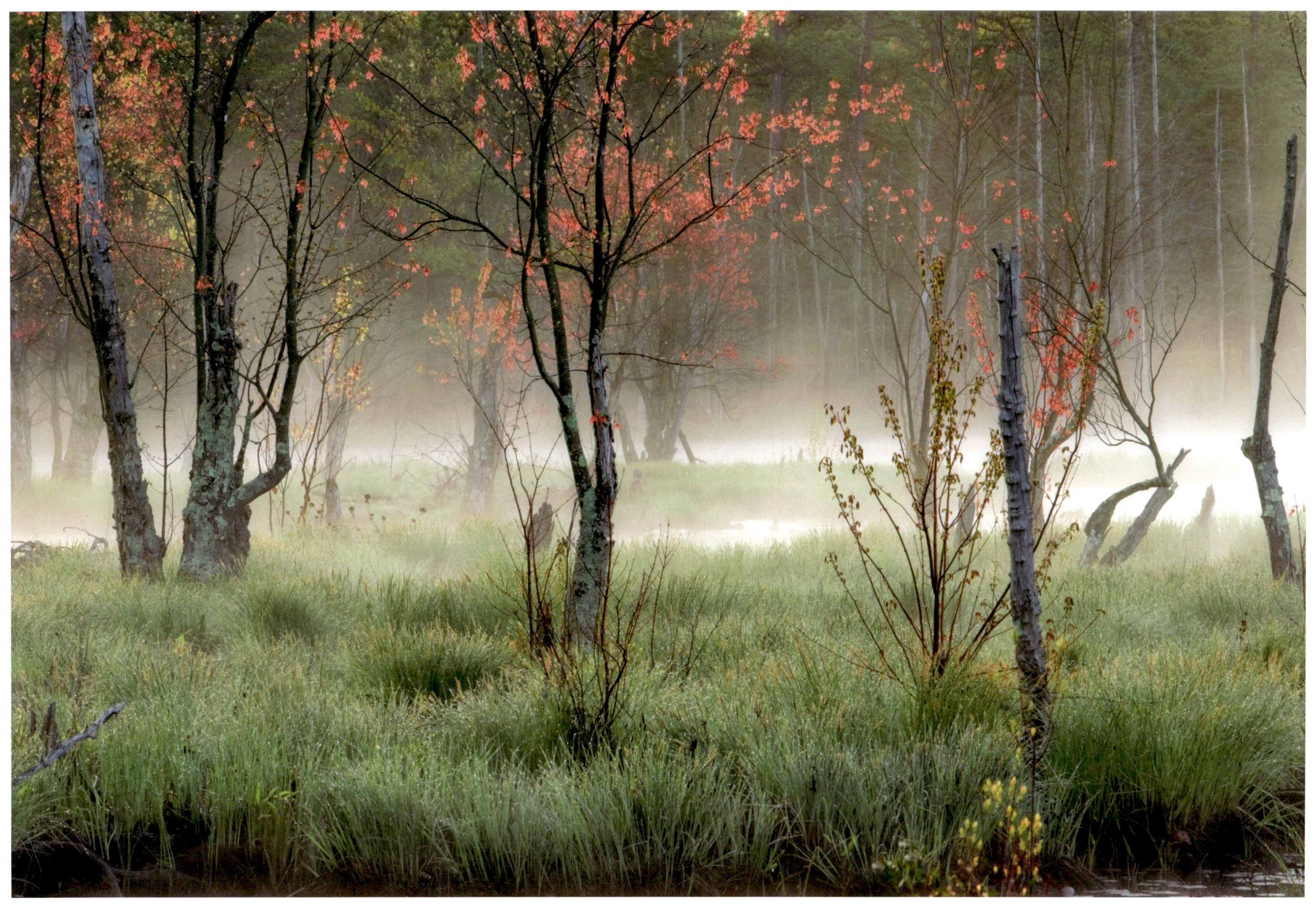

Morning Steam, Mullica River, Wharton State Forest

*"The question is not what you look at,
but what you see."*

—HENRY DAVID THOREAU

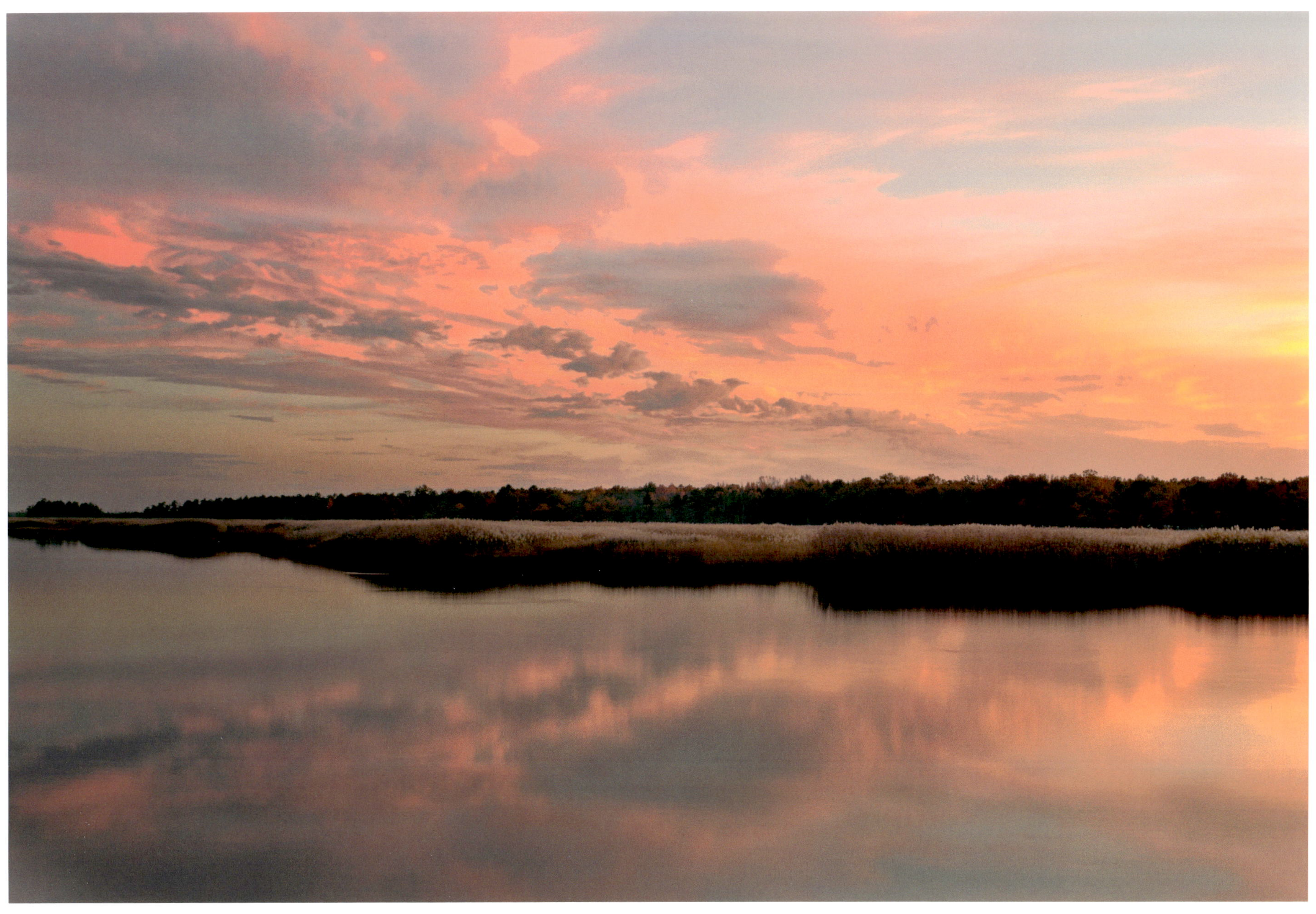

Wading River Sunset, Wading River

Municipalities of the Pinelands

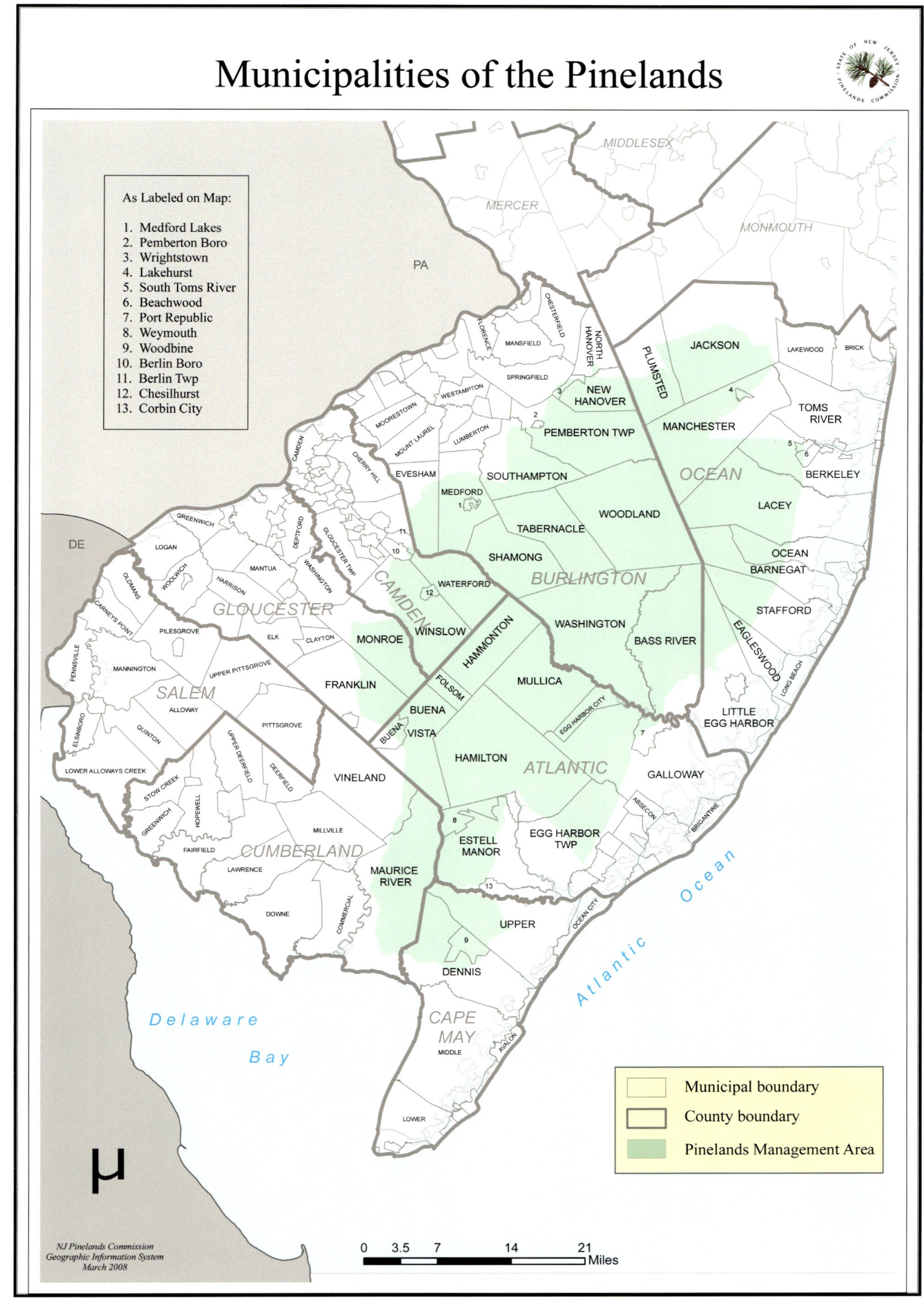

Map courtesy of New Jersey Pinelands Commission

Photographic Technical Data

Page	Image Title	Camera	Lens	f/stop	Exposure	ISO	Taken
13	Sunrise	Canon 1DS MKII	70-200mm	f/11	0.6 sec	50	6/2007
15	Reflections	Canon 5D MKII	70-200mm	f/16	0.8 sec	100	8/2013
17	Half Moon Bog	Canon 1DS MKII	24-70mm	f/10	1.6 sec	100	11/2005
19	Robert's Branch Pond	Canon 5D MKII	70-200mm	F/4.0	2 sec	100	10/2013
20	East Plains Deer	Canon 1DS MKII	70-200mm	f/22	1.3 sec	100	10/2009
21	Great Egret	Canon 5D MKII	100-400mm	F/5.6	1/2500 sec	400	4/2013
23	Batsto Canopy	Canon 1DS MKII	70-200mm	f/22	5 sec	100	10/2009
25	Job's Creek	Canon 1DS MKII	24-70mm	f/11	3.2 Sec	50	10/2007
26	Breaking Through	Canon 1DS MKII	70-200mm	f/22	0.8 sec	50	5/2009
29	Savanna	Canon 1DS MKII	50mm	f/32	30 sec	200	7/2009
31	Cedars at Calico Ridge	Canon 1DS MKII	24-70mm	f/16	8 sec	100	3/2007
32	Shroom	Canon 1DS MKII	16-35mm	f/20	1.3 sec	400	10/2008
33	Pinelands Lowlands	Canon 5D MKII	24-70mm	f/16	1.6 sec	200	5/2011
35	Fire!	Canon 1DS MKII	100-400mm	f/20	0.6 sec	50	5/2007
37	Friendship Trees	Canon 1DS MKII	70-200mm	f/11	1/4 sec	100	4/2007
39	Blue Curl	Canon 5D MKII	50mm	f/22	0.6 sec	50	8/2012
41	Meadows Beaver Morning	Canon 5D MKII	100-400mm	f/22	1 sec	100	5/2013
43	Spring Bog	Canon 5D MKII	70-200mm	f/22	1/55 sec	100	4/2013
45	Retreating Storm	Canon 5D MKII	16-35mm	f/16	0.5 sec	800	8/2013
47	Mullica Maples II	Canon 5D MKII	70-200mm	f/16	1.3 sec	100	10/2013
48	Between Two Pines	Canon 1DS MKII	70-200mm	f/22	0.8 sec	50	4/2010
49	Morning on Chatsworth Lake	Canon 1DS MKII	70-200mm	f/16	1/4 sec	100	5/2009
51	End of Fall	Canon 5D MKII	70-200mm	f/22	13 sec	100	10/2010
53	Green Wood Orchid	Canon 5D MKII	50mm	f/16	0.6 sec	200	7/2012
54	Falling While Rising	Canon 1DS MKII	70-200mm	f/16	1.3 sec	50	1/2010
55	Trunk	Canon 5D MKII	70-200m	f/32	1.3 sec	100	10/2010
57	Ferns	Canon 1DS MKII	24-70mm	f/20	2.5 sec	50	10/2007
58	Lodges	Canon 1DS MKII	100-400mm	f11	1/6 sec	50	3/2007
61	Upper Batsto River	Canon 1DS MKII	24-70mm	f/11	1.6 sec	100	10/2006
62	Standing Alone	Canon 1DS MKII	70-200mm	f/22	1.3 sec	50	12/2009
63	Wading River Reflections	Canon 1 DS MKII	70-200mm	f/16	0.4 sec	100	10/2009
65	Fall Chaos	Canon 5D MKII	70-200mm	f/22	13 sec	200	11/2010
66	Pine Barrens Gentian	Canon 5D MKII	50mm	f/22	0.3 sec	100	10/2010
67	Fall Meadow	Canon 1DS MKII	24-70mm	f/22	13 sec	100	10/2008
69	Morning Mist	Canon 1DS MKII	70-200mm	f/16	0.6 sec	50	5/2008
71	Quietude	Canon 1 DS MKII	70-200mm	f/22	0.6 sec	50	5/2009
72	Chartreuse Grove	Canon 1DS MKII	24/70mm	f/22	6 sec	50	11/2007
73	Sleeper Branch	Canon 1DS MKII	24-70mm	f/16	1 sec	50	3/2007
75	Red Maple	Canon 1DS MKII	70-200m	f/22	1.3 sec	200	10/2009
76	Friendship Mist	Canon 5D MKII	70-200mm	f/22	4 sec	200	4/2013

Page	Image Title	Camera	Lens	f/stop	Exposure	ISO	Taken
79	Flooded Maples	Canon 5D MKII	100-400mm	f/16	1/6 sec	100	3/2012
81	Crescent Moon	Canon 1DS MKII	70-200mm	f/16	2.5 sec	100	4/2010
83	Martha Pond	Canon 1DS MKII	50mm	f/32	10 sec	200	3/2009
84	Preener and Hen	Canon 5D MKII	100-400mm	f/5.6	1/320 sec	200	4/2013
85	Blooming Bladderwort	Canon 1DS MKII	24-70mm	f/22	8 sec	100	5/2009
87	Mullica Maples	Canon 5D MKII	70-200mm	f/8	1.6 sec	100	10/2013
89	Super Moon Over Franklin Parker	Canon 5D MKII	70-200mm	f/16	3.2 sec	200	6/2013
91	Oswego Spring	Canon 5D MKII	70-200mm	f/22	1.3 sec	200	4/2013
93	Wading River Point	Canon 5D MKII	70-200mm	f/16	0.3 sec	100	4/2013
94	Tres Trees	Canon 5D MKII	70-200mm	f/5.0	1/13 sec	100	1/2013
95	Forest Floor	Canon 1DS MKII	50mm	f/32	13 sec	100	2/2009
97	Fall Tunnel	Canon 5D MKII	70-200mm	f/22	4 sec	100	11/2010
99	Mullica River at Lower Bank	Canon 1DS MKII	24-70mm	f/8	0.6 sec	50	12/2006
100	Pickering's Morning Glory	Canon 5D MKII	50mm	f/20	0.3 sec	100	6/2012
101	Summer Morning	Canon 5D MKII	24-70mm	f/22	1.0 sec	400	7/2010
103	Summer Sunrise	Canon 5D MKII	70-200mm	f/16	2.5 sec	200	7/2013
105	Pinelands Fall	Canon 5D MKII	70-200mm	f/11	5 sec	100	10/2010
107	Wading River Reservoir	Canon 5D MKII	70-200mm	f/16	1.3 sec	200	8/2013
109	Mullica Bend Sunrise	Canon 5D MKII	24-70mm	f/9	13 sec	200	10/2011
111	Morning is Coming	Canon 5D MKII	24-70mm	f/16	5 sec	100	4/2011
113	Fallen Leaf Road	Canon 1DS MKII	24-70mm	f/13	3.2 sec	100	10/2005
114	The Female	Canon 1Ds MKII	100-400mm	f/5.6	1/250 sec	200	3/2013
115	St. Andrews Cross	Canon 5D MKII	50mm	f/16	1/4 sec	200	7/2012
117	Batsto Tunnel	Canon 1DS MKII	24-70mm	f/22	13 sec	100	10/2009
119	Mullica Bend Maples	Canon 5D MKII	70-200mm	f/11	2.5 sec	100	10/2011
120	Fire Fog	Canon 1DS MKII	24-70mm	f/8	1/8 sec	200	4/2009
121	Cedar Canyon	Canon 1DS MKII	28-200mm	f/32	4 sec	100	4/2007
122	Looking Back	Canon 1DS MKII	100-400mm	f/5.6	1/250 sec	200	3/2013
123	Eagle Reservoir	Canon 5D MKII	70-200mm	f/22	0.4 sec	100	8/2013
125	Wading River Fall	Canon 1DS MKII	24-70mm	f/9	1.0 sec	100	11/2005
126	Curly Grass Fern	Canon 5D MKII	50mm	f/4	1/40 sec	200	7/2012
127	Clearing Fog	Canon 5D MKII	24-70mm	f/22	3.2 sec	100	10/2010
129	Friendship Moon	Canon 5D MKII	70-200mm	f/16	2.5 sec	200	4/2013
131	Morning on the Meadows	Canon 5D MKII	100-400mm	f/16	1.0 sec	100	5/2013
133	East Plains Sunrise	Canon 5D MKII	24-70mm	f/18	1.3 sec	100	10/2011
135	Clearing Storm	Canon 5D MKII	24-70mm	f/16	3.2 sec	200	6/2013
136	The Grove	Canon 1DS MKII	70-200mm	f/16	25 sec	150	11/2007
137	Gentle Wading	Canon 5D MKII	16-35mm	f/22	8 sec	50	10/2010
139	Morning Steam	Canon 1 DS MKII	70-200mm	f/22	2 sec	100	4/2010
141	Wading River Sunset	Canon 5D MKII	50mm	f/16	2.0 sec	50	10/2010

ABOUT THE AUTHOR

Medford Lakes, New Jersey, resident **ALBERT D. HORNER** has been acquainted with Pinelands National Reserve for most of his life. A self-taught photographer living in its shadow, he has been capturing its intimate landscapes in fine-arts images since 2005. Horner's work is shown in local galleries and exhibitions. He also conducts workshops and lectures about the Pinelands. His work can be viewed at www.pinelandsimagery.com.

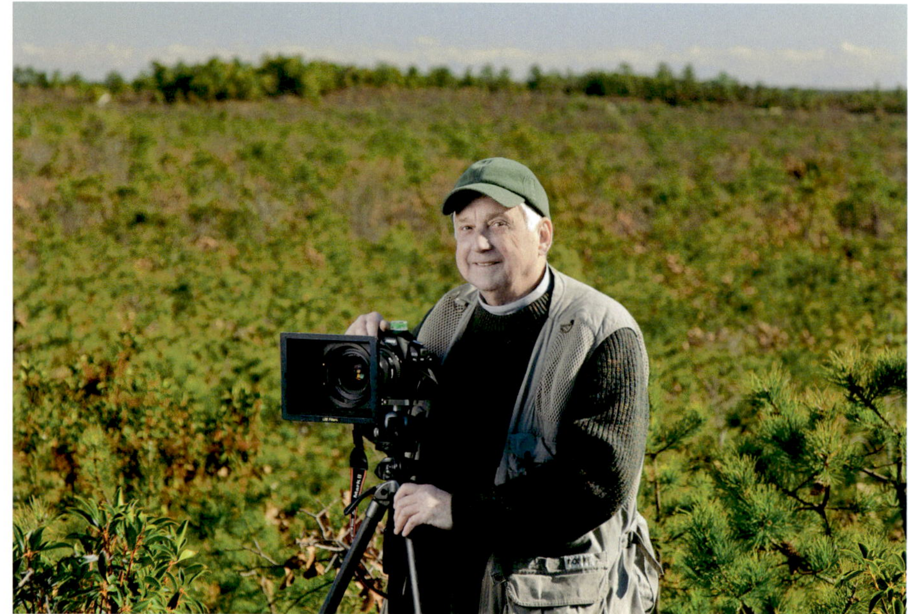

Photo by Steve Greer

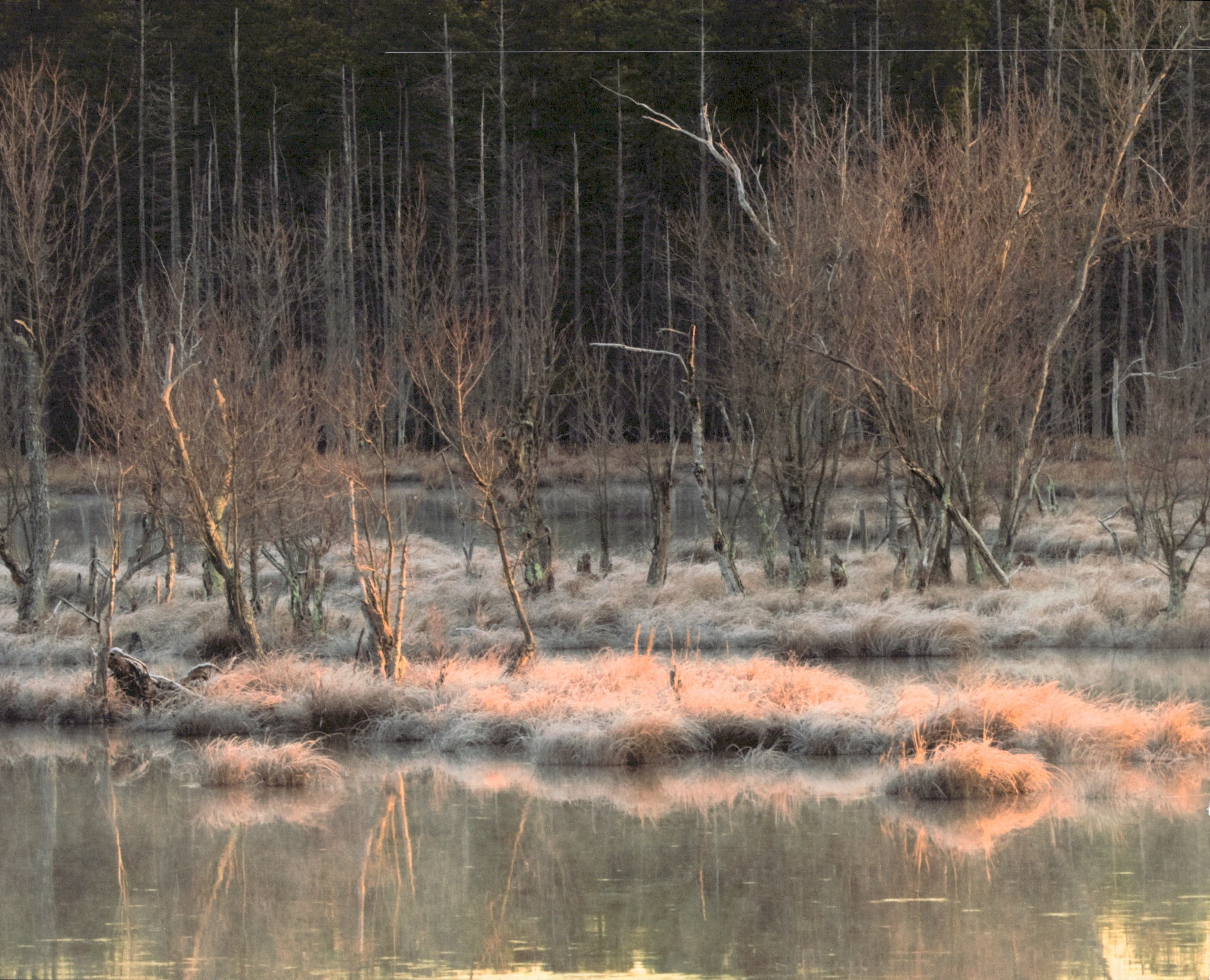